BEWARE
the
BANSHEE'S
CRY

© Photo by Jordan Rolfes

About the Author

Steven J. Rolfes is the author of numerous books on Ohio and Cincinnati, including *Historic Downtown Cincinnati* (with Kent Jones), *Cincinnati Theaters*, and *Supernatural Lore of Ohio*. Passionate about history, Rolfes has been published in various magazines and hosts a summer radio program telling ghost stories. He has worked as a teacher, border patrol agent, salesman, jeweler, former ESL teacher for Spanish-speaking immigrants, and detective. He is a volunteer at the Cincinnati History Museum and is a retired employee of the Southwest Ohio Regional Transit Authority.

BEWARE
the
BANSHEE'S
CRY

*The Folklore & History
of Messengers of Death*

STEVEN J. ROLFES

LLEWELLYN
WOODBURY, MINNESOTA

FIRST EDITION
First Printing, 2024

Book design by R. Brasington
Cover design by Kevin R. Brown
Interior illustrations by Llewellyn Art Department

Llewellyn Publications is a registered trademark of Llewellyn Worldwide Ltd.

Library of Congress Cataloging-in-Publication Data (Pending)
ISBN: 978-0-7387-7827-3

Llewellyn Worldwide Ltd. does not participate in, endorse, or have any authority or responsibility concerning private business transactions between our authors and the public.

All mail addressed to the author is forwarded but the publisher cannot, unless specifically instructed by the author, give out an address or phone number.

Any internet references contained in this work are current at publication time, but the publisher cannot guarantee that a specific location will continue to be maintained. Please refer to the publisher's website for links to authors' websites and other sources.

Llewellyn Publications
A Division of Llewellyn Worldwide Ltd.
2143 Wooddale Drive
Woodbury, MN 55125-2989
www.llewellyn.com

Printed in the United States of America

Other Books by Steven J. Rolfes

The Cincinnati Courthouse Riot

Supernatural Lore of Ohio

To Mark S. Rolfes, 1962–2024.

CONTENTS

Acknowledgments

I would like to thank my editor, Amy Glaser, and Sami Sherratt and Terry Lohmann at Llewellyn; a special thanks to the very patient people at the University of Cincinnati Library and the Cincinnati and Hamilton County Public Library. I would like to thank Mr. Doug Weise for his assistance. This work could not have been created without the tireless help of my son, Jordan Rolfes, who proofread and handled the technical issues. My wife, Terri Rolfes, and daughter, Selena, also were of great assistance. Thank you, everyone.

PREFACE

To welcome thee—Imagination's child!
Till on thy ear would burst so sadly wild
The BANSHEE'S shriek, who points with
   withered hand.
In the dim twilight should the PHOOKA come,
Whose dusky form fades in the sunny light…

   —CROKER, *FAIRY LEGENDS*

It was supposed to be a calm night—a hot, breezeless August evening, sticky and unpleasant. The men were trying to get some sleep in the fetid hellhole of the jail, locked in cages with other inmates. No one was prepared for what was soon to happen.

Some of the prisoners, secure in their cells for the night, believed in the reality of the supernatural. These were men who believed in God, although they had wandered onto a wrong path. Despite their tribulations, they clung to their faith in that which they could not see. It made perfect sense to them that the world of the spirit could sometimes intrude into our own rational, sensible world.

Other inmates, cynical from a life of hard knocks, with their last bits of human compassion wrenched from them after years of causing suffering to others, did not believe in the supernatural. They had spent their days causing pain to others, stealing what others had worked so hard to earn. For them, there was only this world—no God, no spirit, no judgment, no supernatural. To believe otherwise would mean that someday they would face an even higher court than the one that had sent them here.

But reality can be a funny thing. It does not depend upon one's personal beliefs, and that includes the supernatural. This night was different from the others; before the sun would rise, every single prisoner in that jail would believe in the supernatural.

The year was 1876, the place was the Montgomery County Jail in the heart of the city of Dayton, Ohio. Everyone was a bit quieter that evening out of nervousness and perhaps even a bit of respect. Every prisoner knew that when the sun rose, their number would be reduced by one. When the inevitable morning arrived, a young man in their company, an Irish lad named James Murphy, would be marched out and hanged. This was to be his last night on earth.

As the men lay in their bunks, some snored, some rolled about in the heat, a few prayed for the soul of their fellow prisoner who would, in a matter of hours, walk up the thirteen steps to the scaffold.

In his cell near the death chamber, the frightened James Murphy played the scene over and over in his mind. It was such a stupid thing, so foolish, so meaningless …

Deputy Sheriff Tom Hellriggle, the officer in charge of the jail that evening, came by and spoke to him for a few moments, asking if there was anything he could get him. Hellriggle was the main guard that evening, and he did not like it. You could feel the tension and the fear among the other prisoners.

Murphy didn't feel much like talking to him, so the deputy moved on to keep an eye on the others. He would be back a few more times that evening to check on him.

Murphy lay on his bunk, listening to the click of the guard's boots recede down the hallway. He wanted desperately to sleep, but it just would not come. With each second, he grew closer to his date with the scaffold, the same scaffold he had heard them working on in the room next door. Right through that door …

To heck with sleep. There would be more than enough rest after tomorrow.

He wanted to think of other things, but the scene replayed itself over and over in his mind. It had certainly not been Murphy's first encounter with the law. He had been the leader of a vicious street gang known as the Chain Gang. Every night for him was one of violent fights, small-time robberies, and mistreating both men and women.

In his fear he could not help but think of his mother. An honest woman who knew where the church was, she had tried so hard to raise him to be a good Catholic, to have faith in the Lord and respect for the law and for others. How many times over the years had his behavior brought her to tears? She was his last connection to decent society, but she had died when he was still a boy. She had been the last person to love and accept him unconditionally. Without her futile guidance, he had spun out of control with no one to catch him.

As much as he wanted to think about the good times, the time when his mother loved and cared for him, his memory kept going back to the night that had brought him to this cell and his date with the hangman. After years of violence and breaking the law, it finally climaxed on that terrible evening.

The scene played itself out over and over in his head. It started as a regular night. James and his fellow gang members had gone to a dance, where they were busy causing trouble and bullying people. Before long, the alcohol they had was nearly depleted, thus they had to come up with another way to procure some booze. Then someone mentioned that there was another dance going on at Barlow's Hall. This seemed like a good place to visit next.

When they arrived, they found that there was indeed a dance at the bottom level. To their delight, there was also a wedding reception taking place upstairs, and a fancy one at that. All the Chain Gang members knew darn well that at such high-class affairs, the liquor would be flowing like a waterfall.

It was time for the Chain Gang to extend their best wishes to the newlyweds. Of course, James and the members of the Chain Gang were not in the wedding party; indeed they knew neither the bride nor the groom. Nor were they exactly dressed for the event.

They did not care in the least. There was booze and pretty women in revealing formal gowns—that was good enough for them. They would simply invite themselves to the wedding reception.

The group strolled up the stairs to the doorway of the ballroom. Unfortunately, there was a gatekeeper sitting at the door. He asked the young men in rough clothing, who obviously were not part of the wedding, if they had a pass to enter. When they answered no, they were told they would have to go back downstairs. This was a private party.

The tumult at the door had attracted the attention of Colonel William Dawson. A wealthy and powerful man, he was the superintendent of the Champion Plow Works. Dawson had fought in the Civil War, enlisting as a private, but he'd raised himself to the rank of colonel, commanding the Thirtieth Indiana Volunteer Infantry.[1] He was also the man who was paying for the reception. It was one of his best employees who had just been married, and this reception was his gift to the new couple. Little did he know that this particular wedding gift would become a tragedy, a very ominous start to a marriage.

Murphy and the other members of the Chain Gang were already starting to head downstairs. Colonel Dawson, followed by some other men in fine clothes, suddenly appeared at the entrance.

Dawson, who apparently had imbibed a bit himself, was not content to let the matter go so easily. Although the intruders were walking back down, Dawson grabbed Murphy by the shirt and demanded that he and his friends go downstairs ... which they were already in the process of doing.

Seeing the other men watching the proceedings, Murphy did the only thing he could to save face in front of the other gang members: he laughed in the colonel's face. The colonel released the shirt and the party crashers continued down the steps.

It would have been good if they had simply left the hall and looked for trouble elsewhere. But fate wanted blood that evening. Once downstairs, they met another friend who said he could sneak them into the reception through a back entrance. Hearing the happy

---

1. *Cincinnati Enquirer* (August 26, 1876), 1.

music upstairs, the conversation, and having had a glimpse of the pretty ladies in their formal attire, the group readily agreed.

The Chain Gang went back upstairs, but this time, not past the man at the door. Before they knew it, they were in the private party, where they headed straight to the bar. Amazingly, the group was keeping a low profile, wanting to get as much free booze as possible before someone discovered them. But it was only a matter of time.

Standing some distance away with his back to them, in a circle of influential men, was Colonel Dawson, a drink in his hand. Although the colonel was too busy with his conversation to notice the reappearance of the intruders, Murphy saw him. In a low growl he told his fellow gang members he was going to get even for the insult. No one laid hands on James Murphy and walked away in good health!

Dawson and a friend, Mr. Meyers, soon left the reception to go downstairs to the regular bar. They were unaware that Murphy and the Chain Gang had followed them. The two went outside, not realizing that the hooligans were following.

Once outside, the Chain Gang split up, one group going around to circle in front of the two victims. Murphy and gang member Petty reached Dawson and Meyers first as they tried to enter a locked gate. Murphy sucker punched Dawson twice while Petty went after Meyers.

Almost immediately the remaining members of the gang arrived and started beating Dawson. That was when Murphy, obviously caught up in the moment of violence, pulled his concealed knife out of its sheath and, without a pause, thrust it into Dawson.

The Colonel did not die immediately but hobbled up and started to run away. He collapsed, a puddle of blackish liquid growing under his body. With this, the other members of the Chain Gang scattered, running away in different directions. This was more than they had signed up for.

James Murphy was now a murderer, standing alone in the darkness, holding a bloodstained knife.

As Murphy lay alone on his bunk, reliving the terrible scene over
and over in his head, the peace of jail was suddenly shattered. An
extremely shrill, piercing scream erupted through the air. It was the
unmistakable sound of "a woman crying weirdly and wildly in the
darkness, and so loudly that the sound filled all the jail room, and
that many of the men awoke and shuddered."[2]

Murphy sat up in his bed, terrified. There were no women in the
jail. The sound had seemed to come from everywhere, from the air
itself, but it was definitely not from the outside of the building. That
wailing, as Murphy well knew from those silly stories he had heard
all his life, was the ghastly sound of a banshee, the ancient messenger
of death. It would sometimes appear when an Irishman of a certain
family was soon to die.

And one of those "certain families" was his.

Deputy Tom Hellriggle had heard it too. Unfortunately for him,
so did every prisoner locked in their cells! Those men who were so
hard they did not believe in the world of the spirit had what is now
known as a paradigm shift—and they were not at all happy with their
new outlook. The entire jail was in an uproar, knowing that a supernatural creature was loose among them. Some men were screaming;
some were panicked, shouting to be let out; others, the sensible ones,
were on their knees praying.

James Murphy was quiet, sitting on his bunk with his mouth
open and his eyes wide in terror. Everyone else in the jail had merely
heard the banshee. He, however, was actually seeing it!

A phosphorescent figure was slowly appearing in his jail cell.
The glimmering shape gradually took the form of a woman wearing

2. *Cincinnati Commercial* (August 26, 1876), 1.

black mourning attire. Even worse, he recognized the apparition as it became ever clearer. It was his own mother.

The morning came too swiftly. He was visited by a Catholic priest, also named Murphy. After the confession and last rites, the prisoner handed Deputy Hellriggle a shank he had been concealing with the intention of cheating the hangman by committing suicide. After the conversation with the priest, he'd changed his mind.

When he handed the knife to the deputy, he said, "I would not take my own life now, though I were to be hung twice over."[3] File this under *be careful what you wish for*.

The grim act of killing a human being by hanging can go two ways. If everything goes correctly, the weight of the body, the force of the drop, and the position of the rope on the neck instantly snaps the bones of the vertebrae, supposedly causing immediate and painless death. This, at least, is the intention.

Unfortunately, the process is far more difficult than one might assume. The length of the drop had to be correctly determined, or one of two horrible consequences would follow. If the drop was too long, the weight of the body would decapitate the victim, causing a bloody spectacle for witnesses. For the condemned, this would be the preferable of the two. Death would be immediate.

However, if the drop was too short, as was often the case, the neck would not break. The victim would then kick and struggle as the weight of their body choked them slowly to death. It was an extremely painful and horrific manner of dying.

But there was a rare third way of screwing up a hanging, one that was infinitely worse than the first two. This horror was the fate destined for James Murphy.

---

3. *Cincinnati Commercial* (August 26, 1876), 1.

The scaffold had been erected in the next room, part of the jail hospital. It was determined, based on the weight of the victim, that a drop of three and a half feet would suffice to do the job correctly without decapitating him. The rope had been tested numerous times, dropping such heavy items as a barrel filled with nails. The hemp rope was strong, in no danger of breaking.

The night before, to remove any elasticity from the hemp, a bucket filled with water had been suspended for the entire night. What no one noticed on that fateful day was that the calm rotation of the bucket had caused friction and, bit by bit, had worn the rope at the crossbeam.

At one o'clock James Murphy was removed from his cell, where he was smoking a cigar and now talking to two priests. He was escorted to the next room, where he saw a number of reporters, policemen in dress uniform, Sisters of Charity, and others. He also saw the black walnut coffin set off to the side. This had been paid for out of the pocket of Sheriff William Patton.

Murphy's arms were tied by a black cloth at the elbows. He was then led up the thirteen steps and placed over the trapdoor. The noose was placed over his head.

Everyone present was watching the prisoner. No one looked up to the crossbeam; no one saw where the rope was now badly frayed.

For a brief moment the gang member regained a bit of his cocky attitude. He even danced a little Irish jig on the trapdoor. This dance of death ended abruptly when a deputy placed the black velvet hood over his head.

Once the deputy stepped back, there was very little delay. The officer, on silent orders from the sheriff, pressed a control with his foot. With a loud bang the trapdoor opened. James Murphy plummeted through the opening—and kept going.

The unthinkable had happened, that horrible third option. The frayed rope had broken under his weight. Murphy's body, tied and hooded, crashed to the ground below. The onlookers gasped as the deputies scrambled to him.

The hangman told his assistant to grab the backup rope. He quickly secured this in the place of the broken rope as the deputies brought Murphy to his feet and started to walk him to the steps again. He could be heard exclaiming under the black hood that he was still alive. They had to nearly carry him up the steps, although he insisted that he could walk. It was obvious, however, that he could not. Father Murphy helped hold his head as they were taken a second time to the place of death.

The hangman had everything ready when Murphy was returned to the platform. The young murderer began to cry out, asking what they were going to do. The priest whispered for him to be brave and die like a man.

At exactly 1:44 the fresh noose was placed around his neck, and for a second time the deadly switch was activated.

Murphy fell the required three and a half feet, then the new rope jerked a bit, but remained in one piece. The limp body of the criminal swayed a bit as the doctors came forth.

He was mercifully unconscious but not dead. Dr. Crum, the physician in the jail, checked his pulse. He announced a pulse of 100, but kept checking, calling out lower and lower numbers.

Seventeen minutes after the fall, Dr. Crum could detect no pulse. He checked the heart with his stethoscope and officially pronounced James Murphy to be dead.[4]

Earlier, as the men and women gathered about the place of execution waiting for the prisoner to arrive, there was a great deal of quiet

---

4. *Cincinnati Commercial* (August 26, 1876), 1.

conversation. The night guards had told the officers, who now whispered it to the doctors, the reporters, the Sisters of Charity, and anyone else they could find. Word was spreading quickly. Every prisoner in the rest of the Montgomery County Jail was also talking about it.

Everyone asked the same question, a question they all knew the answer to: What was that wailing woman whose voice everyone in the jail had heard the previous evening?

Father Murphy, and many others, had no doubt as to what it was. It was a banshee. An Irishman was to die soon, and as had happened for generations, that death was heralded by one of the most frightening denizens of the spirit world.

Let us now take a journey to the Emerald Isle to meet this mysterious and terrifying entity known as the banshee—and her kith and kin.

INTRODUCTION

See the space within my dwelling—
'Tis the cold, blank space of death;
'Twas the Banshee's voice came swelling
Slowly o'er the midnight heath.

—Croker, Fairy Legends

It did not happen in some gothic fantasy of a tiny cottage on a fog-shrouded moor, but rather in Derry, a major city in Northern Ireland. It was the 1940s, on a quiet side street known as Fulton's Place. The lane was quite near an old churchyard—the famous church known as the Long Tower, part of St. Columba's.

That winter one of the residents of the street, an elderly man, was lying in his bed; his health was failing quickly. Friends and relatives came to him, fearing they would never see him alive again. Of course, the priest came to administer the final sacraments that the old Irishman would receive in his days on this earth.

Then there was a knock on the door … probably more people arriving to pay their respects. Strange thing is, only one person, a teenage girl, heard the knock. Everyone else wondered what the heck she was talking about.

Then she saw the doorknob rattle and heard more knocking, more insistent than before. After this there was an eerie moaning sound, a low and sad lamenting from a woman. The girl wondered, *Why isn't anyone letting her come in?* She was obviously in some kind of distress.

The girl would take it no more. Even though it was not her house, she scurried to the door and swung it open. Then, as the other guests watched in horror, she screamed and fainted dead away.

When she was revived, she told them she had seen an old hag with very long white hair. The crone was standing out in the cold, wringing her hands and crying out plaintively. The bizarre woman saw the door was opened for her and started to move toward it.

That was when the girl screamed. As soon as she did, the ghostly woman vanished.

The old man left this world a little later that evening.[5]

---

5. *Derry Journal,* "Ghost Stories Special."

Meet the banshee.

Everyone has heard of this specter, a ghostly Irish woman who cries out at night to predict the deaths of members of a family. There is the old expression "to wail like a banshee." However, beyond that, most people know little or nothing about this grisly herald of the grave.

The banshee is a bewildering entity that defies all attempts to analyze it. Like a will-o'-the-wisp, it moves about, always changing, always just out of reach. When you think you know what it is, it is something else. Just when you think you have a hard-and-fast rule, it breaks it. There is always an exception.

A banshee is a female spirit who informs people of an upcoming death, often by crying out before a person dies. However, sometimes it does not give the classic screech, but instead washes the victim's bloody clothing in a nearby stream. We know that it is an ugly old crone—except when it is a beautiful maiden with long golden hair. We know the cry is frightening and discordant, except when it is soft, sweet, sometimes even accompanied by a traditional Irish harp.

Even the most basic question is difficult to answer: What exactly is a banshee? Is it a remembrance of a powerful Celtic goddess from pre-Christian Ireland? We will see examples of that. Is it a fairy, one of the supernatural beings known properly as the Tuatha Dé Danann? We will see examples of that. Is it a ghost, an ancestor who returns from the world beyond to warn people of their upcoming demise? We will see examples of that. Is it a ghost of an ancestor who loves the family and wishes to help them through the sadness of death? We will see examples of that. Is it the ghost of someone who had been terribly wronged in the past, now returning to take delight in announcing their tormentors' deaths and sorrow? We will see examples of that.

What, then, is the banshee? In the pages that follow, we shall see her in all her manifestations, as well as many of her kith and kin from other lands. We shall follow the twisting trail of mythology, folklore, and a surprising number of documented cases to try to answer that question.

Perhaps we are asking the wrong question. Instead of *what*, why don't we ask *why*? Why does this entity, and others like it, exist in our myths and legends and, from time to time, seep into our sane world?

Who better to explain it than St. Paulinus? One night he was sitting at a banquet table, trying to explain his new religion to King Edwin of Northumberland. The monarch asked a number of questions, not only about this new God, but about the meaning of life.

The monk paused for a moment, took a sip from his goblet, then answered with an excellent metaphor. Pointing up to the walls, he suggested the king should imagine that a single little bird, a sparrow, flew out of the darkness outside and into the hall through that window over there. For just a brief few moments, the bird flew across the banquet room, then without the slightest pause, flew out of the other window, back into the dark night.[6]

And in the saint's brilliance, we are all like that sparrow, flying in out of darkness when we are born. We are here only for a short time, then we, too, fly out of the other window.

The banshee tells us that leaving the banquet hall of life should be acknowledged. She wails and cries out for the little bird, helping it on its journey.

Banshees are connected to certain purely Irish families and will wail only for them—with, of course, one exception. In County Clare, near the village of Corofin, there have been many reports of a solitary banshee who sits at a crossroads wailing. She is not crying out

---

6. Sellar, *Bede's Ecclesiastical History of England*, 117.

for members of a specific family, but rather for any prisoner in the nearby workhouse who is soon to die.[7]

And there we have it: this spirit is not concerned with family or social rank. Whether prince or peasant, she will cry out for the forgotten, the lost, the low who are burdened by sin ... the people no one will miss. The banshee believes no little bird should fly out of the banquet room window without at least one person shedding a tear.

Now, let us go on a journey to seek out the wailing spirit in all her various forms. It will be a wild and thrilling trip.

---

7. Westropp, "A Folklore Survey," 191.

Chapter 1
CÚ CHULAINN
AND MORRIGAN

But something rustled on the floor,
And someone called me by my name:
It had become a glimmering girl
With apple blossom in her hair
Who called me by my name and ran
And faded through the brightening air.

—Yeats, "The Song of Wandering Aengus"

Throughout the realm of fairy lore, there is no specter of the shadow world more frightening—and more fascinating—than the banshee. This mysterious harbinger of death, with her nightly wailing, is perhaps the best known of the Irish spirits, but unlike other denizens of darkness, the average person knows very little about her. Everyone has heard the expression "to wail like a banshee," but few know little beyond that.

The banshee does not feature prominently in folk and fairy tales, but she does make an occasional appearance. This sullen, lonesome phantom has little interaction with the mortals who fear her cry. Usually, she is only heard as a sad wailing in the distance, but sometimes, she can be seen. She cries out a grief-stricken screech, a somber prediction that one of a family is soon to make their way to the grave. Then she is gone … at least until the next person in the family is about to die.

She is the herald of death. She does not take the soul herself, but rather, she announces to the family that one of their loved ones is destined to leave this world. There is nothing to be done to stop her; nothing can change her prediction. In this way, she is one of the most dreadful of all supernatural creatures.

So let us now take a furtive glance behind the veil and gaze with trembling breath upon the dreaded aspect of the banshee. To begin this journey, we must keep in mind that, like most Irish fairy lore, the origins of the banshee are shrouded in the mist of the deep pagan past, where myth and history blend together. We begin our journey in ancient pre-Christian Ireland, a time of powerful gods, alluring or frightening goddesses, bloody battles, and mighty heroes.

Fráech and Finnabair

One of the earliest tales with supernatural maidens attending a dying hero is found in the *Táin Bó Fraích*.[8]

In the saga, Fráech is the most handsome and desirable young man in all of Ireland. The princess Finnabair decides she wants him to be her husband, even though she had never actually laid eyes on him. She had only heard people describe his good looks and charm, but for her, this was enough.

The two do meet, significantly when Finnabair is bent over engaged in washing her hands in a stream. Fráech is immediately smitten with her beauty and asks her to elope. Although she had been desperately in love with this previously unseen man, she refuses his offer. Oh, she still wants to marry him, and she lets him know it. But she wants this done right. As a sign of their new troth, she gives him a thumb ring that her father, King Ailill, had given her.

Fráech goes to the court and formally asks King Ailill and Queen Medb for the hand of their daughter. The king demands a very high price for his bride, more than the young man can possibly afford to pay.

Later, the king and the prospective son-in-law are by the water. Fearing that the young man would decide to skip the formalities of paying the bride's price and simply elope with her (which was his original intention), the king takes the thumb ring and throws it into the water. It is immediately swallowed by a figure known well in Celtic mythology, a salmon.

Later, Ailill claims to be desperately ill. He tells his followers that the only way he can be cured is for someone to bring him some rowan-berries. He then gives the young hero directions to where the berries are growing, which by the strangest coincidence is right where a dragon dwells.

---

8. Faraday, *Cattle-Raid*.

Fráech and Finnabair join forces to slay the monster, but Fráech is grievously wounded in the fight. As he lies dying, one hundred fifty maidens clad in crimson and green come and carry him off. They take him to the fairy mound, where after some time they heal him of his wounds. This is a rare case where the "women of the mound" bring healing instead of announcing death.

Once he is healed, they escort him back to the palace so that he can claim his bride. Now the king becomes haughty and demands proof that this is the same young man his daughter was originally to wed. The only way to do this and satisfy the king is for him to see the ring his daughter had given him. To his shock, without the slightest hesitation, the young dragon slayer produces it. As it turns out, he had gone fishing and caught the exact same salmon that had swallowed the prize.[9]

One can easily see the mythical motif here of the women carrying the dying hero off to the Otherworld, just as the three maidens did to King Arthur after the Battle of Camlann. Here, this ancestor of the banshee does not predict death—but that is about to change.

Cú Chulainn and Morrigan

There is no doubt that the greatest Irish hero of all time is Cú Chulainn, sometimes shortened as Cuchulainn. Some call him the Irish Heracles, while others (myself included) call Heracles the Greek Cú Chulainn.

He is the mythical hero in the same vein as Heracles, Samson, Hildebrand, the Persian Rostam, and many others across different cultures and their myths. Indeed, the similarities are so profound that it has been suggested there was, in prehistoric times, a single Indo-European legend that was changed as the various tribes settled

---

9. "Fráech," *Oxford Reference*.

in different regions, each one developing their own peculiar version of a solitary tale. As time passed, these stories of the great heroes became the cultural icons of many different nations.

There is a great deal to say about Cú Chulainn, literally the "Hound of Culann." Numerous books have been written studying and analyzing this awe-inspiring character. Sadly, in this work, we must defer all of that for another day and concentrate on Cú Chulainn's encounter with a banshee—most likely the dark goddess Morrigan herself.

Queen Medb had invaded Ulster to steal Donn Cúailnge, the Brown Bull of Cooley. Through witchcraft, all of Ulster's warriors suffered from labor pains of childbirth. However, Cú Chulainn was immune and alone fought the invading army. He met the heroes of Medb's army one by one at a river ford. With each battle, he was victorious. Then, during a lull in combat, the dark goddess of war, Morrigan, interfered.

As the hero sat catching his breath, he heard the sound of footsteps. Someone was approaching him. Was the enemy engaged in some manner of treachery?

He stood up and waited, ready to draw his sword and confront his foe. But it was not an enemy warrior walking toward him. It was a dark-haired woman, possibly the most beautiful woman he had ever seen, wearing a dress of many different colors.

Cú Chulainn was immediately suspicious. He demanded to know who she was.

The woman, in a sultry, seductive voice, replied that she was the daughter of Buan. She also said that she brought not only treasure but her cattle with her. What she wanted from him was obvious.

But Cú Chulainn knew this would not be the first time an army used a beautiful woman to defeat an opponent they could not conquer in a fair battle. He dismissed her.

""The time at which you have come to us is not good. For our condition is evil, through hunger. It is not easy to me to meet a woman, while I am in this strife."" [10]

Morrigan did not appreciate having her advances spurned, even if, as he had clearly said, "The time at which you have come to us is not good." Furious at the rejection, while he was engaged in desperate combat with Lóch mac Mofemis, the goddess attacked him three times in different animal forms: as an eel, a wolf, and a heifer. This did no good, as Cú Chulainn severely wounded each of the creatures, driving them off so he could concentrate on the task at hand.

The hero was victorious but exhausted. As he walked, he encountered Morrigan again. This time she had assumed the form of a hag milking a cow. She was now blind and lame, the exact same wounds he had given to the various animals during combat. He asked her for a drink of the milk.

When Cú Chulainn tasted the milk from the first teat, he blessed the old woman, invoking the gods and non-gods (those worshipped by common people). The moment he pronounced the blessing, the wound in her head was healed.

She gave him milk from the second teat. He thanked and blessed her in the same way. Immediately the blindness left her and she could see again.

The same thing happened with the third teat, after which her leg was healed.

She now revealed herself as the dark goddess Morrigan.

"You told me," said the Morrigan, "I should not have healing from you for ever."

---

10. Faraday, *Cattle-Raid*.

> *"If I had known it was you," said Cuchulainn, "I*
> *would not have healed you ever."* [11]

Then comes the banshee, almost certainly Morrigan in yet another disguise. Cú Chulainn was on his way to his final battle. First, he visited his mother, and there he was offered a drink of wine. It does not go well.

The sorcery of Morrigan was following him, right to his own mother. Trying to relax just a bit before the tremendous battle, he thought he was beyond the reach of the dark goddess. But that was not to be.

His mother, as expected, offered him a goblet of wine. Smiling, he took it, talking of unimportant things to prevent his mother from being too concerned.

But as soon as he tasted it, he spit it out. The wine had turned to blood in the goblet.

He exploded in a rage. "'My grief!' he said, 'my mother Dechtire, it is no wonder others to forsake me, when you yourself offer me a drink of blood.'" [12]

She looked at it, just as horrified as her son. She poured it out, then poured another goblet. The hero could see that it was wine coming from the pitcher. But when he raised it to his lips, it was human blood.

The goblet was tossed away a second time, then refilled again. As before, at first it was wine, but when Cú Chulainn was about to drink, it was blood again, a presage of his own death.

After this less-than-encouraging start, Cú Chulainn goes off to war. On his way to the battle, Cú Chulainn experiences one of the

---

11. Faraday, *Cattle-Raid*.
12. *Cuchulain of Muirthemne*, 335.

greatest encounters with a banshee ever recorded. He is in the company of the great druid priest Cathbad, the man who had given Cú Chulainn his name.

The two men approach a ford in a stream. There, to their horror, they see the banshee, once again most likely Morrigan.

She appears as a beautiful woman, quite thin, with very long golden hair. She is busy washing clothing in the stream and crying out in a frightening lament with each move. The water is becoming crimson from her washing, as the clothes are saturated in fresh blood.

She pays no notice to them, but continues to wash and cry out in anguish.

Cathbad speaks to his companion, warning him of what he is seeing.

"'Little Hound,' said Cathbad, 'do you see what it is that young girl is doing? It is your red clothes she is washing, and crying as she washes, because she knows you are going to your death against Maeve's great army. And take the warning now and turn back again.'"[13]

Cú Chulainn, run away from a battle in fear for his own life? That would never happen, and the young hero tells him so. He even correctly identifies the person he sees as not being human, calling her "the woman of the Sidhe" (which, as we shall soon see, is the direct translation of *banshee*). If Cathbad wishes to turn around, that is his business. He even mocks, saying that the banshee will have plenty of washing to be done soon enough.

With that, the two walk on toward the battle and certain death.

The hero, who had a taboo against eating dog meat, then encountered a trio of hags (quite possibly the Morrigan now divided into the three goddesses). They invoked the law of hospitality and demanded that he eat with them, even though they were poor.

---

13. *Cuchulain of Muirthemne*, 335.

Under this profound obligation, he had no choice but to accept their offer. It was a trap to force him to break a taboo and bring about misfortune. The dinner did not go well:

"Then he went over to her. She gave him the shoulder blade of the hound out of her left hand, and he ate it out of his left hand. And he put it down on his left thigh, and the hand that took it was struck down, and the thigh he put it on was struck through and through, so that the strength that was in them before left them."[14]

As predicted by the banshee in the water, Cú Chulainn did not survive the battle, but his actual death is quite fascinating and deserves a quick mention here.

Cú Chulainn knew that his time in this world was over; the banshee has assured him of that. But behind him were his loyal warriors, brave men who looked to him for inspiration. If they saw him fall, it would dishearten them and probably lead to defeat. He knew that whatever happened, he could not let them see him go down.

Ahead of him, with spears and arrows and swords, was an equally large force of men charging his way. As much as the men behind him wanted to see him standing and fighting, the men coming toward him wanted to see his bloody body lying lifeless in the grass.

Giving an encouraging shout to his men, he performed his last great act of defiance.

Cú Chulainn stepped calmly up a hill to where an ancient standing stone stood. Everyone knew this was a sacred place, a place where spirits dwelled. He took his belt and tied himself securely with his back to the stone. Thus, when the inevitable happened, his men would not see his body touch the earth. The spiritual power in the ancient stone would possibly give him strength, and the belt would keep him standing—no matter what.

---

14. *Cuchulain of Muirthemne*, 336.

He heard the war cries, the bloodthirsty shouts, he could feel the ground shaking as they charged toward him. Battle rage overcame him; he slashed with his sword like a wild man. One by one the enemy fell. Blood dotted Cú Chulainn's face and clothes.

Arrows whizzed through the air, many lodging in his body. He paid them no mind. Spears pierced him, but despite the pain and the growing weakness, he would not stop. He could feel the strength draining out of him with the blood pouring from his many wounds, but he kept fighting. Ever more slowly, he slashed away at the spear tips as they were thrust at him.

Finally, he stopped. There was no more air; all went black. The end had come. With a defiant gaze, he looked up to the sky, to that single black bird flying overhead.

Then his head fell back against the stone. The great hero Cú Chulainn was dead—but still standing.

The enemy, frightened to death of this valiant warrior, could not tell if he was dead or just resting his head for a moment. They were hesitant to come too close, to dare to step over the dead bodies of their comrades into his range. Was he just catching his breath for a moment in the desperate battle … or was he truly dead?

But the goddess flying above in the shape of a crow, the sinister Morrigan, knew better. To demonstrate to the warriors that their opponent had truly fallen, she flew down and, in a mocking action, perched herself right on the shoulder of the dead man. With that, the forces knew they had accomplished the impossible: they had killed the hero.[15]

Morrigan had announced to Cú Chulainn before the battle that she would soon have her revenge on him for spurning her advance, that this would be his last battle. He knew what she had prophe-

---

15. *Cuchulain of Muirthemne*, 340.

sized. But despite her machinations, despite her victory, his dead body never touched the ground.

It is quite significant that his final act is to tie himself to a standing stone, a menhir. These stones are found throughout Europe and are always considered places of supernatural power, closely connected to fairies, and are often believed to be an entrance to the Otherworld. Should you have the good fortune to be in Ireland and you wish to visit the standing stone that Cú Chulainn tied himself to as he died, you will find it in County Louth. It is known as *Clochafarmore*, "Standing Stone," and is near Knockbridge.[16]

Morrigan

Once again, we see the washerwoman aspect of a pagan deity in the *Reicne Fothaird Canainne* from the ninth century.[17] This is, again, the dark goddess Morrigan, happily washing blood-soaked clothing and armor by a mass of gory entrails.

Of the pagan Irish goddesses, Morrigan is possibly the darkest and, in many ways, the most mysterious. Sometimes she is referred to simply as Morrigan, at other times she is *the* Morrigan. This is because she was actually three different goddesses: Nemain, who brought panic to warriors on the battlefield; Macha, who "revelled amidst the bodies of the slain"; and most significant to the banshee, the bloodthirsty Badb.[18] It was when these three goddesses were combined that they became one deity, the dreaded Morrigan.

Appearing as a black-haired woman, this tripartite goddess loved slaughter. She would take great delight in the carnage below as she flew around the battlefield in the form of a raven, crying out to encourage

---

16. *Irish Identity*, "Death-Place."
17. Lysaght, *Irish Death Messenger*, 199.
18. Hennessey, *Irish Goddess of War*.

the butchery. She was often accompanied by a flock of natural ravens, birds who would feast upon the corpses of the slain lying on the field after a great battle.

There are scholars who have tried to identify her with the Norse valkyries, who were also connected to birds and were quite fond of battle.[19]

The name in Old Irish was *Morrígan* (the Great or the Phantom Queen), quite possibly derived from *Mor*, a word translated as "phantom." It has been suggested that the word is from the same root as an Anglo-Saxon word *maere*, from which we derive the English word *nightmare*.[20]

In *Táin Bó Cúailgne* (*The Cattle Raid of Cooley*), two of the three goddesses who make up the Morrigan, Badb and Nermain, now as separate beings, let out a banshee screech for all of the men of Ireland. Everyone who hears it is filled with fear, and about a hundred of the men die of fright just from listening to the cry.[21]

Cormac

One of the members of this dark trio, the one most closely associated with the banshee, is the bloody war goddess Badb. In *The Hostel of Da Choca*, the hero Cormac encounters her by a river.

They were at a place called Druim Airthir, tending to their chariots. Suddenly they heard a curious sound in the water nearby. Going to look, they saw from a distance a strange woman clothed entirely in scarlet. She was standing in the river next to a chariot and was washing it, the cushions, and the horse's harnesses. However, whenever she pointed her hand down, the water in which she was standing

---

19. *Publications of the Modern Language Association of America*, 1–12.

20. Stokes, "Second Battle of Moytura," 128.

21. *Táin*, 239.

suddenly became crimson with blood. But when she raised her hand up, the water returned as it was.

With a smile, she then raised her hand up high. Through some strange magic, the water receded, and the forces of Cormac simply walked across.

Having crossed, Cormac and his companions began to discuss the strange thing they had seen, and how horrible the woman was. Some of the men were frightened of this omen. Everyone was asking what message this would portend.

Cormac called up a loyal messenger and told him to go to the lady and ask her what she was doing and why.

The messenger rushed off. After a while he came back with a frightened look on his face.

At the time he approached she was washing a harness, dripping blood in the water. The messenger asked her who she was and whose harness she was washing the blood from.

She replied that the harness she was washing was that of a king.

Cormac, seeing the effect this strange apparition was having on his men, marched to the stream himself. The woman was still there, still washing the harness, still standing in crimson water.

He demanded to know whose harness it was, what king did it belong to? She looked up at him from the water and said with an evil grin,

> *"This is thine own harness, O Cormac,*
> *And the harness of thy men of trust."* [22]

---

22. Stokes, *The Hostel of Da Choca.*

When the party reached the hostel of Da Choca, Badb appeared again to them, once again prophesying doom.

They watched her approach, now an old hag with long gray hair that drooped below her knees. She was dirty with soot and squinting with her left eye. Her cloak was quite worn and of a dark color.

The crone leaned against the doorpost and made a prophecy of death:

> "Sad will they be in the Hostel:
> bodies will be severed in bloods,
> Trunks will be headless,
> above the clay of Da Choca's Hostel." [23]

We find another of the Morrigan trio prophesying doom in *The Destruction of Dá Derga's Hostel.*

Conaire

It was after the sun had gone down. King Conaire and his men had settled in for the night when they suddenly heard a loud knocking at the door. The keeper of the hostel rushed forth as a woman's voice from outside demanded to be admitted.

The door was opened to reveal a foul-looking old hag with long gray hair that went to her knees. She leaned against the doorpost, neither inside of the building nor outside, and glared at the king and his young men, possibly casting the evil eye.

Conaire, however, was not frightened of her. He called out to her, stated that if she was a seer, which she certainly resembled, then what manner of prophecy did she have for them?

---

23. Stokes, *The Hostel of Da Choca.*

She replied to him right away, but did not give the answer they wanted to hear.

"'Truly I see for thee,' she answers, 'that neither fell nor flesh of thine shall escape from the place into which thou hast come, save what birds will bear away in their claws.'"[24]

The king was not at all happy with her divination and told her so. Angry, stating that he was not familiar with her, he demanded to know what her name was.

"'Cailb,'" came the simple reply.

He laughed at that, stating that it was hardly a name. But she hissed back that she had other names as well.

He wanted to hear them, and she immediately obliged.

"'Samon, Sinand, Seisclend, Sodb, Caill, Coll, Díchóem, Dichiúil, Díthím, Díchuimne, Dichruidne, Dairne, Dáríne, Déruaine, Egem, Agam, Ethamne, Gním, Cluiche, Cethardam, Níth, Némain, Nóennen, Badb, Blosc, B[l]oár, Huae, óe Aife la Sruth, Mache, Médé, Mod.'"[25]

Note that the names listed here include Badb as well as Némain and Mache. With all three names identifying a single entity, this is undoubtedly the one name she does not use: Morrigan.

The dark trinity of the goddess(es) Morrigan is reflected much later in the middle of the fourteenth century. Seán mac Ruaidhri Mac Craith, the hereditary historian, wrote *Caithréim Thoirdhealbhaigh* (*Triumphs of Torlough*). In it, he mentions a trio of banshees with rather interesting names.

The first of these is young and beautiful. She is known as the Sovereignty of Erin. Her two companions are old hags, Dismal and

24. Stokes, *Destruction of Dá Derga's Hostel*.

25. Stokes, *Destruction of Dá Derga's Hostel*.

Water Dismal. Dismal is also known as Bronach, or Hag of Black Head.[26]

Morrigan was not the only goddess to become a banshee after the arrival of Christianity. There are others, including one who is very famous as a death messenger.

---

26. Westropp, "A Folklore Survey," 187.

Chapter 2
FROM GODDESS TO BANSHEE

A shriek, that made us thrill as if our very hearts were pierced by it, burst from the hedge to the right of our way. If it resembled anything earthly it seemed the cry of a female, struck by a sudden and mortal blow, and giving out her life in one long deep pang of expiring agony.... the moon started suddenly from behind a cloud and enabled us to see, as plainly as I now see this paper, the figure of a tall thin woman, with uncovered head, and long hair that floated round her shoulders, attired in something which seemed either a loose white cloak or a sheet thrown hastily about her.

—Croker, Fairy Legends

One of the most powerful and beloved of the pagan Celtic goddesses, the nature deity Áine, later became the banshee for the Fitzgerald family.[27] This divinity was in charge of all the good stuff: summer, wealth, love, passion, and, of course, fertility. She is still said to reside in a fairy mound near Knockainey in County Limerick.[28]

Áine being the most beautiful of the Celtic pantheon, was, of course, married. Some say that her husband was the great sea god Manannán mac Lir. Other tales of their relationship have a more interesting soap opera twist.

According to the rather saucy version, Manannán mac Lir was married to someone else, a goddess whose name is not recorded. Áine's brother, Aillén, wanted to spend some quality time with Manannán's wife. The problem was convincing the great god of the sea to go somewhere else for a while.

Áine obliged her brother's lust and convinced Manannán to go on a little trip alone with her. The sea god was more than happy to agree; he made up a story and took the lovely Áine on an excursion to Tír Tairngire, a magnificent paradise translated as the "Land of Promise." While he was out playing around, his wife and Aillén were able to sneak away as well for a little paradise of their own.[29]

Áine also was said to have a lovely singing voice. Evans-Wentz mentions how, around 1700, the beautiful music of Thomas Connellan, a famous minstrel of his day, was repaid from the other side at his funeral. As the procession made its way toward New Church, the mourners heard the most wonderful singing from a woman. The people looked about, and to their surprise, standing on a nearby boulder, was a tall woman of angelic beauty. They knew from the old

27. Lysaght, *Pocket Book*, 21.

28. Lysaght, "Banshee Traditions," 94.

29. *Oxford Reference*, "Áine."

stories that this was none other than Áine herself. She was apparently saying farewell to a fellow musician.[30]

The area around Lough Gur is still frequented by the ancient goddess Áine. One of the many legends concerning her tells how a king in the eighth century, Ailill Olom, fell asleep on the sacred hill of Cnoc Áine as his people were engaged in celebrating the rites of Samhain. When he awakened, he had a frightening vision. He was alone on the fairy hill and, looking about, he saw a scene of desolation. All the grass in the area was gone.

Unable to understand this disturbing omen, he consulted a seer, Fergus mac Comáin. The two went up to the hill, where King Ailill Olom promptly decided once again that it was nap time. Fergus paid little mind to the snoring monarch but scurried behind some bushes and hid himself.

Later that evening, the goddess and the king of the fairies were seen strolling in the moonlight. The seer rushed out and, for some reason, murdered the fairy monarch. At the sound of this commotion, the human king awoke and saw Áine. Somehow forgetting where he was, he thought that the lovely maiden was a mortal, indeed the most alluring mortal woman he had ever seen. He just had to have her! Ailill rose from the ground and attacked her, raping her.

However, the former goddess, now fairy queen, had the last laugh. In the struggle, she managed to bite off one of his ears. This may seem insufficient given the outrage of the deed, but in that culture, it was extremely serious. To ensure the fertility of the land, no man could, by law, be an Irish king unless he was whole in body. By disfiguring him, and in a way that could not be hidden from his subjects, she had effectively robbed him of his kingship.[31]

---

30. Evans-Wentz, *Fairy Faith*, 81.

31. *Emerald Isle*, "Lough Gur."

This was not the only time she had an unwanted lover. There is a variation of the swan maiden legend featuring the former goddess Áine. An earl of Desmond was strolling by Lough Gur when, like Ailill Olom before him, he saw the most beautiful woman he had ever seen. She was sitting naked by the lough, combing her hair. Her rich clothing was lying next to her; obviously, she had been swimming.

Being an earl, he was used to having whatever he wanted, and right now, he wanted her. He approached her from behind, overpowered her, and started to have his way.

Surprisingly, she permitted him to proceed, but only after giving him a stern warning: a child would be born, the product of this union. It would be his responsibility to raise the child. But take heed: one day, the child would do something amazing—something impossible. When this happened, the earl must show no surprise or emotion at all.

He readily agreed to this condition, and, with the custody matters settled, continued with the business at hand. It was only later, as he made his way back to the castle, that he wondered what manner of devil contract he had entered into.

What she said came true. Nine months later, a beautiful woman, as pregnant as she could be, appeared, knocking on the door of the castle. There she gave birth to a son who was named Geréid ʻIarla. After giving birth, the woman left the castle.

The young man grew up to be handsome and wise, everything a father could hope for. All the maidens of the court had their eyes on him. But as the years passed, the earl was quietly waiting for the strange thing that he was not to show surprise at. It never came. Everything about the child seemed completely normal.

One night, by the time the earl had almost forgotten about the strange condition set by Áine, there was a fetching maiden who was a guest at a banquet. Probably as a way of gaining the attention of Geréid, she ran toward the banquet table and cleared it in one leap.

With the other guests cheering her feat, with a seductive smile on her face, she asked Geréid if he could do that. The youth grinned, said, "Hold my wine goblet." He then took an even greater leap than the maiden. He cleared the banquet table with no problem.

But it did not end there. Still flying through the air, Geréid impossibly landed inside a bottle. His whole body somehow went in, after which he immediately leaped out again!

Everyone in the banquet hall was ready to faint. His father stood up, speechless, his jaw wide open.

Geréid at once gave him an angry look. The young man declared that his father had broken the agreement with Áine as he had shown surprise at something remarkable he did. Without a word to anyone, he turned and walked out of the castle. Those who followed him watched from a safe distance as he made his way to Lough Gur. Once he arrived at the shore, without the slightest pause or even a last look around, he stepped into the lough. The instant his foot touched the water, he turned into a goose. With that, he flew out over the lough, no doubt on his way to join his mother.

There is an ending to the tale that both Áine and Geréid 'Iarla returned one more time to the castle, when the old earl was lying in his deathbed.[32] In some versions of the tale, Áine remains with the earl as his wife, but in typical swan maiden style, she leaves along with her son when he breaks the pact.[33]

Reverence for Áine survived long after the pagan gods had been vanquished. There remained for many years, well into the nineteenth

---

32. Fitzgerald, "Popular Tales," 186–188.

33. Squire, *Celtic Myth*.

century, the following yearly ritual, a tradition that obviously harkens back to the pre-Christian era.

The festivities would correspond to the feast day of St. John the Baptist, which occurs at the same time as the summer solstice. People would come from all about the countryside to take part.

Once assembled, they would be formed into ranks. The organizing of the participants was performed by an older man who had charge of the ceremony. The marchers were then given poles with burning hay atop.

These torches were then "carried in procession round the hill and the little moaî on the summit, Mullach-CrocdinIdmh-lé-leatf-an-Triâir (the hillock-top near the grave of the three)."[34]

What is most interesting is what happened after the parade. The participants, still holding the flaming torches, would run away in all directions, spreading the light of the torches through all the fields and by the cattle of the area. This ceremony was to bring good luck and prosperity, i.e., fertility to the fields and animals.

As the story goes, one year the man in charge of this ritual became very ill at the last minute. No one else knew how to organize the proceedings, so it was decided that they would simply not be able to enact them this year.

However, later that night, the villagers saw the torchlights on the hill just as usual. They also heard a woman's voice shouting orders to the participants. Apparently Áine herself was conducting the midsummer rite. The fertility goddess was making darn sure the crops would grow.

There is an extremely fascinating note to this. It is said that, should there be someone visiting the area, they were advised to look at where they were and relate that to the moon. If they failed to take

---

34. Fitzgerald, "Popular Tales," 186–189.

this precaution, they would soon become lost and may never be found again.[35]

This connection to the moon is rather puzzling, but as we shall see, the banshee is very hard to pin down. We know that she appears in one of two forms. The first is the manifestation most familiar to us today, the phantom woman who shrieks in the night to warn a family of an upcoming death. At other times, as we have seen in the saga of Cú Chulainn and in many other old tales, she's a washerwoman.

This grisly version of the banshee is usually an old hag kneeling by a stream, washing bloody clothes—or in older times, the armor—of a person destined for death. In this aspect, she is sometimes referred to as the "Washer at the Ford."[36]

Clotha

One goddess who performed this washing activity with great delight was a very dark and little-known deity called Clotha, or Sile na Gig. She was, as strange as it seems, a fertility deity, although she also had a lust for battle. She brought life and, at the same time, was very helpful in taking it away. She would not only wash the bloody clothing in the water, but it is said that she also spent many a happy day sewing burial shrouds.[37] Some believe that River Clyde in Scotland takes its name from this dark deity.[38]

Aoibheall

Another pagan goddess who was later turned into a banshee is the goddess Aoibheall (also known as Aibhill or Aibhinn) in County

---

35. Fitzgerald, "Popular Tales," 186–189.

36. Lysaght, *Irish Death Messenger*, 197.

37. Wells, "Some Irish Vampires."

38. Curran, *Mysterious Celtic*, 276.

Clare: "The ancestors of the Dalcassians may have worshipped Aibhinn on her holy hill, and her equally lovely sister Aine, crowned with meadowsweet, on the tamer mound of Knockaney." [39]

Aoibheall was said to control the weather and, interestingly, possessed a magic harp. This harp, the instrument sometimes played by banshees, was said to have a dark power: anyone who heard its sound would soon die. Taking it a bit forward, it is now said that anyone who hears the instrument being played in the night will suffer a death in the family.

Aibhinn is sometimes considered to be the queen of the banshees. She has been observed with twenty-five other banshees in attendance, all washing bloody clothes in a lake in the Inchiquin district of County Clare. [40]

She is, or rather was, found in the rock Crag Liath (Craglea). I say "was" as some state that she left the neighborhood in anger when the people cut down all the trees in the vicinity. Fairies are spirits connected to nature, not highways and strip malls.

The Coming of Christianity

These were only a few of the deities worshipped by the Irish Celts, but despite this rich heritage, things were destined to change. By the fifth century, the ways of the old gods were being steadily superseded by the foreign religion of Christianity. Indeed, there was a small Christian presence in Ireland as early as the third century—no doubt from slaves captured in Roman Britain. Their masters didn't care who they prayed to, just so long as they did their work.

39. Westropp, "A Folklore Survey," 187.
40. Westropp, "A Folklore Survey," 187.

But slavery always carries within it the seeds of societal destruction. In this case, the vile practice resulted in the uprooting of an entire religious system.

Things changed completely in the fifth century. In 430, Pope Celestine sent Palladius, a bishop in Britain, to Ireland to convert the pagans to Christ. He was as much help as a fan in a hurricane, as he returned to Britain having accomplished very little.

Sometimes God works through the Church, and sometimes God works in spite of the Church. What a high and mighty British bishop could not do was soon accomplished by an escaped slave.

Patrick was a Christian Englishman who had been captured by Irish pirates and sold into slavery. One day, while tending his master's flocks, he received a vision from God. In it, he was told that he was to escape from his bondage, go back to Britain, but then return to bring Christ to the Emerald Isle. Although this command would put him in great peril, Patrick did not hesitate to follow it.

Miraculously, he managed to convert much of Ireland, vanquish the old gods, and in the process he gave all the snakes an eviction notice. (In truth, there were no snakes in Ireland.) This ecclesiastical accomplishment is celebrated in America every March 17 by raising a mug of green beer.

He was not alone in his zeal. The work of St. Patrick was taken up by numerous missionaries, including the beloved St. Brigid.[41]

But what of the old gods? The common people of Ireland had lived their lives as their parents and their grandparents many generations back had: by worshipping Lugh, Manannán mac Lir, Crom Cruach, Áine, Brigid, and, with a fearful eye, the Morrigan. Could this new God possibly take the place of all these deities so loved and feared by the common people?

---

41. Ganley, "Medieval Ireland."

Survival of the Celtic Pantheon

As had happened in countless other parts of the world, the answer is yes—but conditionally. In truth, the old gods of Ireland never really left. They retreated into the mounds and have been there ever since. While a passionate Christian missionary may be convincing the king at a banquet to adopt the new faith (often, the monarch would agree to this for political reasons and alliances), the common farmer laboring in the fields, dependent on the whims of weather and nature, would often continue to practice the old ways.

Bit by bit, generation after generation, the old belief system faded—but it never completely disappeared. The once powerful deities with grand tales now became fairies. Remnants of the old ways, as we see in the midsummer ritual on Mullach-CrocdinIdmh-lé-leatf-an-Triâir, lingered on in what Evans-Wentz called the fairy faith.

Mortal dealings with the former gods and tutelary spirits have created some of the most beloved literature of all time, the Irish folk and fairy tales. There are countless exciting and sometimes humorous narratives of people dealing with the dwellers in the fairy mounds that dot the Irish landscape.

As in the pages of such works as the Welsh *Mabinogion* and other literary pieces from ancient times, if one looks closely enough, the reader can see the faces of the old gods peeking out between the pages. For example, in the tale of "Pwyll Prince of Dyfed," the *tylwyth teg* (fairy) Rhiannon is none other than the Celtic horse goddess Epona. Her second husband, Manawydan, is a Christianized version of the powerful sea god Manannán mac Lir. Even the mysterious horned nature deity Cernunnos makes a guest appearance in this cryptic work.

As we shall see in the next chapter, the most literal translation of the word *banshee* is "woman of the mound." Despite the new faith ruling the Emerald Isle, these women of the mound were still around.

Battle of Clontarf

Whether Christian or pagan, there were still bloody battles to be fought, and the old goddesses would often be there predicting death and bloodshed. Aoibheall made an appearance in one of the most famous battles ever fought on Irish soil. In 1014, the Irish, led by Brian Boru, were ready to face an overwhelming Viking army at the Battle of Clontarf, a place near Lough Derg near the rock Crag Liath—the traditional dwelling place of the goddess Aoibheall. This sacred area was soon to gain the bloody title "where shields were cleft."[42]

The night before the battle, the ancient goddess, now a banshee, appeared to the Christian king Boru and told him he was going to die the next day. Also fated to die were his son and even his grandson. All those mentioned in her grim prophecy did indeed die, as did the Viking leaders Sigurd and Brodir.[43] As it turns out, the next day was Good Friday, a propitious time for Christians to do battle against heathens.

In the midst of fighting, as the battle raged outside, the elderly Boru was in his tent on his knees in solemn prayer, preparing to rise and go out to join the fray. A messenger rushed in to inform him that his son's standard had apparently fallen. Perhaps they should retreat?

Boru rose slowly and replied in a calm voice, "Oh, God! Thou boy, retreat becomes us not, and I myself know that I shall not depart

---

42. Westropp, "A Folklore Survey," 186.

43. History Ireland, "Battle of Clontarf."

alive, for Aibhill of Crag Liath came to me last night, and she told me that I should be killed today."[44]

It is said that Brian Boru did not rush out with sword in hand, but as a Christian king, he remained in his tent on his knees in prayer. The banshee had declared that he was to die, and there was nothing he could do to stop it. He decided that his last minutes on earth would be spent not in killing, but rather, in prayer for victory over a heathen enemy.

Thus, it was there, as he was praying in his tent on Good Friday, that he was slain by Viking warriors loyal to Sigurd of Orkney. The Irish forces prevailed as they held the field, but both sides were trapped by a high tide.[45]

An entity described as Aibell, sometimes rendered as *Eevin*, also appeared to the mighty Irish warrior Dunlang O'Hartigan before that same battle of Clontarf. She presented to him a *fe-fiada*, a mantle that would render him invisible. He used this powerful device to great success in the fight. But he felt that it was cowardly for him to use such a magical advantage and threw it away. Now visible to his enemies, Dunlang was slain soon thereafter.[46]

Centuries later, Aibell was seen once sitting on a stile. The witness, a man driving a coach, stated that she was quite small, had very long hair, and was dressed in a red cloak.[47]

Lough Rasg

Among the deities to take shelter in the fairy mounds is the bloody goddess Badb, one third of the battle-loving Morrigan. Thus, it

44. Westropp, "A Folklore Survey," 186.

45. O'Hart, "Battle of Clontarf."

46. Joyce, "Irish Sorcerers."

47. Neligan and Seymour, *True Irish Ghost Stories*, 199.

comes as no surprise that one of the many names for the banshee is *badhbh*.

Amid the Anglo-Norman wars, in 1317, Badb was up to her old tricks, appearing to Donogh O'Brien at Lough Rasg. The narrative shows the banshee in her most hideous form.

The ghastly description of the banshee is a classic portrayal of a wicked witch from a fairy tale. Every feature of her body was distorted and marred, made as disgusting as possible.

The creature's forehead was a mass of bumps. Her disheveled hair was said to be reddish, but mixed with gray. Her eyebrows were the same color, but also described as being like fishhooks. These sat above two evil eyes, both said to be as red as berries. These evil eyes were, naturally, glowing like a fire. Her nose was said to be a vile shade of bluish green, with nostrils such as on a wild beast. Her mouth was extremely wide, with the upper lip turned upward toward the oversized teal-colored nose. A handkerchief was in order as from this nose "a copious stream flowed down her furrowed face."[48] Her tongue was pointed like a spear, but like a serpent's was darting in and out.

Of course, the most grotesque feature was an attribute known on every elementary school playground: "She had two long slender and sharp and green-coloured teeth in her head, which were never cleansed since the day of her birth."[49]

She was, in true banshee style, standing in the water, busy washing. Her laundry consisted of human skin, heads, bones, and other body parts. Floating in the liquid gore, the water had been stained deep crimson, and masses of human hair congealed like scum on the surface.

---

48. Clare County Library, "Ordnance Survey Letters."
49. Clare County Library, "Ordnance Survey Letters."

To keep his men from panicking, the king himself walked toward her and demanded to know her name and from what tribe she came.

She identified herself as Bronach of Burren, and her tribe was the Tuatha Dé Danann. In other words, she was a denizen of the fairy kingdom.

He then asked her about the bloody heads she was washing in the stream, demanding to know whose they were.

With an evil cackle she replied, "'Yours are the heads which I have here in a litter, and thine own, O Fair King! in the very centre of them! For though thou carriest it, it is not thine own, and though proud your march to the field of contest, soon shall ye all perish with the exception of very few.'"[50]

Needless to say, this was rather bad for morale, so the commander returned to his men and quickly dismissed it: "'Heed not the flowing prediction of the dire sprite' said Donogh to his brave hosts 'for she is only a friendly Bádabh to the lordly Clann of Torlogh, who is endeavouring to strike dismay into your minds by pretended predictions of your deaths. Wherefore my nobles, be not terrified, but proceed on your undertaken journey with firmness and valour to meet your enemies.'"[51]

They did—and her prediction proved to be true. He did indeed perish at the battle fought near the Abbey of Corcomroe, at a place now known as the Hill of the Gallows.[52]

This particular banshee has been reported many times in the district, and is sometimes referred to as *Caileach Cinn Boirne*, the aforementioned Hag of Blackhead.

---

50. Clare County Library, "Ordnance Survey Letters."

51. Clare County Library, "Ordnance Survey Letters."

52. *The Illustrated Dublin Journal*, "Corcomroe Abbey."

The very next year, the Norman Wars were still in full swing. The Anglo-Norman commander Richard de Clare was in a campaign against Conchobhar Ó Deághaidh, chief of the Cineal Fearmaic—but his true encounter would be with a banshee.[53]

He and his army were crossing River Fergus when they saw her. The banshee was again an old hag. She introduced herself as *dobar-brónach*, which means "the water-dismal one." She was washing armor stained with fresh blood, a certain sign that de Clare and his sons were destined to die in the upcoming battle.[54]

Like Donogh O'Brien, he tried to convince his men that this was a trick to frighten them. Once again, the banshee was absolutely correct.

The washerwoman banshee was seen again before the Battle of Aughrim in 1691, during the Williamite Wars. She was seen twice: first, washing the bloody clothes while situated underneath a bridge; second, crying out in a bog near the battlefield.[55]

Battle of the Boyne

In 1690, the exiled King James II, trying to regain the English throne now occupied by King William III, made alliances with both the Irish and the French. This resulted in the bloody conflict known as Battle of the Boyne, along River Boyne in County Meath.[56]

On the night before the battle, a banshee was seen on the battlefield.

One of the soldiers was on the field. He suddenly noticed there was someone else near him. Ready to raise his weapon, he saw that it was not an enemy soldier, but a beautiful woman.

---

53. Simms, "The Battle of Dysert O'Dea."
54. Lysaght, *Irish Death Messenger*, 200.
55. Lysaght, *Irish Death Messenger*, 398.
56. National Army Museum, "Battle of the Boyne."

She was quite different from the banshee that appeared to Donogh O'Brien before the bloody battle at Lough Rasg. This was "a woman, swathed from head to foot in a mantle of some dark flowing material … her mantle looked costly, and her hair—of a marvelous golden hue—though hanging loose on her shoulders, was evidently well cared for … Its beauty electrified him. Her cheeks were as white as marble, but her features were perfect, and her eyes the most lovely he had ever seen."[57]

Of course, he wondered who the heck she was, but quickly figured that she was either a relative or a special female friend of one of the nobles. It was best not to interfere.

But things became stranger. He saw she was jerking about. Was she laughing? There didn't seem to be anything to laugh about the night before a battle.

But no, she was not laughing; she was weeping. He was about to ask her if he could help her when one of the other sentries shouted out to him, asking what the heck he was doing standing there staring off into space.

He turned around to look at the guard. Obviously, the man had not been able to see the woman. He turned back to the lady, but she was starting to melt away before his eyes. In a moment she had vanished altogether.

The truth was apparent: there was no doubt she was a banshee.

He saw the banshee a second time that night, bending over a handsome young man with curly hair. In the next day's fighting, that same boy died.[58]

Amidst the madness of the Napoleonic Wars, there was the report of multiple banshees being heard in the English camp before

---

57. O'Donnell, *The Banshee*, 125–126.

58. O'Donnell, *The Banshee*, 125–126.

the fighting. The commander was amazed, as he did not believe he had any Irish soldiers. He asked his aides, who assured him there were quite a few young Irishmen ready to shed their blood to defeat Napoleon's older brother, Joseph Bonaparte. Many of the Irish soldiers died in the fighting. The battle, for all its waste of young men's lives, did not present a clear-cut victor.[59]

Although not as common as the wailing banshee, this washerwoman manifestation has continued, particularly in the region in and around County Galway. The banshee will always find a stream or river near the home of the person they are washing the grave clothes of.[60]

In County Clare, there is a small river known locally as the Daelach, or the Banshee's Brook. The water is often red. While scientists state that it is because of iron, many people believe that it is from the banshee washing the bloody clothes of those destined to perish violently.[61]

We have followed her across battlefields and in streams, stained scarlet from her washing. But what, exactly, is this strange entity known as the banshee? Once a powerful goddess, she is now a dark messenger of death, the one who summons us to the grave. Let us get to know her a bit better.

59. O'Donnell, *The Banshee*, 128–130.

60. Lysaght, *Pocket Book*, 61.

61. Westropp, "A Folklore Survey," 191.

Chapter 3
THE WOMEN
OF THE MOUND

Wail no more, lonely one, mother of exiles,
*   wail no more,*
Banshee of the world—no more!
The sorrows are the world's, though art no
*   more alone;*
Thy wrongs, the world's.

—Todhunter, "The Banshee"

Perhaps the first question to be answered when examining the lore surrounding this uncanny spirit is this: What exactly is the name of this specter? The most correct rendering of the word in traditional Irish would be *an bhean sí*, or in some parts of the Emerald Isle, *badhb*.[62] However, as with everything connected to this entity, this is just the beginning of a very confusing trail.

We also find her referred to as the *bean chaointe* and *bean chaointe*, undoubtedly a variation of *bean chaoint*, which designates not a ghost, but a keening woman, a professional mourner.[63]

The connection to the ancient war goddess Badb is seen in a name from southeast Ireland, *badbanshee*. In this form, she is often described as having long golden hair flowing down her back.[64]

Professor James MacKillop has collected a number of variations of the name of this entity in his article "Politics and Spelling Irish, or Thirteen Ways of Looking at 'Banshee'" published in *The Canadian Journal of Irish Studies* in 1991.

Among his findings are a few from old Irish, including *ben side* and *ban side*, as well as a more Scottish *ben síth*. In unreformed Modern Irish, we find *bean sídhe*, sometimes combined into one word as *beansídhe*. In Scotland we find *bean sith*, *bean-shith*, and *ban-sith*. He does not mention the term most often used by folklorists: *caointeach* or *bean nighidh*.

Located between the two lands in the middle of the Irish Sea, we find the marvelous Isle of Man. Stories tell us that it was once an enchanted island. It may be true, as it is certainly rich with legends of fairies and the supernatural, including the wailing death messenger. Here, the word he records for this dark entity is *ben shee*.

---

62. Lysaght, *Irish Death Messenger*, 15.

63. Lysaght, *Irish Death Messenger*, 29, 33.

64. Lysaght, *Pocket Book*, 37.

Finally, Professor MacKillop proceeds to English, from which he relates what is essentially a pronunciation spelling: *banshee* or *banshie*.

It all becomes very complicated. You have no doubt noticed that all these titles are quite similar with just minor variations. It would be best for us to break them down to their two components.

The *ban* or *bean* refers to a woman. The *si*, *shith*, *sidhe*, or *shee* means "a mound," in this case, a fairy mound. Thus, the meaning of the many variations of this creature's name can be rendered as "the woman of the mound." This can be a bit confusing; the word *sidhe* with its variants refers specifically to a fairy mound, supposedly the entrance to their underground palaces. A simple mound, say a common mound of dirt, would be translated as *dumha salachar*.

If there is one thing everyone can agree upon, no matter what spelling one chooses, it is that this *baen-sidhe*, the "woman of the mound," is a spirit who announces death. In this office she is contrasted to her opposite, the *leanan-sidhe* (fairy lover), a spirit of fertility who brings life.[65]

And just to make certain that everything is as confusing as possible, Keegan in his 1839 article suggested that the word comes from *bawn shee*, which, by his reasoning, would mean "white fairy."[66]

Now, before proceeding any further, we must choose which of this multitude of terms we will be using. In this study, as it is the most familiar to readers, we will generally use the phonetic term (which admittedly is the worst of the litter): *banshee*.

What Is She?

With that settled, we must ask the most important question of all: What exactly is the banshee? Is it a fairy, as the connection to the

---

65. Wilde, *Ancient Legends*, 135.

66. Keegan, "Legends and Tales," 368.

mound certainly implies? Or is she the ghost of a human woman, once alive in a physical form, but for some reason now doomed forever to follow certain families and announce death and sorrow?

As we shall see, once again the answer is not so clear. We have seen in the previous chapter examples of the ancient goddess turned into fairies who performed the office of a banshee. We shall soon see mortal women who have taken on the same mantle after their death. Some perform this task out of love and devotion for their family. Others take a sadistic delight in their grim announcement, seeking eternal vengeance on the descendants of someone who had done them a terrible wrong centuries ago.

Keening

To properly understand the banshee with her nocturnal death cry, we must pause for a moment and take a quick look at a dying piece of folk tradition in Ireland: keening.

This is the practice of hiring professional mourners at a funeral. These women would begin by singing songs of lament. Eventually, this would erupt into loud crying, wailing, clapping their hands, pulling their hair, and other theatrics. This curious practice was not exclusive to Ireland, but was, and in some cases still is, practiced in different parts of the world. It is mentioned in the bible (Jeremiah 9:10–11; Judges 11:38, etc.), is practiced in the Middle East, and was part of the culture of ancient Rome.

The act of keening is traditionally referred to in the Irish language as *caoineadh*, or sometimes *caoine*. It is now suggested that the original word in ancient Irish was actually *cine*, quite similar to the Hebrew term *cina*.[67]

---

67. *The Keening Wake*, "The Keening Tradition."

The practice, as would be expected, was extremely ritualized. When done in its full glory, there would be at least four keeners, two at the head of the coffin and two at the feet. The head keener would begin with a low song, sometimes accompanied by a harp. From there, the cries of the other women joining in would become a wild and sorrowful performance. The person who was in the coffin would be asked a series of questions as to why they died.

The keening would take place at the wake, on the way to the cemetery, and sometimes even at the side of the grave. Notice that the keening would cease when the body entered the church.

The Roman Catholic Church in Ireland strongly discouraged this ancient practice—discouraged, but did not forbid it. Their objection was quite reasonable. It was not because of the racket the women were making, but because these mourners were paid and sometimes had little or no connection to the deceased. The funeral was a sacred process that should have been emotional and spiritual, not commercial. In short, while being dramatic, keening was not genuine. It was the belief of the Church that it would be far better for a single tear to roll down the cheek of a truly sorrowful person than to have all the wailing and hand-clapping theatrics of the professional keeners, who may not have ever met the person they were crying for.

Certain wealthy families had their own keeners, a sign of status. Thus, possessing such a troupe was, in truth, pure vanity. Some of the professional mourners feared that, after death, they would return to the family they had served during their life and continue their curious profession as a banshee. They would thus be forever bound to the wealthy family that supported them in life.[68]

Partrick Johnston of County Westmeath was the son of a woman who made her living as a keener. Although she was quite good at

---

68. Lysaght, *Irish Death Messenger*, 50.

her profession, she secretly detested the job. The spiritual dangers were evident to her, as she often stated that she hoped she would not become a banshee after she died.

In County Waterford, it was believed that one did not become a banshee for being a good keener, but rather, for being a bad one. Those who neglected their duties or did not put forth a good effort were punished after death by becoming the dark messenger.[69]

But times are changing. The professional mourners of old are dying off and even the people who remember hearing them are disappearing as well. Today, the curious practice of keening has been relegated to the dominion of the folklorist. Thankfully, some of it has been preserved as part of the Irish cultural heritage. There are a few recordings of traditional Irish keening; an interesting example of traditional keening is found at "Six authentic recordings of keening from Ireland and Scotland (1955–1965)" on the YouTube channel The Folk Revival Project.[70]

In modern Ireland, the old custom has largely disappeared. However, we see a ghostly echo of this practice in the wailing of the banshee. As mentioned earlier, the mortal keening woman known as the *bean chaoint* is closely related to the banshee, who sometimes is referred to as the *bean chaoínte*.

Family Connections

Returning to our supernatural keeners, one interesting feature of the banshee of old Erin is that she is Irish through and through. If you are wondering, when it is your time to leave this world, if a banshee will come to wail for you … well, your last name had better be Irish. She will not keen for anyone who is not of pure Milesian—that is, old Irish—stock. There is a famous poem that seems to be the creed of this specter:

By Mac and O, you'll always know
True Irishmen, they say;
But if they lack
Both O and Mac
No Irishmen are they.

There was an instance recorded in 1936 in the city of Dingle, County Kerry. In the middle of the night, the residents were awakened by the horrific wailing of a woman, the sound going up and down the street. They knew immediately that it was the banshee they were hearing, and of course, everyone was terrified that the specter was lamenting to foretell their own death. As it turned out, they had nothing to worry about. The keening stopped abruptly and they heard the ghostly voice of a woman scolding them, saying that she would not bother to cry for the likes of them! She was there for the Hussey family. Just as she predicted, one of that old family was found dead by the time the sun came up.[71]

These select families have one particular banshee who follows them. In some cases, we know the names of these death messengers.

The old goddess Áine is associated with the Fitzgerald family, but her name also crops up as being connected to the O'Corra clan. Another goddess, Aoibhell, is connected to the Dal-gCais of Munster. Cliodhna wails for the MacCarthys and a few others. The O'Carrolls have a banshee named Una.[72]

---

71. Lysaght, *Irish Death Messenger*, 59.
72. Wood-Martin, *Traces of the Elder Faiths*, 364.

A small sample of other Irish families that have the services of a banshee includes those with the name of Barrett, Bradley, Caldwell, Cartwright, Cody, Cole, Conway, Cox, O'Daly, Devereaux, Doyle, Finnegan, Gallagher, Graham, Hussey, Jordan, Lawless, Lynch, Monoghan, Murphy, MacIntyre, O'Donnell, O'Neill, Ryan, Sheridan, Walsh, Westropp, and many, many more.[73]

Even if the Irish leave their beloved homeland to emigrate to another country, and then to fit in with their new neighbors drop the O or the *Mac* from their last names, this will have no effect upon their family's supernatural follower. The banshee always knows her own and will still wail for them as if they had not changed their name.[74]

One curious exception to this rule is the Lyons family residing in County Limerick. They somehow merited a banshee, even though the family was of English descent.[75]

Lady Fanshawe

Possibly the most famous banshee encounter is the one involving Lady Fanshawe, a case in which the banshee is both seen and heard.

The lady was visiting the home of a man who was the leader of a *sept*, an old Irish word referring to a family. This home was a medieval castle that even included the traditional moat.

After an enjoyable evening, she retired to bed. However, her rest was not to be pleasant that evening.

In the midst of the night, she was startled awake by the most horrible screaming. She looked about. She felt the screaming was very close, but obviously there was no one in her room.

73. Lysaght, *Irish Death Messenger*, 261–280. Entire list is found here.

74. Lysaght, *Irish Death Messenger*, 58.

75. Lysaght, "Banshee Traditions," 111.

She looked to the window and received quite a shock: there was a strange woman floating in the night air staring through the window at her. Lady Fanshawe described the entity in minute detail: "A female face and part of the form hovering at the window … The face was that of a young and rather handsome woman, but pale, and the hair, which was reddish, loose and dishevelled. The dress … was that of the ancient Irish."[76]

This Irish woman with uncombed copper-colored hair could not have been standing on anything, but she was hovering in the air like a balloon. The window was too high up, and there was the old moat besides.

The apparition stared in, seemingly as curious about the lady inside as the lady was about the woman floating outside her window. The ghostly maiden then pulled back a bit from the window and simply vanished into the night. But as she did, there were two more screams, exactly like the ones that had woken Lady Fanshawe in the first place. This made for a total of three screams in all.

The next morning Lady Fanshawe went downstairs to breakfast—and to get some answers to the mysterious happenings of the night before.

Her host had a sad look on his face as he confessed the truth. As she had arrived the night before, the family went to lengths to conceal the fact that a member of the family was in another part of the castle, and not expected to live much longer. To reveal this would most certainly have caused her to excuse herself from their hospitality in the time when their attention should have been devoted to the dying person.

---

76. Croker, *Fairy Legends*, 132.

Of course, they did not know that the person was going to die that very evening. Then came the sound that she had heard and the face she had seen floating in the air outside her window.

It was the family banshee.

The most astonishing part of the discussion came when the host described how this woman Lady Fanshawe had seen had become the banshee: "She is believed to be the spirit of a woman of inferior rank, who one of my ancestors degraded himself by marrying, and who afterwards, to expiate the dishonour done to his family, he caused to be drowned in the Castle Moat."[77]

We shall see this scenario again and again throughout Ireland and the rest of Europe, this sad story of the spurned woman of lower class having been seduced by a young man of noble birth sowing his wild oats. This one is unique in that the young man fulfilled his moral obligations by marrying the woman, but his family believed that in so doing he had "degraded" himself. He tried to erase the "dishonour" by drowning his young wife. One would think that murder would be a bit more dishonorable than marrying beneath your station! Of course, they had no idea that the ghost of the young lady would forgo to leave the family.

The young woman may have become a banshee, but the humans about her were devils.

Banshees and Their Irish Families

The family banshee is as loyal as a hound and completely nonjudgmental. Once attached, the spirit remains with its family, no matter where they travel to, and no matter what the station of society they occupy: "Although, through misfortune, a family may be brought down from high estate to the rank of peasant tenants, the Banshee

77. Croker, *Fairy Legends*, 132.

never leaves nor forgets it till the last member has been gathered to his fathers in the churchyard."[78]

Thus, while attached to prominent families, some banshees are not in the least bit impressed with social standing. As Thomas Westropp recorded:

"Mr. Casey of Ruan heard a banshee cry at the death of his father. The late Dr. MacNamara of Corofin was similarly honoured; indeed, when his family lived at Ballymarkahan, near Quin, there were numerous 'authentic instances' recorded. The Corofin banshees, however, did not lag behind the age by maintaining aristocratic prejudices, for one, at least, used to sit near the cross road leading to the workhouse and foretell the deaths of the poor inmates."[79]

Elliot O'Donnell had a sharp word for those foreigners who understandably wanted to pass themselves off as true Irish, but were not. While you may fool some people, you can't fool the woman of the mound. "Such a pretense, however, does not deceive those who are really Irish, neither does it deceive the Banshee, and the latter, I am quite sure, would never be persuaded to follow the fortunes of any Anglo-Saxon, or Scotch, Dick, Tom, or Harry, no matter how clever and convincing their camouflage might be."[80]

Clíona

Banshees are always connected not just to certain pure Irish families, but also to certain locations. They have fairy mounds or great stones where they reside between their forays into the mortal world. The McCarthy clan, for example, has a family banshee known as Clíona. If you wish to pay her a visit, she is said to make her dwelling in a

---

78. Dyer, *Ghost World*, 275.

79. Westropp, "A Folklore Survey," 191.

80. O'Donnell, *The Banshee*, 13.

magnificent palace hidden beneath the great rock *Carraig Chlíona* in County Cork.

Clíona has quite a bit of mythology and history behind her. As with most of the famous banshees, she was once a goddess, indeed the daughter, of the great sea god Manannán mac Lir.

She had two great passions. She would bestow the gift of inspiration on poets, and she would seduce desirable young men. Throughout the ages, she compiled a large collection of living young men as lover's conquests.

Once, when she was madly in love, she defied her father and stole away from the abode of the gods to elope with an especially attractive young fellow. She did not think this through—the two attempted their escape in a boat, somehow forgetting that her father was the god of the sea. A great wave capsized the boat, thus putting an abrupt end to the romance.

Caitlin and Clíona

Perhaps the most interesting of the many medieval tales regarding her overzealous romantic pursuits concerns a youth named Seán. He was at an engagement party for the Fitzgerald clan. He was astounding the ladies with his good looks and dancing skills when he suddenly collapsed to the floor. The people rushed up to help him, but he was apparently dead.

One of the ladies, Caitlin Óg Ceitinn, who was hopelessly in love with him, was not convinced of his untimely demise. She figured, rightly so, that Clíona had wanted him, and had spirited him away to the Otherworld so that she could have him all to herself.

Caitlin, although just a mortal girl, ran as fast as she could to *Carraig Chlíona*. She stood at the base of the massive boulder in the moonlight and loudly demanded the return of the man she loved. She then, in grand Irish style, began to wail her complaint in the form of fine poetry.

This was a challenge that could not be ignored. Clíona, from her palace beneath the stone, answered her, also in poetry, and in the exact same meter.

Caitlin, with her Irish temper, knew the contest was on. Thus did the struggle begin. For hours, the mortal woman and the lustful goddess traded barbs, all in exquisite poetry, never once changing the meter.

As this was apparently not working, Caitlin pulled out the ace card. Okay, if the goddess wanted him so badly, she could have him … but as tradition dictated, Clíona now had to pay her a dowry. The price she demanded was considerable.

This brought the poetry contest to a panicked stop. Clíona thought to herself, *Yeah, the guy is hot and all, but if this is going to cost me money …*

Apparently he was not in the budget. In an instant, Seán was standing in front of Caitlin.[81]

Clíona's banshee activities include a rather nontraditional form of death messaging. In the harbor of Glandore, close to the village of Skibbereen, in County Cork, there is on rare occasions a thundering, bestial roar heard among the rocky crags and oceanside caves. Whenever this happens, people know one of the kings of southern Ireland is about to die. This phenomenon is called *Tonn Cleena*, or Cleena's Wave.[82]

---

81. Daly, "The Legend of Clíona."
82. Wood-Martin, *Traces of the Elder Faiths*, 371.

Mary Anne and Sheridan Le Fanu

There is the case from the countryside of County Sligo of a young man calmly talking to an older man. As they passed the time, they heard a wailing sound rush down the road and settle at the house where they knew a woman, Mary Anne, was lying extremely ill. The sound remained at the house, moving about, going around the building a few times and even over the top. After a few moments, all became calm again.

The young man was quite frightened, but the older knew better. He sadly said that it looked like poor Mary Anne would leave this world very soon. When asked how he knew, he replied that Mary Anne's maiden name had been Flynn. Since as long as anyone could remember, a banshee had followed the Flynn family.

Of course, he was absolutely correct. Mary Anne died that very evening.[83]

Although it may seem a bit bizarre, having a family banshee gives the members of that clan certain bragging rights. A case of this was related by the niece of the great horror writer Sheridan Le Fanu.

"Miss Elizabeth Sheridan … firmly maintained that the Banshee of the Sheridan family was heard wailing before the news arrived from France of Mrs. Frances Sheridan's death at Blois … A niece of Miss Sheridan's made her very angry by observing, that as Mrs. Frances Sheridan was by birth a Chamberlaine, a family of English extraction, she had no right to the guardianship of an Irish fairy, and that therefore the Banshee must have made a mistake!"[84]

One may feel free to insert a "meow" after that last statement.

It should also be noted that on one occasion, the former goddess Aibhill, who was connected so closely to the O'Brien clan, was heard

83. Lysaght, *Pocket Book*, 31.
84. Croker, *Fairy Legends*, 131.

wailing in County Galway for a person of English descent with an English name.[85]

Musicians

The one major exception to the old Irish family rule is the case of those skilled in music.[86] One famous example of this was from the eighteenth century.

Charles Bunworth, whose name was certainly not an *O* or a *Mac*, was the rector of the Church of Ireland, in Buttevant, County Cork. He was a kind and generous man, beloved by the community.

His one great passion in life was the Irish harp. He played it well himself, collected rare harps from old times, and, most importantly, gave food and lodging to traveling harpists as they made their way around Ireland. These people never had much money and would often find themselves sleeping in fields or, if they were lucky, in a farmer's barn. They depended on the generosity of people for food and shelter.

One person they knew they could always depend on was Reverend Bunworth. Not only would they have a good meal, a little something for the road the next morning, and a warm bed, they would also be able to spend the night talking by the fire, passing along their secrets of the harp to an eager student who shared their passion.

Such was Bunworth's love for this instrument that, no less than five times, he was chosen to be the president of the local *cúirt éigse* (meeting of the bards).

In 1772, the old rector became ill, and soon it was obvious that he was not long for this world. It was then that there were appearances of the banshee.

85. Neligan and Seymour, *True Irish Ghost Stories*, 199.
86. Wilde, *Ancient Legends*, 135.

The first occasion was a week before he died. There was a curious sound in the hallway, described as the shearing of a sheep. Of course, no one would shear a sheep in the rectory hallway. When the servants and family went to investigate, there was nothing there.

Then his health became worse, and it was obvious the old harpist was soon to go on to his final performance. A group of men who had known and loved him were in his bedroom that night. A small group of relatives and friends was sitting in a parlor close to the open door of the bedroom. Prayers had been said, idle conversation was not appropriate. The group sat there in silence; a few fingers went silently through the rosary beads. Beyond that, all was quiet and solemn.

Then there was a curious noise. Just outside the window was a large rosebush. It had grown so much that it brushed up against the window. Now there was the sound of it being pulled away. Then they heard it: "A low moaning was heard, accompanied by clapping of hands, as if of a female in deep affliction. It seemed as if the sound proceeded from a person holding her mouth close to the window."[87]

The woman who was sitting with Mr. Bunworth suddenly rushed into the room with a panicked look on her face. For a moment she said nothing, then in a low voice she asked if those present had heard the cry of the banshee.

The men were astonished, but some were skeptical. They had seen the rosebush by the window. Thinking they were about to capture an intruder who was playing a rather tasteless prank, they rushed outside.

There was no one there. They saw the rosebush had recently been planted, and there was fresh mulch. This would certainly have the

87. Croker, *Fairy Legends*, 113–114.

footprint of the prankster. The mulch was undisturbed, and no mortal could possibly reach the window without standing in it.[88]

The O'Connor Banshee

The banshee connected to the O'Connor family also has quite a story behind her. While the tale has doubtlessly grown in the telling over the centuries, it would certainly make a great opera.

One day Phelim, the solitary son and heir to the O'Connor family, was out hunting. In the course of this hunt, the nimrod was terribly wounded by a stag.

He was taken to a remote cabin in the woods and nursed back to health by the woodsman and his beautiful daughter. At first, as he regained consciousness, he thought that he had died and gone to heaven, as there was obviously an angel attending him.

No, she replied with a laugh—he was not dead. He just had a slight problem with the business end of some antlers. He would live, but it was going to take a while to heal.

It took enough time for him to fall in love with her. Before he left, they secretly wed.

Eventually, the son was well enough to return to the castle. To his new wife's amazement, he did not take her with him. He said that he had to break the news to his father first. What he did not tell her was that his dad wanted him to marry a noblewoman so that he could have a political advantage. Marrying for love was not an option for people of a certain rank.

The son went home. At first, everyone in the court was happy he had returned. He was about to inform his father that his new daughter-in-law was a poor peasant girl with no social standing.

---

88. Croker, *Fairy Legends*, 111–114.

Unfortunately, Phelim wasn't any better at diplomacy than he was at hunting. He chickened out.

Soon, the father began to press his son to be married, preferably to the princess of Munster. The son kept putting him off, still too frightened to tell the truth. When it seemed as if Dad was about to make the match himself, the son had no choice but to confess what he had done while recovering.

His father was not much better at diplomacy. In his rage, he shouted that he wished he had a second son so that he could kill this idiot.

There were ways around this little stumbling block. The father secretly sent out some men to find the girl. Soon, it was reported throughout the countryside that the young bride had mysteriously vanished. It was assumed that no one would ever see her again. The problem was solved.

Or was it?

Phelim searched the entire kingdom; he asked everyone he could find, but no one knew anything, or if they did, they were not talking. Finally, giving her up for dead, the son allowed himself to be forced into an arranged marriage with a princess of the kingdom of Munster.

But just as he was about to be wed, who should rush in but his peasant wife! As the bishop and the bride-to-be looked on in confusion and anger, the girl called him her husband.

The truth was revealed. She had been confined in one of the dungeons below the entire time. But tonight, due to the wedding, the guards were able to have a little drink, then a little more … and before the vigilant sentries knew what was happening, the girl was free and running up the stairs.

But the hardships she had endured in the dungeon had taken their toll. She let out a bloodcurdling scream and fell over, dead.

Phelim ran to her, bent over her lifeless body, and began to weep, crying out for his beloved wife.

This certainly fits the requirements for the "does anyone have any objection?" provision. The bride, embarrassed and seething, stormed out before the marriage could be completed.

Things were not too happy between father and son after that. At the first opportunity, Phelim went off to war. Besides hunting and diplomacy, he was also no good at warfare. He died almost immediately.

However, on the night he died, the people in the castle heard a familiar scream. It was the anguished cry of his true wife, the same exact scream she had made before collapsing to her death. There was no doubt that she had become a banshee. She has been attached to the O'Connor family ever since, no doubt taking great delight in heralding their deaths.[89]

---

89. "The Banshee," *The Dublin Penny Journal*, 3.

Chapter 4
THE CRY
OF THE BANSHEE

Who sits upon the heath forlorn,
With robe so free and tresses worn?
Anon she pours a harrowing strain,
And then she sits all mute again!
Now peals the wild funereal cry,
And now—it sinks into a sigh.

—DYER, GHOST WORLD

As the vast majority of encounters with a banshee involves hearing rather than seeing it, it is certainly a fair question to ask: What exactly does this entity sound like?

There are numerous instances of the phantom being heard but not seen. Many times witnesses will go to the door or window to see who is making the eerie sound in the middle of the night, only to find that there is no one there.

On some occasions the banshee is seen as well as heard, but these are comparatively rare. There are only a handful of cases of someone destined to die seeing a banshee with the specter remaining silent. She is almost wholly an auditory creature.

O'Donnell's Experience

Noted author Elliot O'Donnell heard the cry of the banshee himself, and definitely stated that he did not want to hear it ever again. "Sometimes by wailing, and sometimes by uttering the most blood-curdling of screams, which I can only liken to the screams a woman might make if she were being done to death in a very cruel and violent manner."

He continues, "I, for one, have heard the sound, and as I sit here penning these lines, I fancy I can hear it again—a Satanic chuckle, a chuckle full of mockery, as if made by one who was in the full knowledge of coming events, of events that would present an extremely unpleasant surprise."[90]

Another connection of banshee belief and ancient mythology has survived in County Mayo, where it is often held that, not only will a person or their family hear the banshee, but that the individual will not be allowed to leave this world until the spirit has announced their departure. It is further held, at least in a number of families, that a bird must first crash against a window before the death can

---

90. O'Donnell, *The Banshee*, 17.

occur. This is reminiscent of the Morrigan in the form of a crow.[91] As we shall see later, an old legend in England states that the messenger of death for one family is a white bird.[92]

As O'Donnell stated, sometimes just to hear the cry of the banshee is a horrific experience. There is the instance of two women from County Kerry who were walking along a country road one night. The two were having a normal conversation, with little care in the world. Suddenly, the stillness of the early evening was shattered by the shrieking cry of a woman. The sound was so petrifying that one of the two girls suffered a mental breakdown—and as a result of this died within a few days.[93]

Lady Jane Wilde described the sound thusly: "The cry of this spirit is mournful beyond all other sounds on earth, and betokens certain death to some member of the family whenever it is heard in the silence of the night."[94]

Cat Screeching

Sometimes the sound is described as that of a cat screeching. In 1983 a Dublin woman, Anne Hill, reported this to a researcher. Obviously sensitive to such phenomena, it was actually the second time in her life that Anne had heard the banshee. The lady was in her house going about her business when she suddenly heard a racket outside as if a cat was shrieking madly.

She looked about to see if her own cats were having a little disagreement. Nope—they were sleeping through the whole show.

---

91. Lysaght, *Pocket Book*, 49.

92. Croker, *Fairy Legends*, 133.

93. Lysaght, *Irish Death Messenger*, 66.

94. Wilde, *Ancient Legends*, 135.

She then rushed to the window to look outside: first, to see if there was a local feline addressing some strongly held complaints; second, in the event that it actually was a banshee, she might actually get a glimpse of it. She had been told that the specter would sometimes be seen as a doll-sized woman sitting on the windowsill and combing her hair. This would certainly be something to see.

There was no cat, nor was there a tiny woman in a cloak with a comb. But there was still that eerie sound—fading away, then coming back.

Frightened, she asked her mother what she thought of the sound. Her mother looked at her as if she were batty. What the heck was she talking about? There had been no sound.

Once again, just one person in a household could hear the banshee's wail.

The sound ended; life returned to normal, at least until the next day. Anne was walking up the street toward the house when her mother, who had heard nothing the night before, came running out to her. Her aunt had died at the same time that Anne had heard the screeching sound.[95]

Variations of the Wailing

While the sound may vary slightly with the individual spirit making it, there are two major variations of the banshee's cry: beautiful singing or horrific screeching. This difference may shed some light on what a banshee actually is. D. R. McAnally Jr. postulates that the "Banshee is really a disembodied soul, that of one who, in life, was strongly attached to the family, or who had good reason to hate all its members, such as the banshee reported by Lady Fanshawe or the

95. Lysaght, *Irish Death Messenger*, 239–242.

one following the O'Connor family. Thus, in different instances, the Banshee's song may be inspired by opposite motives."[96]

There is evidence to support this, as with the old story of a poor woman of great beauty but no social standing. Seduced by a young lord then abandoned, possibly even murdered, she would have great animosity toward his descendants. Such a specter would take delight rather than sorrow in announcing their deaths.

McAnally continues, stating how the old Irish believed the souls of the dead were always near at hand. He states that the spirits of ancestors would certainly be at major events in one's life, such as at a wedding. They would also be present at funerals.

Sometimes their presence could be detected in the faint sound of voices in the air. Sometimes there would be barely audible music.

There was a great difference in the character of these ancestral spirits: "The spirits of the good wander with the living as guardian angels, but the spirits of the bad are restrained in their action, and compelled to do penance at or near the places where their crimes were committed."[97]

However, while the cry of the banshee is generally described as horrid, much like the disturbing wail of the keeners of old, there are many other occasions in which the cry is beautiful singing.

The Singing and Harp-Playing Banshee

Sometimes the banshee's cry is just singing in the night wind; other times, the fascinating song is accompanied by the sound of a harp. Very often, the wonderful singing is heard before the saddest of occasions, like the death of a child. One such case of this was the little brother of the celebrated Irish poet Dr. Kenealy.

96. McAnally, *Irish Wonders*, 110.

97. McAnally, *Irish Wonders*, 111.

As the boy was being examined by a physician, the assembled group heard what they described as the most beautiful singing they had ever beheld.

The adults stepped aside to assess the grim situation. Speaking in hushed tones, they agreed the young man was seriously ill and would probably not live much longer. In the midst of this grim discussion, one of the adults in the party commented that the singing outside was absolutely wonderful, he had never heard such a melody or voice in any concert hall.

There was silence for a moment. Another man in the group looked at him in wonder. He stated that, yes, the singing should indeed be beautiful beyond the capacity of a mortal woman—that was because it wasn't made by a mortal woman. He had just heard a banshee.

The poet, a look of horror on his face, turned back to the bed. His little brother had just died.[98]

The banshee who follows the Baily family near Lough Gur in County Limerick also has a pretty voice she uses to gently serenade the dying. The previously mentioned minstrel Thomas Connellan, whose funeral was serenaded by the goddess Áine, had been at Lough Gur Castle when he died.

On another occasion, a young woman of the family was lying on her deathbed in the same castle. Suddenly, the group sitting with her noticed the most wonderful singing they ever had listened to. It was very loud, coming from just outside. The angelic voice rose into the air and passed right over the top of the ancient structure.

Soon after, the young woman died.[99]

---

98. O'Donnell, *The Banshee*, 25.

99. Evans-Wentz, *Fairy Faith*, 81.

Sometimes, instead of mournful howling or singing, there is the sound of a harp. This may accompany the singing or, in rare cases, play alone.

The Badajoz Banshee

A banshee's harp was played alone once during the Napoleonic wars just before the horrific slaughter of the Siege of Badajoz, Spain, in 1812. In the initial fighting, a soldier named O'Farrell had been captured by the French. Being Irish, he was granted a bit of liberty, but, of course, he could not leave the town and return to his lines. Not wishing to suffer the conditions of the other prisoners, O'Farrell readily agreed.

He soon found another Irish family in the town, the McMahons. To his delight, they had a lovely daughter named Katherine. He would often visit the family, enjoying the company of fellow Irish, and especially enjoying the company of Katherine. He even had fantasies of making her his wife; however, he was only a poor soldier, and the McMahons were wealthy.

One night, he chanced to arrive a bit too early at the house and was asked by a servant to wait on the veranda. He did so, and while sitting there, enjoying the peace of the Moorish garden, he suddenly heard the sound of an Irish harp and a wailing song accompanying it. The music was enchanting, but quite sad.

Later that evening, he asked Mr. McMahon about this. To his surprise, the old man suddenly looked quite alarmed. Quickly gathering his composure, he replied that it was undoubtedly some street musicians, and he should not concern himself with it—nor should he mention it to anyone else.

O'Farrell had heard the sound, and he knew darn well it was not street musicians. Since when did Spanish street musicians carry a harp? But he let the matter drop, as the man obviously did not want to discuss it any further.

Soon thereafter, Arthur Wellesley's forces stormed the city. Amid the carnage, the entire McMahon family was killed.[100]

Words of Doom

Banshees usually do not speak, they merely wail. However, on very rare occasions, they will converse with the intended.

Lady Wilde records the instance of a young woman who was rather athletic and in the optimum of health. She loved to ride horses and was quite skilled at it. She was equally ecstatic about dancing. Everything about her made her the ideal example of a sound and fit young woman.

But one night, she awoke to hear a ghostly woman's voice at her window. It growled, "In three weeks death; in three weeks the grave-dead-dead-dead!"[101] As happens so often with these omens, the words were repeated twice, making a total of three.

The poor girl was frightened, but soon thought nothing of it; probably just a bad dream. She rolled over and went back to sleep.

But soon she became ill with a condition that quickly worsened. Then "the angel of death entered the house with soundless feet, and he breathed upon the beautiful face of the young girl, and she rested in the sleep of the dead, beneath the dark shadows of his wings."[102]

This tale from County Westmeath offers another narrative of what was, certainly, a banshee talking to the victim.

The widow Dysart was poor and raising a daughter on her own. The daughter was quite attractive, young, and full of life. But that

100. O'Donnell, *The Banshee*, 131–135.

101. Wilde, *Ancient Legends*, 137.

102. Wilde, *Ancient Legends*, 137.

was not the way she looked when she dragged herself down the steps that morning. Her mother knew at once that something was wrong and asked her what on earth was the problem.

She said she felt tired and rather sick. Something was off, and it seemed to be somehow connected to the lady she spoke to during the night.

Lady? What lady? Was her daughter talking foolishness?

The daughter, leaning back in her chair and catching her breath, muttered that, in the middle of the night, a beautiful woman dressed entirely in white had appeared in her bedroom. She revealed that there was a treasure buried in a field nearby, and she would show the daughter where it was. But the girl was frightened of the apparition and simply rolled over and went back to sleep.

Her mother was silent for a moment, then she was furious. How could she raise a daughter so darn stupid? This morning they could be wealthy, sitting at the same table counting piles of gold coins. Why didn't she go with her and see where the treasure was?

The daughter just stared listlessly.

The mother was fuming. She demanded that if the woman in white came to her again, then no matter how bad or frightened she felt, she should rouse herself from the bed and follow her. They needed the money. Whatever happened, she should follow the woman!

That night, the woman in white did indeed appear again. However, instead of being picture-book gorgeous as she had been the previous evening, the woman now looked older; her skin was too pale, her eyes were a bit sunken. She looked like someone who had once been pretty but had just recently died ... and nature was starting to take its course.

Now in a raspier voice, the ghostly woman repeated that there was a treasure buried in a nearby field, and that the daughter should climb out of bed and follow her to it.

If she had been frightened when the woman was pretty, the daughter was utterly terrified now. She rolled over and cried out that she did not want to speak to her and certainly did not want to go for a stroll with the dead. The woman in white vanished.

The next morning, the daughter had to struggle merely to make her way to the table. The widow Dysart, who had been contemplating the matter, did not even ask how her daughter was—it was obvious that now she was quite ill—but immediately questioned her as to whether or not the woman in white had appeared.

The daughter replied truthfully but told her mother that the woman was starting to look like a corpse. She was too frightened to follow her.

The mother was in a rage. She had figured it all out. This ghost was obviously some ancestor of theirs from long ago, wishing to help the poor widow struggling to raise a daughter. No matter what, should the mysterious woman have the patience to return a third time, the daughter must go with her.

She did. The widow Dysart found her daughter lying in bed the next morning, dead. Now she understood the true meaning of the treasure buried in the field—it was the churchyard.

Now she called out to her, weeping and hating what she had done to her beloved child. "But the ears of her darling child would hear no human sound again, for Death had claimed her as his own, and for her all the riches of the earth were but dross and vanity." [103]

While this banshee was dressed in white and appeared to the victim before death, there is a case from Dublin in the 1850s of the

---

103. Bardan, *Dead-Watchers*, 74–75.

death messenger being dressed in green, a color often associated with fairies. It was the sad instance of a young boy named David. Unlike most boys, he was quiet, dreamy, interested in things such as fairy tales. To no surprise, he had few friends beyond his imagination and was often lonely.

One day, his sister Isa walked by his room and heard what sounded like a conversation from inside her brother's room. Who could possibly be in there with him?

Without knocking, she walked in. He looked up, startled, and a little disappointed. David told his sister that he had been conversing with a beautiful woman dressed in green. He asked his sister if she thought the pretty woman would come to visit him again.

Isa had no answer to that, as she thought David had made it up with that wild imagination of his. Yet … she was certain she'd heard two people talking, one of them being a woman. Was he that good at impersonating voices?

A few days later, the sister heard conversation from the room again. Once again, she barged in, and just as the first time, there was David sitting by himself. This time he said that, just like before, as soon as Isa entered, the pretty lady in green just vanished into thin air.

He told his sister what had transpired. During their conversation, the lady promised him he would never be lonely again. She was coming back for him, and when she did, she would take him away to a place where he would be happy.

A few nights later, Isa was awakened in the middle of the night by the sweet sound of a lady singing. The music was beautiful, the voice celestial. But where was it coming from? It seemed to be floating in the air about the house, but as Isa (being very practical) knew, such a thing was impossible.

The next day, David fell into a cistern and drowned. The lady in green had indeed taken him to a much happier place.[104]

In a curious instance of a banshee speaking to mourners, there is the case of the unmarried young woman who gave birth to a son. She swore up and down that the boy was sired by a member of the Finnucane family. The Finnucanes vehemently denied this allegation for years.

Sadly, the illegitimate child died when he reached twenty years. There was, of course, a funeral. The mother wondered and asked all those in attendance why the Finnucane banshee had not wailed for him.

Her question was answered. At that moment, in front of everyone, a ghastly face appeared at the window. To the horrified attendees, the hag cried out that she was not about to cry for a descendant of the Ó Bodhrán clan.[105]

While there is the screeching and wailing or angelic singing, sometimes there are other manifestations of the banshee's presence. One of the most common of these is either tapping on a window (usually three times) or rattling the doorknob of a locked door as if the banshee's trying to force its way in.

This is what happened to a group of young people in County Cork. They were making their way in from the fields, talking to each other as normal. Suddenly they heard a long mournful wail.

At first, they paid little attention, figuring that it was a dog howling. But after it continued and they heard it longer, they realized no dog ever sounded like that. There was no mistaking it—they were hearing a banshee.

After crossing themselves, they sighed. Someone in the area was not long for this world. Their conversation was now, "Who could it be?"

---

104. O'Donnell, *The Banshee*, 29–34.
105. Lysaght, "Banshee Traditions," 113–120.

That night, the informant was in a room with some of the others, sleeping. Suddenly, the latch on the door rattled, as if someone were struggling to enter. One of the residents, probably more asleep than awake, stirred and opened the door. No one was there.

In the morning, they received word that one of their relatives, Lizzie Carey, had died in America. From what they could gather from the letter, she had died at the exact same time they'd heard what they'd thought had been a dog.[106]

Knock, Knock

In County Mayo, there is a variation of the banshee who walks along lonely country roads at night carrying a lantern. She is not looking for an honest man, but rather for a soul to take.

Once she arrives at the intended house, she knocks on the door and tries to make her way in. Quite often, the family will go so far as to press themselves against the door to prevent her from fulfilling her mission.[107] Sometimes the banshee communicates by neither a gentle knock on the window nor the tapping of a door knocker, but rather by a loud crashing sound.

In County Wicklow, in the 1700s, there was a nurse in the service of a wealthy merchant attending to the man's wife. The wife was extremely ill and not expected to live very long.

One day, the nurse was sitting in the room. Seeing that her patient had fallen asleep, the caregiver quietly left the room, leaving the door open, and headed downstairs for a cup of tea. It had been an exhausting day.

As she sat, resting a bit and sipping tea, she suddenly heard a terrible crash from the floor above. She knew the kitchen was directly

---

106. Lysaght, *Irish Death Messenger*, 66.
107. Lysaght, "Banshee Traditions," 102.

underneath her patient's bedroom and now greatly feared the poor woman had rolled over in her sleep and fallen out of bed. The nurse raced back upstairs as fast as she could.

She breathed a sigh of relief as she rushed into the room. The sick woman was lying there in bed, just as the nurse had left her, still asleep. It was as though nothing had happened. The nurse looked around to see if there had been some damage that had caused the noise. Did something heavy collapse or fall off a shelf? No; there was nothing amiss. All was normal.

Later that day, she reported the sound to one of the relatives. The response was a sad look and a nod. The relative explained that the family had a banshee, and the same sound she had heard always occurred before a member of the family died. Sure enough, the banshee was correct: the old woman died the very next day.[108]

Selective Hearing

Sometimes, only one person in a group can hear the cry of the banshee. Such is the case of a brother and sister in County Cavan. They went out one evening to care for the dogs. While they were outside, the sister heard the frightening wail she knew at once to be the banshee. She asked her brother what he thought it was, but the young man looked at her. He could hear nothing. He was, in fact, thinking his sister was going a little batty. His mind changed, however, when they received the bad news: there was indeed a death in a nearby house.[109]

One woman was in her bedroom when she suddenly heard a woman weeping just outside her window, as if the crier was sitting on

108. Neligan and Seymour, *True Irish Ghost Stories*, 215.

109. Lysaght, *Pocket Book*, 29.

the windowsill. She looked out, but there did not seem to be anyone there.

She immediately called the servants and ordered that they go out on the lawn and see what was going on. From the plaintive cry, it appeared someone might need help. The servants looked at each other, took a deep breath, then did as they were told. After a few minutes of wandering around the lawn, they returned inside. No; there was no one out there. Perhaps she had just heard the wind?

Of course, the servants knew darn well what the sound was. The next morning, the woman did not come down to breakfast. The maid went to check on her and found that she was lying in her bed, dead.[110]

Although the banshee is generally regarded as a solitary spirit, on exceptional occasions the entity will combine with two or three others of her kind. This is done only when the person being wailed for is exceptionally holy or famous.[111]

The O'Flaherty Banshee

There was a literal choir lamenting the passing of a very pious and kind woman of the O'Flaherty clan. The problem was, the woman was not sick—at least, not when she heard the ghostly messengers. However, soon after the serenade, she suddenly contracted pleurisy and died.[112]

The O'Flaherty clan has long had a very active banshee. In olden times, the chieftain was leading his men out of the castle to meet the enemy in battle. As soon as they departed, they heard the unmistakable howl of the family banshee. The men looked at each other and,

---

110. Wilde, *Ancient Legends*, 136.

111. Yeats, *Irish Fairy and Folk Tales*, 116.

112. O'Donnell, *The Banshee*, 18.

knowing full well what the sound was and what it meant, promptly turned around and decided to go out and play another day.

The next day, the party set off as before, and once again, the cry of the horrible messenger greeted them; they turned around and decided to sit this one out as well.

The third day, the same party ventured forth. They departed slowly, listening as hard as they could and looking about. This time there was no sound. Ah, at last. This must be the day.

It was indeed the day. When they returned that evening from the battle, they were carrying their slain chieftain on a bier.

The Quality of the Cry

Thus, there is no easy answer to the question of what exactly the sound of the banshee is. Like the appearance of the entity, there is a wide variety of sounds.

As we have seen, the cry can be generally divided into two major types. One is sweet and pleasant, like angelic singing, mixed with crying and mourning. While somewhat mortal sounding, this voice is described as being not quite human; it's ghostly, less distinct than a regular person.

The other possibility, found usually in the parts of Ireland where the banshee is known as the *badhbh*, the cry is violent, sometimes even threatening. This most certainly reflects the nature of the ancient goddess Badb, the patroness of battle and slaughter.[113]

As with the group of young people in County Cork, initially mistaking the howling of the banshee for the sound of an animal is fairly common. Oftentimes people think it is the screeching of cats. In County Clare outside of Coolmeen, there is a rocky area known locally as *Creagán na gCat*. A banshee who follows the Lynch fam-

---

113. Lysaght, *Pocket Book*, 26.

ily haunts the region, sitting on the hill and screeching like an angry alley cat. Of course—like those who mistook the banshee for a dog—before long, it would be understood that it was certainly not an angry tomcat, nor a hound, or any other animal from this world.[114]

The wailful sound is reportedly maddening to listen to. It goes on for a long time, almost like a siren. No living creature could possibly cry out like that so loud and not take a breath. This is one of the ways people realized that what they were hearing was not from a natural source.[115]

The sound is also unnaturally loud, so much so that in urban areas, the neighbors hear it as well. There is even an instance from County Down where a woman who was nearly deaf, Ellen Burns, heard it quite clearly.[116]

Three Times and Location

The cries of the banshee will often come in groups of three. A case from County Waterford in 1913 illustrates this. A woman was awakened in the middle of the night by the shrill scream that she thought might just be a banshee. But before accepting this dark conclusion, she knew that after the first wail, two more would invariably follow. She was right, as almost immediately there was a pair of similar screeches.

Now she knew that it was indeed the banshee, and that someone whose family had a banshee would die. The very next day, she learned that one of the Colbert family had left this world.[117]

114. Lysaght, *Irish Death Messenger*, 125.
115. Keegan, "Legends and Tales," 368.
116. Lysaght, *Irish Death Messenger*, 76.
117. Lysaght, *Irish Death Messenger*, 79.

This grouping of three may also include instances when the sound goes in a circle around the house of the doomed person. It will always circle the building three times. In a case from County Clare, people reported that the sound of the keening descended from the sky above then went in a circle around the house three times.[118]

The sound of the banshee would almost always be heard at the home of the doomed person. This will happen even if, as is most often the case in modern times, that victim is lying in a hospital room some distance away. It would appear that the spirit is informing the family rather than the patient.

An instance of this occurred in County Galway. Seán Mahon was lying seriously ill in a hospital bed. A man, a close friend of the family, went by the house to give a courtesy visit and inquire as to how Seán was progressing.

The wife, Cáit Mahon, gave the bad news that poor Seán was extremely ill and may not survive. At about that point, the servant boy, Feardaf Ó Luachra, came running in, pale and terrified. When they were able to calm him down, they learned that he had just heard the horrible sound of a woman wailing in the hills near the house. Cáit and the visitor looked at each other in horror, then scurried to the back door. Sure enough, they could clearly hear the lamenting of a woman but could not see anyone. It was just like the keening of days of old.

The next day, Cáit learned that she was a widow, and that her husband had passed away in the hospital at about the exact time they had heard the banshee.[119]

---

118. Lysaght, *Irish Death Messenger*, 83.

119. Lysaght, *Pocket Book*, 31–32.

War

Young Irishmen in uniform have died in many lands in the midst of terrible wars. These battles have occurred in every part of the world "from North America, the West Indies, Africa, Australia, India, China; from every point to which Irish regiments have followed the roll of the British drums."[120]

And, of course, there are loved ones, wives, children, parents, sitting by the peat fire in their cottage, knowing only that their soldier is facing an enemy in service of a nation that is not their own. Sometimes, outside of their window, long before the dreaded telegram arrives, the banshee delivers the ultimate bad news.

This may occur at the family home, or it may be heard right on the battlefield the night before the fighting.

Once again, the banshee does not care about social status or military rank. The wailing may be for the lowest of privates to the commanders. The Irish-born Arthur Wellesley, duke of Wellington, the hero of Waterloo, died in September of 1852. When he died, a banshee wailing was heard at his ancestral estate.[121]

When a number of Irish soldiers are fated to perish on the battlefield, more than one banshee can be heard in a dark choir. One can only shudder to think what it must have sounded like before the Battle of the Somme.

In 1798, in the mountains of County Galway, a terrible battle was fought in a glen that bore the name *Áth nag Ceann*. However, the night before the bloody conflict, a chorus of screaming women was heard up in the mountains. This was understandably having a bad effect on morale. A soldier was sent up the mountain to investigate. He was never seen again.

---

120. McAnally, *Irish Wonders*, 118.

121. *Ireland's Lore and Tales*, "Banshee."

An officer told his servant to look into the strange situation and promised him riches if he spied out the activity and returned with the information. The boy refused to accept any money for what he believed was simply doing his duty. He did, however, say that he would only do it with the help of God.

He crept up the mountain pass and beheld a scene of horror. As he hid behind a rock, he watched as a group of hideous banshees was cavorting with a pile of skulls. Each one was lamenting for the skulls of those in her family.

In a moment, he found that one of the hags had separated unnoticed from the group and was now standing right above him. In a ghastly voice, she declared that if he had not sought the help of God in this mission, he would have met the fate of the earlier intruder.[122]

Young Irishmen dying in combat was not always overseas. Their own homeland was often a battlefield; guerilla resistance against British rule was a major conflict lasting for many generations. The bloodshed resulted in countless casualties, some of which were announced by the banshee.

Peggy Rilehan, who was working as a maid, heard the banshee one night as the time approached for her cousin to be executed, the result of an attack on a barracks in Churchtown.[123]

There is an old Irish folk belief that if you hear the banshee, you can make the sign of the cross three times. This will stop the wailing and send the spirit back to wherever it came from. However, this does not mean the person destined to die will live. The banshee merely announces the upcoming death, she does not cause it.[124]

---

122. Lysaght, "Banshee Traditions," 101.

123. Croker, *Fairy Legends*, 133.

124. Lysaght, "Banshee Traditions," 97.

Another case from the old days involves a chieftain in County Mayo. It was the familiar story, played out so many times before. The chieftain was powerful and had wealth. He professed to love a poor but beautiful girl of the peasant class. She was desperately in love with him, being quite naïve about such matters. Naturally, she was devastated when she was discarded like a used plaything. She died soon afterward. The chieftain, for political rather than romantic reasons, married a wealthy woman from another clan.

Soon thereafter, the people in his castle heard a strange crying outside the door. The guards ran out to investigate, but there was no one there. Perplexed, figuring it was probably some crazy or drunk woman, they went back in.

That evening, the wailing started up again. The guards asked if they should go out and look again. The chieftain told them not to bother. There was no doubt now as to what the sound was. What was in doubt, however, was exactly who the crying was for.

It was for him. Apparently, his kind and generous nature extended to dealing with his subjects. The very next day, he was brutally attacked by a group of common people and assassinated.

The poor girl he had discarded had returned from the dead as a banshee—and there was no doubt she was enjoying her new line of work.[125]

Reacting to the Banshee

In County Roscommon, there was the case of a young man, a farmer, who had spent a long night helping the cow to calf. When it was finally completed, the exhausted fellow went back into the house to clean up and rest for a while.

---

125. O'Donnell, *The Banshee*, 36–37.

After a bit, he decided that before turning in, he would go back out to the barn to make certain that the cow and her new calf were doing well. But before he could leave the house, he suddenly heard the pitiful wailing in the area around the farm. When it ended, he heard the heavy footsteps of his father coming down the steps very quickly. He saw that his son was about to step outside and demanded to know where he thought he was going. The reply was logical: to check on the new calf.

To his surprise, he was ordered not to check on the livestock, but to go to bed instead. The son obeyed, realizing by now that the ghastly sound he had heard was the banshee. His father knew more about these things than he did.

Bad news came from America a few days later. One of their cousins had passed away.[126]

The sound of the banshee can sometimes be heard traveling down roadways and streams toward the intended house. In County Clare, a man named Michael McMahon heard the cry in his own backyard. Needless to say, he was not happy with this. But he was relieved when the sound quickly passed through his property and moved up the street.

He listened to see if he could determine where it went. He was able to determine that it stopped and remained stationary at the house of his neighbor John Keane. John died that very night.[127]

It should be noted that there is a multitude of superstitions from around the world concerning strange knocks that come in a grouping of three. These are always believed to be a presage of death: "The

---

126. Lysaght, *Pocket Book*, 46–47.
127. Lysaght, *Irish Death Messenger*, 116.

original idea is that the spirit of Death, by these raps, is knocking for admission." [128]

Another case of a death being predicted by a mysterious door knock came from Dublin. Near Christmastime, a family was interrupted one night by a knocking on the hall door. The lady of the house went to open it but found that there was no one there.

Some in the family thought it was merely some children, but she said a strange knocking always preceded a death in the family. The banshee was apparently a bit ahead of schedule. It took until summer, but the woman's mother-in-law, who lived in the same house, passed away. [129]

In another grouping of three, Reverend D. B. Knox related a strange tale. He was in attendance as another clergyman's wife was dying. As the group sat in the parlor, they suddenly heard the door knocker. Thinking that it was a neighbor or relative coming to pay respects to the dying woman, one of the men went to the door. When he opened it, there was no one there.

They returned to their conversation, when after a few minutes, the knocker clacked a second time. Again, the door was opened, and again, there was no one standing there.

After this, one of the guests positioned himself so that he could look out the window and watch the front door. If some children were exhibiting extremely bad taste and disturbing a family when one of them was dying, he would see it.

He saw it—but it was not rude children. He stared in horror as the knocker rose a third time, but no one was there. It was as if an

128. Bergen, Beauchamp, and Newel, *The Journal of American Folklore*, 19.

129. Neligan and Seymour, *True Irish Ghost Stories*, 215–216.

invisible hand had raised it. It came down and everyone heard the dreaded third knock. A few days later, the woman was dead.[130]

Protective Banshee

There are rare instances when a banshee does not predict a death, but instead acts like a guardian angel and warns of an impending disaster. The dreaded banshee has now become a sentinel spirit of the family, heralding a warning of calamity rather than death.

There was the instance of a man and his son in County Clare returning from a fair. As they walked along the road in the dark, they heard the plaintive wailing that could only be a banshee. They could even see her—a small old woman walking slowly away from them.

They rushed home, and to their relief, they found that everyone was fine. Still, they had heard the dreaded messenger of death, but who could the lament have been for? No one was ill. Needless to say, the family found it hard to sleep that night.

Which was a very good thing. That very night, their house burned down around them. Thankfully, everyone in the family made it to safety—and who should they thank? If they had all been asleep rather than worrying about the banshee, some might not have escaped.[131]

One type of banshee wails people living on a coast definitely do not want to hear is the sorrowful moan coming in over the waves. This may be for just one person, but it may also foretell a shipwreck in the vicinity.[132]

It is interesting to note that unlike other messengers of death, particularly the Teutonic *Weiße Frauen* (who we shall meet later),

130. Neligan and Seymour, *True Irish Ghost Stories*, 215.

131. Lysaght, "Banshee Traditions," 113–114.

132. O'Donnell, *The Banshee*, 136.

the Irish banshee does not ever enter the dwelling she is crying to. She may circle the house, go over the top on occasions, or more often than not sit on the windowsill and utter her cry. But she always remains outdoors.[133]

Who Can Hear the Banshee

It is a curious fact that sometimes in a group of people, only one person will be able to hear the banshee cry. This may mean that the person who hears it is in some ways psychic, or at the least is more sensitive to such things.

This may be the reason some people have multiple occasions of hearing the banshee. One may well include Jenny McGlynn of Mountmellick in County Laois in this class. In 1976, speaking to a folklorist, she calmly related how she had heard the banshee before they received the sad news that a cousin in Dublin had passed away from an asthma attack.

But this was not the end of it. She related that only two days before, she had heard the banshee on Chapel Street. As her brother-in-law was a sexton, she later was informed that a man from that street had just died.[134]

At the same time, there are many instances of the person who is destined to die not hearing the cry, and sometimes not seeing the creature when others do.

There was a group of young women working in a bog near Killeeny in County Longford. Suddenly, their work was interrupted by a maddening scream that seemed to be traveling in a circle around them.

---

133. Lysaght, *Irish Death Messenger*, 135.
134. Lysaght, *Irish Death Messenger*, 239.

The girls were frightened, knowing full well what it was. As they started to discuss the ominous message, one girl in their party was asking what the problem was—she had heard nothing.

The others looked at each other but said nothing.

After work, the girls went to a nearby stream to wash the dirt from their hands, just as they always did. The girl who could not hear the sound suddenly lost her footing on the muddy bank, fell into the water, and drowned.[135]

Who Is Being Summoned to the Grave?

Mr. Duggan of County Sligo was fond of telling people how, when he was a boy, he was walking through a forest in the company of two grown men. As they made their way through the peaceful woodland, the stillness of nature was suddenly shattered by the piercing scream of the banshee. All three of the fellows clearly heard it.

One of the men was not particularly effected. Instead, he lit his pipe and said calmly that someone was about to die. When things were back to normal, the trio continued their journey.

The next day, one of the men was traveling through the forest again. He came across a fellow who was busy chopping down a tree. Seeing the stranger nearby, the woodsman warned him not to come too close, as the tree could fall at any time. He thanked him, made certain he was far enough away, and continued his business.

At that exact moment, there was a huge cracking sound. Realizing what was happening, he ran away as fast as he could. Unfortunately, that was not fast enough, and the tree was quite large. When informed of the accident, the others understood who the banshee was wailing for.[136]

---

135. Lysaght, *Irish Death Messenger*, 144.

136. Lysaght, *Irish Death Messenger*, 118.

In 1900, a family was attending to the mother of the household who was dying. Without warning, there came the sound of a woman wailing. The people who heard it were looking everywhere, even under the mother's bed. No one could place where it was coming from.

Curiously, some of the people in the group could hear the sound while others, including the dying woman, could not. What is more, some neighbors rushed over, for they had heard the wailing too. A servant summed up the matter. "'Did you hear the Banshee? Mrs. P. must be dying.'"[137]

In a boarding school in the 1890s, a boy was sick and confined to a room by himself. During the day, the doctor visited him. Suddenly the sick boy stood up and asked the doctor if he heard it.

It was the cry of the banshee—the boy had heard the same sound before and knew what it meant. He feared he would not recover from the illness. Happily, he did recover. Tragically, the headmaster received a telegram informing him that the brother of the sick boy had been accidentally shot and had died from his wounds.[138]

Sometimes the only one to hear the cry is the one it is intended for, whether they know it or not. This was not the case with Joe Condon of County Waterford. He was busy digging potatoes and happened to mention to his friend that he had heard the banshee the last night, and that somebody was about to die.

He was absolutely right. What he did not suspect was that the doomed person was … Joe Condon.[139]

It is held in some areas that, not only is the cry of the banshee a presage of death, it is actually necessary for the death to occur. Thus,

137. Neligan and Seymour, *True Irish Ghost Stories*, 204.

138. Neligan and Seymour, *True Irish Ghost Stories*, 204.

139. Lysaght, *Irish Death Messenger*, 116.

it is said by some that a person cannot leave this world until the banshee has cried for them. Their horror and fear are then mixed with a morbid expectation, so that a desperately ill person may suffer no longer.[140]

The Rossmore Banshee

It is quite unlikely that an Irish banshee would cry for a Scotsman who commanded military forces in Ireland—however, the Scots have a strong banshee tradition of their own. Just as Irish banshees would be heard in America, Canada, and other lands, so, too, a Scotsman may well hear his family's banshee while living in Ireland.

Such a person was Lord Rossmore, who married a wealthy Irish woman and purchased a grand estate in County Wicklow.

One night Lord Rossmore was entertaining some guests, Lady Barrington and Sir Jonah. In the middle of the night, the guests heard a strange sound.

No matter how hard he listened, the bizarre sound could not be identified. It was like no sound on earth; it would rise in tone, then slowly descend, only to return more forcefully. Not only could it not be identified, but even the place where the sound was coming from seemed vague.

Sir Jonah awakened Lady Barrington, who had been sleeping through the entire performance. The two could both hear the sound, but neither could identify it. The lady's suggestion that it was perhaps an Æolian harp was quickly dismissed. This was no harp, at least not a natural one.

Then, after a half hour, the sound took a more sinister aspect. It suddenly ended in a very grim sigh. It then cried out in "sharp, low

---

140. Lysaght, *Irish Death Messenger*, 115.

cry, and by the distinct exclamation, thrice repeated, of 'Rossmore!—Rossmore!—Rossmore!'"[141]

The people gathered and looked out of a large window that overlooked the garden to see what the source of this cry was, but there was nothing to be seen.

Lord Rossmore called in a maid to see if she could recognize the sound. Apparently, she did, as she ran out of the room in terror, no doubt muttering something about not getting paid enough for this.

The sound continued for about a half hour. The lord asked his guests to refrain from telling anyone about this, for fear that he would become a laughingstock.

Being humiliated was not going to be a big problem for him. The next day the guests were informed that Lord Rossmore had died in bed at about 2:30 in the morning.[142]

Reacting to the Cry

The reaction to hearing the messenger of death varies. To some people, it is a terrifying experience. Others simply accept the banshee as part of the Irish flora and fauna. It is understood that everyone who comes into this world will someday leave it. Such witnesses do not exhibit fear, merely sad resolution.

One woman in County Cavan had a very Christian reaction to hearing the banshee. She was on her way into town when she heard the wailing. She knew not only what it was, but who it was for.

There was a man in town she had quarreled with for years and had no use for. She also knew this man was lying in bed and was not expected to live. She went immediately to the man's house and spoke to him. She told him honestly what she had heard and made peace

---

141. O'Donnell, *The Banshee*, 77.

142. O'Donnell, *The Banshee*, 75–78.

with him for all the years they had been on bad terms. She left the house feeling much better about herself and the peace she had made. It was not long after that she learned he had died.[143]

This is actually a practice known in Ireland as *maith in agbaidb an oilc*, which may be translated as "good in the face of evil." It is an old belief that, when one is dying, old scores must be settled and put to rest—partially to prevent the deceased from coming back to do so from the other side.[144]

Skeptics

Sometimes, as in the case of Con Egan, those who profess not to believe in the banshee experience what is sometimes referred to in modern parlance as a paradigm shift. One of these was a clergyman in Newtowncunningham, a village in the far northwest of Ireland in County Donegal. This man of the cloth rejected all the old people's superstitions of fairies, leprechauns, pookahs—and, of course, those crazy stories about this noisy spirit called the banshee. He was too educated to believe in such nonsense.

He was summoned to the home of the Dunn family, where a young lady was quite ill and not expected to live. With the family he gathered over her bed, he gave her what comfort he could, and joined with the others, leading them in prayer.

As they spoke to God, in the distance, they could hear the shrieking of a woman, as though her heart were going to explode. The young woman did indeed die. The family calmly informed him afterward that the sound he'd heard was no ordinary woman, but the family banshee.

---

143. Lysaght, *Irish Death Messenger*, 148.
144. Lysaght, *Pocket Book*, 68.

He walked out of that house a changed man, muttering the famed words from Shakespeare's *Hamlet*: "There are more things in heaven and earth, Horatio, than are dreamt of in your philosophy."[145]

Then there was the woman in County Roscommon who swore up and down that she did not have time for superstitious nonsense and most certainly did not believe in the banshee. It was just a ruse invented by her mother to keep her from staying outside after dark.

That was until the night her grandfather died. She heard the cry and looked out the window to see the entity she swore did not exist. It was sitting there on the sill, wailing, just as her overprotective mother had described.[146]

Calm before the Departure

Some react to the sound with denial or mistaking it for a more natural human cry. This is what happened in County Cork to a woman named Mrs. Broderick. She was out for a little boat ride with a young woman named Mary and two young men. There was a local boatman doing the rowing.

The man took them to an old wreck that was abandoned in the water near the rocky coast. The two men and Mary wanted to go aboard and catch a better look at it. Mrs. Broderick had no desire to go prancing about the deck of a ruined ship where the timbers may be rotted from exposure to the elements. She and the boatman remained in the small boat as Mary and her two friends happily climbed aboard for an adventure.

The two wandered about the wreck for a while, satisfying their curiosity. Then they decided to take a look below. They told the two

---

145. *Hamlet*, act 1, scene 5; Lysaght, *Irish Death Messenger*, 221.
146. Lysaght, *Pocket Book*, 84.

in the small boat what they were doing, then quickly disappeared down the steps.

Things seemed normal for a while, Mrs. Broderick chatting with the boatman. Suddenly, they heard the bloodcurdling sound of a woman screaming. Mrs. Broderick was ready to rush onto the wrecked boat, thinking the two men were trying to murder Mary.

But the boatman, after making a solemn sign of the cross, told her to relax. Mary was fine. What they had just heard was the sound of the banshee. He sighed and said in a sad voice that his own mother had been ill lately, and many felt she was not long for this world.

Mrs. Broderick was still staring in disbelief as they heard the excited conversation of Mary and the two men onboard. When the trio returned to the small boat, they were told about the banshee, and how the boatman's mother may have been the one intended.

Yes, the mother of one of the people on the boat did indeed die shortly after. However, it was not the boatman's, but rather the mother of one of the two young men who had explored the shipwreck with Mary.[147]

Sometimes upon hearing the fateful cry, people seem to be resolved and are calm, knowing their end is near. A case from County Waterford in the 1930s demonstrates this.

John was a man who loved to go visiting at night, often coming home late. One night, he was making his way home quite late when he suddenly heard the horrific screech of the banshee. He knew immediately what it was and began to run home. As he rushed down the road, the sound seemed to be following him.

The shrieking became a duet by the time he reached the door to his house, as by now he was screaming in terror. John's father, who

147. O'Donnell, The Banshee, 145.

did not approve of these late hours his son was keeping, opened the door. Poor John collapsed on the floor as soon as the door was ajar.

When he was revived, it was seen that he was not drunk, but terrified. He asked if he was alive or dead. His angry father assured him that he was alive—at least for the moment. It was then that John explained about hearing the banshee on the road. His father told him to go upstairs to bed.

John told others of his frightening experience, starting with his neighbor, Tomás Tóibín, an elderly man who had been in poor health recently. The old man listened attentively, saying nothing. When the tale was done, he simply smiled and told John that he had nothing to worry about.

The banshee was crying for him. He stated that death must be coming soon, and he was correct. By the very next day, Tomás had left this world.[148]

In a similar case in the village of Dromahaire located in County Leitrim, a woman was lying on her deathbed, fully aware the end was coming. To ease her passing, a number of women had come by and were staying with her.

Suddenly, they heard the wailing outside. Some of the guests were terrified, having no idea what was going on. The dying woman smiled and told them to relax. It was only the banshee.[149]

While some people greet the wail of the banshee with a calmness and acceptance, others react to it in confusion. These are families in which everyone, as far as they know, is perfectly healthy. This may mean the cry is meant for another family, a relative living elsewhere—or worst of all, that someone in the household is destined to die violently in an accident or other mishap.

---

148. Lysaght, *Pocket Book*, 28–29.

149. Lysaght, "Banshee Traditions," 106.

The stoic calmness may be a mistake when it is assumed the cry is for someone else. There was an instance from County Kerry where a young woman named Norah was in love with the dashing Michael O'Lernahan. Michael could have any young woman in the area, but he had chosen Norah. The two were apparently deep in love, and the families gave their approval for the wedding. Norah could not have been happier.

As the two sat out one night in the moonlight, stealing a kiss and inching as close to each other as the propriety of the time would allow (to say nothing of the family members keeping an eye on things from the cottage window), they suddenly heard the dreaded cry of the banshee. The sound traveled through the air and even went right over the top of them, pausing for a moment when directly above the lovers.

The two were startled but paid this little mind. Yes, they had heard the call of the banshee, but they were both young, strong, and in the best of health. It was obviously meant for some elderly or sick person in the area. Sure, they felt sorry and made a quick sign of the cross, but their lives had to go on. They were the future; the people of past years were always fading away one by one. It was the way of things, especially when your yesterdays outnumber your tomorrows.

All seemed well for Norah, excited about her upcoming marriage. However, Michael suddenly stopped coming around. She had gone from dreaming of her wedding gown to wondering where the heck he was.

Then the news came. He was still very much alive—and engaged to be married to someone else.

Norah felt as though she had just been kicked in the face by a mule. There had been no meeting with Michael; he did not have the fortitude to tell her face-to-face. He just made himself scarce and let her find out through local gossip.

The shock was devastating. After setting a world record for crying, she found she had no appetite. Soon she became very ill, quite literally dying of a broken heart.

As she lay in her bed, becoming weaker with every day, the family heard the banshee cry out again. This time, Norah could not hear the wail, but she could hear something rattling her window.

Soon after, everyone understood who the banshee had originally keened for.[150]

Another case of this confusion was reported in County Offaly. The wailing was heard, but no one in the family had the slightest idea who it was intended for. A few days later, one of the family was working in a tree and fell out, dying from the impact.[151]

Who Is She Wailing For?

The banshee always knows who is destined to die, even if the members of the family have no idea. The sad case of Anastasia Doyle in County Wexford illustrates this. She was a perfectly healthy woman who had not been ill, nor was she in an accident. The banshee was heard—and once again, no one in the family had the slightest idea who it was intended for. Anastasia was later putting on her hat when she suddenly collapsed dead on the spot.[152]

There is no getting around it: when the banshee cries, someone is destined for the grave. A little girl in County Roscommon heard the wail and asked her mother what that strange sound was. She was informed that it was indeed that terrible being known as the banshee. This meant someone was to die, but there was no idea who. Oh sure,

---

150. O'Donnell, *The Banshee*, 26–28.

151. Lysaght, *Pocket Book*, 49.

152. Lysaght, *Pocket Book*, 50.

there was an uncle who was ill, but it was no big deal. He would certainly pull through. It must be for someone else...

But once the banshee cries for you, there is no escape. The uncle did not pull through, and soon, the little girl and her mother were attending a funeral.[153]

In County Leitrim, a man named Matt Gaffney as well as the rest of his family all heard the pitiful screaming around their house. Perplexed at this unexpected situation, he called his neighbors. They listened, and yes, they could hear it plainly. It was definitely a banshee, and it was definitely at the Gaffney house.

With that settled, he had no idea what he should do. Of course, there was nothing he could do. Someone in the family was about to die, but who? They thought of all the elderly and sick relatives, wondering who was the unfortunate one.

Turns out, it was none of them. It was only a few days later that Matt suddenly became violently ill. Then the family knew who the banshee had been crying for.[154]

People who are nearby can often hear the banshee and sometimes even see her. Patrick Organ along with his friend Patrick McMabon were walking home late one night in County Clare. Suddenly, they heard the sad lament of a woman. They looked about and saw a woman in white, apparently with wings, coming down the hill toward them, crying her heart out.

The two knew what they were dealing with and fled as quickly as they could. Later on that evening, they heard the exact same cry, this time from Shannon's Mountain. They knew that someone in the district was going to die very soon, but they had no idea who it was.

---

153. Lysaght, *Pocket Book*, 48.

154. Lysaght, "Banshee Traditions," 106.

The very next day, they learned that one of the O'Briens had passed away during the night. The family had also heard the banshee wailing—right outside of their house. It was sitting on a bush.[155]

Drunkards and Dogs

While confusion and disbelief may be some people's reaction to the cry of the banshee, there are always a few who greet the death message with hostile arrogance. In 1948, the *Detroit News* printed an article discussing the banshee said to haunt a castle in Laragh in County Wickland. About once a month, the creature would be heard wailing from the old castle.

A local man named Sean Clement, especially after being fortified with a few drinks in the pub, would show the other patrons how a real Irishman reacted to this. He would walk out of the pub and howl right back at her.[156]

While not everyone can hear the banshee, there is no doubt that dogs, horses, and other animals can. They always react to the sound. If pressed to go toward the creature, which may not be seen by human eyes, the animals know it is there and will refuse to approach it. Dogs will often howl, as if joining in on the lamentation.[157]

A woman in County Cork was awakened in the middle of the night by the panicked barking and screeching of every dog and cat in the neighborhood. Suddenly, all the animals became silent. Then there was only one sound to be heard, that of the wailing of the banshee.

Diarmid Bawn

There is a humorous instance of mistaken identity in the Irish folktale known as "Diarmid Bawn, the Piper."

---

155. Lysaght, "Banshee Traditions," 97.

156. *Western Folklore.*

157. Lysaght, *Irish Death Messenger*, 84.

A man had come home and was with his family. Suddenly, they heard the screeching sound outside. "'And that's no lie for you, Pat,'" said his wife; "'but, whist! What noise is that I hard?'" and she dropped her work upon her knees and looked fearfully toward the door.[158]

As they were talking, the wife suddenly looked frightened and dropped what she was doing. She wanted to know what the shrill shrieking sound was.

His daughter answered the question immediately. "'The Vargin herself defend us all!'" cried Judy, at the same time rapidly making a pious sign on her forehead, "'if 'tis not the banshee!'"[159]

However, Pat merely told them to be quiet. Wondering how he came to be blessed with a family of imbeciles, he assured them the sound was merely the rusty hinges of the gate blowing in the wind.[160]

While this is not a true supernatural occurrence, they are soon visited by the squire. Pat, who was skeptical a moment or two before, now tells a wild tale about his wife's grandfather, the celebrated piper Diarmid Bawn and how the fairies transformed him into a horse and rode him through the sky across the sea to Jamaica.[161]

Mistaking the wailing as the cry of animals is well known. In County Wexford, it is said that people will hear the wail three times, and that the wailing sounds like the cry of a fox.[162]

Dogs and Cats

There is the case from County Roscommon where a brother and sister were sitting in the house one night when they were interrupted by

158. Croker, *Fairy Legends*, 267.

159. Croker, *Fairy Legends*, 267.

160. Croker, *Fairy Legends*, 267.

161. Croker, *Fairy Legends*, 267.

162. Lysaght, "Banshee Traditions," 104.

a terrible racket outside. Their first reaction was that a couple of the neighborhood cats had come together and renewed an old animosity. The siblings decided that it would be a good idea to let the dog out the back door and give the felines a little exercise.

It did not work out that way. They did indeed open the door, but the dog just stood in the doorway, frozen in fear, the hair raising on his back. He gave them a look as if to say *are you out of your mind?* and would not move another inch. The two looked at each other—now that they heard the sound, they wondered: Is this the sound of cats?

They very quickly shut the door.

Not knowing what to do, they woke up their father and told him what had happened. Yes, he had already heard the sound and knew there was nothing they could do. It was not cats; it was a banshee.[163]

Apparently, the specter was crying for another household nearby, as no death was recorded in the family.

In another case of an initial mistaken identity, a couple in County Clare heard the cry in the air. They found it unusual but dismissed it as a strong wind. Then they noticed nothing was blowing, and the trees were still. It was certainly no wind they were hearing.[164]

Merely crying out in the vicinity of the doomed person or the family then disappearing may not be sufficient. Sometimes, an ambitious banshee will continue her actions in a cemetery, undoubtedly where the person is destined to be buried.[165]

Such is the famous shriek of the banshee, sometimes sad and sweet, other times discordant and terrifying. But in some cases, the specter is not only heard, it is also seen.

---

163. Lysaght, *Pocket Book*, 34.

164. Lysaght, "Banshee Traditions," 104.

165. Lysaght, *Irish Death Messenger*, 83.

Chapter 5
THE SIGHT
OF THE BANSHEE

*He saw ... the figure of a tall slim girl, in a long,
loose, flowing gown of some dark material, with a
very pale face ... and masses of shining golden hair
that fell in rippling confusion on to her neck and
shoulders ... It was so evil that he felt sure it could
only emanate from the lowest Inferno, and it leered
at him with such appalling malignancy that, brave
man as he had proved himself on the field of battle,
he now completely lost his nerve, and would have
called out, had not both figures suddenly vanished,
their disappearance being immediately followed by
the most agonising, heart-rending screams, intermin-
gled with loud laughter and diabolical chuckling.*

—O'Donnell, The Banshee

While the banshee is usually just heard, on some occasions, she is also seen. Here, once again, just as it is with the sound they make, the appearance of this denizen of the Otherworld can be divided into two distinct varieties. The first is a young, beautiful woman; the second is a ghastly old crone.

The lovely young ones usually are described as having extremely long hair and wearing old-fashioned clothing or a cloak. Like the classic image of a mermaid, she is often seen combing her hair, the color of which is usually—but not always—described as some shade of gold. The color of the cloak is usually a fairy color, such as green. It has been suggested that those wearing a red cloak are predicting an untimely and bloody end for the victim.[166] It has further been proposed that the combing was actually the action of pulling the hair, an action taken by the professional keeners.[167]

Window Sitting

The banshee is often seen sitting on a windowsill (in old Irish houses, these are often much deeper than in modern American buildings). As she combs, she wails her lament.

This is how she was seen by James Clooney of Nemestown, County Wexford, in 1910. He was walking down the street late one night when he heard the plaintive keen coming from the house of Richard Barry. He looked at the house and saw the banshee sitting on the windowsill combing her hair, wailing. She was described as wearing a black cloak and having inky black hair, and she was barefoot. Two days later, Richard Barry was dead.[168]

---

166. Lysaght, *Irish Death Messenger*, 103.

167. Colum, *Treasury*, 397.

168. Lysaght, *Irish Death Messenger*, 67; Lysaght, *Pocket Book*, 40.

The young and beautiful variety of banshee was wonderfully described in a short work of fiction printed in *All Ireland Review*. In it, a young woman traveling alone at night hears keening in a field. She sees something she never really believed in:

> *"Holy Mother!" she gasped, "What's that?"*
>
> *A woman, tall and slender, clad in some loose white drapery—a woman with a thin, beautiful face, long, unbound hair, golden as the light of the dying sun. From her lips issued the mournful croon, and in her hand she held a golden comb.*
>
> *It was the Banshee!*[169]

The Ghastly Ones

The other manifestation of the banshee is that of an elderly hag, often with horrific or deathlike features. She is generally reported as being dressed in a cloak with a hood. When she lowers the hood, the witness, who may believe they are dealing with a mortal old woman, beholds an unpleasant surprise.

What may set the record for ugliness in a banshee was the one who was locked away in a room by two unmarried sisters, Georgina and Harriet O'Rorke.

Like a gothic Victorian horror tale, they actually had a banshee locked in a room. But the lock was not to keep the banshee in—there was no way the sisters could do that. Rather, it was to keep anyone else from walking into the room and seeing the hideous creature.

A maid knew very well that the room was always locked and off-limits. That was fine with her—one less room to clean. But one day,

---

169. J. M., "A Brilliant Idea," 53.

as she walked by the locked room, she heard a terrible tumult from behind the door. Terrified, she ran downstairs to the sisters and said there were violent, loud noises coming from the forbidden room.

Rats, was the initial explanation. Just rats.

The look on the maid's face said that she was not stupid, and those had to be some mighty strong and belligerent rats they had. The sisters looked at each other. There was no choice but to reveal the secret. With a sigh, they confessed what exactly was behind that perpetually secured door.

Georgina explained that the family had a banshee who liked to stay in the room (an extremely rare instance of a banshee actually being inside of a house). For some reason, the spirit had a fascination for a certain antique gold ring, one that no one would now dare to put on their finger. The hideous specter had even been reported wearing it.

The problem was that the creature was so ghastly, some people would die simply by looking at her. Georgina took a breath, sipped some tea, then continued. She stated that while some banshees were described as being beautiful young ladies, and others were simply old crones, their family banshee was grotesque. Indeed, the hideous appearance was so terrifying that some people would go into shock from the sight: "'One of our great-great-uncles, for instance, to who it once appeared, is reported to have died from shock; a similar fate overtaking another of our ancestors, who also saw it.'"[170]

They expected that they would soon have to go about finding a new maid. But to their surprise, the woman was satisfied at the explanation, the banshee being part of the world she had grown up with since childhood. She thanked them, then calmly went back to

---

170. O'Donnell, The Banshee, 49.

her duties, with absolutely no intention of ever peeking through the keyhole into that room.

The sisters sat back, sipped their tea, and debated who exactly the family banshee was making such a fuss about. They did have a cousin who was seriously ill in County Galway … yes, that must be it.

But it was not. It turned out to be Harriet.[171]

The Italian Count

In a rare case of a banshee being seen but not heard, one man of strong Irish descent became a wealthy count in Italy. One day he hosted a few guests, including an army colonel, onboard his private yacht.

As they enjoyed a wonderful day on the water, the colonel suddenly asked his host who the strange woman onboard was. This made no sense, for there was no woman other than the ones they were with at the moment. All females were present and accounted for.

But the colonel persisted, describing her as being dressed like an Irish peasant wearing a green cloak. As he was in the midst of saying this, the officer suddenly panicked, saying that he just saw her again—and she had the face of death. Her skull-like head was covered in long scarlet hair. He said she could have been an attractive young woman, but her expression was hellish.

The count merely sat back with a sorrowful look on his face. He stated that, although his name was Neilsini, he was actually descended from the Irish O'Neill family. His ancestors had fought for King Louis XVI in the French Revolution, but that did not end well and they had to flee France. They made their escape to Italy, where they made their fortune.

An American woman suggested that since the count was of Irish descent, perhaps the grisly lady the colonel had seen was a banshee.

171. O'Donnell, The Banshee, 46–49.

The count had apparently already reached that conclusion, and merely stated that he hoped his wife and his daughter were okay.

They were. However, two hours later, the count died of a heart attack.[172]

What follows is very likely another, slightly different, account of the same story from Elliot O'Donnell, in which once again a banshee appears to others but not the family member, and, once again, does not cry out.

In a luxury hotel in north Italy, a young woman became fascinated by an elderly gentleman. She was part of the young and lighthearted set—wealthy and rather frivolous heirs to family fortunes. They traveled from one high society spot to another, always ready to dance and socialize. However, for some unknown reason, this woman was fascinated by this old man.

There seemed to be an aura of sadness about him. He ate alone at a table for one, then afterward, he would leave the dining room and walk alone on the balcony, standing in silent contemplation while staring out at the sea.

She asked some of the hotel workers who this forlorn man was. She was informed that the man in question was Count Fernando Asioli. He was indeed a sad and lonely man; his wife of many years had recently died. Now he was simply filling his remaining time, going from one day to another, living in dreamy contemplation of the woman he had so truly loved and missed so terribly.

The young woman felt sorry for him and wanted to speak to him, to try to console him. The next night, after dinner, as was his habit, he rose from his solitary table and slowly made his way out to the balcony. Once there, he walked around the corner to his favorite spot where he could watch the sea and remember the good times.

---

172. Neligan and Seymour, *True Irish Ghost Stories*, 204–206.

The woman excused herself from her festive companions and walked out onto the balcony. She was not certain exactly what she would say to this grieving man, but she knew she had to say something.

But, as it turns out, that was not to be. When she turned the corner to where he was standing, she saw to her amazement that he was not alone. A tall, thin young woman with scarlet hair and an exquisite emerald dress was standing next to him, her hand placed lovingly on his shoulder, as if comforting him.

As she hadn't been seen by either of them, she backed away behind the corner and returned to her friends.

The next day, she again inquired of the hotel staff, asking who that gorgeous woman with the red hair was. She had not seen her at dinner or anywhere else in the hotel—and she certainly would have noticed someone like that. The staff looked at her in wonder. The count with a young woman? That was absolutely impossible. She must be mistaken.

She bit her lip and moved on. These blind idiots—she knew darn well what she had seen with her own eyes. She asked another guest, an older society lady who thrived on gossip. She knew everything about everyone. But like the hotel staff, she said that Count Asioli had no one.

The young woman was now determined that the next time she saw the two of them, she would introduce herself, and she would show this old biddy exactly what was going on. She would take her along.

That opportunity came that very evening. As always, the count dined alone, then quietly left for the balcony. The woman, now with the older lady in tow as a witness, followed again.

The older woman gasped. Just as her young friend had said, the count was indeed standing there looking out to sea with a young woman standing next to him. The hand of the gorgeous redhead in a sparkly emerald gown was again on his shoulder. They were together, but neither of them was speaking. Both were just staring at the black water and the stars above the horizon.

This time, the pair walked up to them. The redhead immediately turned toward the intruders, an annoyed expression on her face. The two women looked for a moment at the count, who was now turning about to see who was approaching him in the midst of his reverie. They then turned their attention behind him to the girl—only now, the young lady was not there. The count was standing on the balcony completely alone.

This made no sense. How could she have left so quickly? There was nowhere she could go without being seen. It was as if she had simply vanished.

The count stood and waited to see what his unexpected visitors wanted. The young one expressed her sincerest condolences over the loss of his wife, then asked him about the strange woman with red hair.

He looked at her in a perplexed way. Woman? What woman? He had been standing out there completely alone. Then he took a breath and nodded in understanding. Ah yes, that must be it.

He explained that although he was an Italian count, his heritage was Irish, from the O'Neill family. His family had always had a banshee—and from what they had just said, it would appear she was now coming for him.

The count was right. The very next day business compelled him to travel to Venice, but he never arrived at his appointment. He collapsed at the train station and died.[173]

Unintended Witnesses

The sister of a Catholic bishop related that when she was a little girl, she and her friends were walking down a road in the evening. On a

---

173. O'Donnell, *The Banshee*, 53–60.

large rock by the road, near a house, they saw an old woman. As they approached, the old woman suddenly began to clap her hands and wail like a keener.

The girls did not at first realize they had encountered the dreaded banshee. Some of the girls, thinking the woman might be ill or in some kind of distress, spoke to her. They received no reply; the crone ignored them and continued her mourning. By now, the girls understood something very strange was going on. They headed home as fast as they could run.

The very next day, they learned the man of the house near the rock had died that night, and he'd died at the same time the girls had encountered the old woman.[174]

In County Cavan, there was the case of Lizzie Crowe. Her sister was lying on her deathbed; her time in this world was almost complete. Lizzie went to the door to take in some air. As she looked out, she began to hear the wailing she knew at once to be a banshee.

While she knew the banshee was coming, she did not expect to actually see the entity. But on a small hill in the yard, there was a stack of turf. She watched in amazement as the crying came from an old, bent-over crone, who for some reason was walking around and around the turf. Finally, on one rotation, the old woman reached the other side of the pile, and did not reemerge.[175]

The O'Donnell Banshee

Elliot O'Donnell was not merely a passive researcher of the supernatural. He not only heard a banshee, but also had the misfortune of seeing a wraith that could well have been the dreaded death messenger.

---

174. Neligan and Seymour, *True Irish Ghost Stories*, 202.

175. Lysaght, *Pocket Book*, 25.

When he was a child, his father was away in Ethiopia. That was when his family heard the death messenger.

"It was a windy but fine night, and ... absolutely still. Suddenly, from apparently just under the window, there rang out a series of the most harrowing screams ... fearing ... that it was some woman being murdered in the garden, my mother summoned the servants ... The sounds went on, every moment increasing in vehemence, and there was an intensity and eeriness about them that speedily convinced the hearers that they could be due to no earthly agency. After lasting several minutes they finally died away in a long, protracted wail, full of such agony and despair." [176]

When he was a bit older, he developed a curious fear of the staircase in his home, especially a place where the staircase would bend and the person ascending or descending could not see around. For some reason, he felt certain there was something evil lurking there, as if waiting to ambush them.

He confessed his fear to his older sister, who could be expected to tease him about such a thing. But she was sympathetic and understanding. She admitted that she too was frightened of the same spot. What is more, she was certain she had actually seen something at that same bend in the staircase.

Eventually, the fateful day came when he, too, saw the entity. It was as horrible as his imagination could conjure.

Her hair was light blonde, but wild and uncombed, more like straw than human hair. Her pale skin was "tightly drawn over the bones like a mummy, it looked as if it had been buried for several months and then resurrected." [177] The creature's eyes were intense and filled with hate. As it stared at him with those malevolent eyes,

---

176. O'Donnell, *The Banshee*, 234–235.
177. O'Donnell, *The Banshee*, 237.

the specter had a leering, almost demonic grin. It did not seem to be human, nor was it anything that had ever been human, but rather it appeared "to be the creation of something wholly evil."[178]

He continued to experience the banshee throughout his life. He heard the satanic laugh again when his mother passed away. Years later, he heard the sound of what he described as possibly a skeleton foot walking back and forth in the room above, followed by a terrible crash. Following this omen, the family received word of the death of an uncle.

After that he was married, and with his wife, he moved into a different, less haunted house. But the change of address does not delay the death messenger.

Once again, the banshee returned, but in a more traditional manner. The husband and wife were awakened at night by the sound of a woman screaming and wailing outside. By then, he knew darn well what it was as he had heard it before. He informed his wife that they would soon receive word of another death in the family.

He was right. A few days passed with the new couple being worried every time they brought in the mail. Sure enough, before long, there was word from a relative that an aunt of theirs had died.[179]

It is interesting to note that the family banshee (if indeed that was what the specter was) was lurking not only at a staircase, but in a bend of the steps. Spirits tend to congregate in in-between places; in haunted houses, ghosts are often manifested on staircases. This is an anomalous spot, not on one floor, not on the other. The bend means you are not going this way or the other, you are in between the two directions.

---

178. O'Donnell, *The Banshee*, 237.
179. O'Donnell, *The Banshee*, 238–244.

Wilfred and Ellen

In another sad tale of love and betrayal, we have the instance of Wilfred and Ellen. Both were young and very much in love. However, one day, as they walked arm in arm down a flagstone path through a garden, the serene mood was shattered by the unexpected appearance of an old woman. "It was a broad face with very pronounced cheek-bones; a large mouth, the thin lips of which were fixed in a dreadful and mocking leer; and very pale, obliquely set eyes that glowed banefully."[180] This disgusting creature looked at the young lovers and erupted into diabolic laughter.

When the couple returned to the house, they revealed what they had seen. Who was this old hag wandering about their grounds? But instead of a clear answer, they were advised not to say anything more about this as it might frighten other members of the family. They complied with this and went on with their lives, intent on marriage and having a good life together. The matter was soon forgotten.

Apparently to Ellen, having a good life meant being wealthy … and Wilfred's family suffered some serious financial problems. They were so bad that the family was in dire danger of losing everything.

To Ellen, love was love, but money made her life comfortable and secure. Seeing that her financial future suddenly did not look too good with Wilfred, she discarded him like yesterday's newspaper and quickly married a wealthy Englishman.

Now she had her comfort and security. However, she soon learned the hard lesson that money was temporary and fleeting, but true love could be eternal. Although Ellen was well provided for materially, her new marriage was not at all happy. She had all the luxury money could purchase, but none of the happiness she'd had with Wilfred. She realized too late that she had made a terrible mistake.

---

180. O'Donnell, *The Banshee*, 40.

But there was no time to correct it. As if to mock her, the wheel of fortune had spun yet again, and Wilfred's family was now doing well. He had been in the West Indies on a very successful trading mission for a few years and was now due to dock again in Ireland.

But that night, the family once again heard the mocking, satanic laughter of the hag the couple had encountered on that garden walk so many years before.

The next day, Wilfred's family was waiting to receive him on the dock. Sadly, they learned they were actually there to claim his body. He had died just before docking.[181]

Selective Witnesses and Size

White, the color of a burial shroud, is often worn by banshees. We see this on a case from Rathlin Island in County Antrim, the northernmost point in Ireland. This was also another instance of a banshee being seen by some but not by others.

In the 1950s, a woman's grandmother was dying upstairs. Relatives and neighbors had gathered in the house; many had congregated downstairs to say a rosary.

Suddenly, their prayers were halted by the sound of a woman screaming outside. The group moved to the window and gazed out on the lawn. Some said they could see her quite clearly: the creature was a wee lady dressed entirely in white. Others, however, could see nothing.

The grandmother passed away soon after.[182]

The size of the banshee varies considerably. Occasionally, the beautiful variety is quite tall, sometimes unnaturally so. The old hag variety may be the size of an elderly woman hunched over—or other

---

181. O'Donnell, *The Banshee*, 38–45.

182. Lysaght, *Pocket Book*, 24.

times, she is reported as being the size of a doll, a description often used while discussing numerous members of the fairy kingdom.

This is not particularly helpful, as a child's doll can be very small or knee high to an adult. Either way, it is obvious that this dwarf type is not a natural creature. Some witnesses place the size as that of a child of four. This is larger than most dolls, but certainly smaller than an adult woman.[183]

The Dangers of Curiosity

Pursuing a banshee may not be the smartest idea. It has been recorded that some people, hearing the death cry, decide they want to steal a look at this phantom they had heard about all their life. They start to make their way toward the source of the sound only to find that, just as in the *Mabinogion* tale of the fey Rhiannon, the closer they move toward the source, the farther away it sounds.[184]

Those who are curious—and stupid—enough to want to catch a glimpse of the spectral messenger of death are advised to look for those rock formations nature has fashioned into the likeness of a chair. There are a number of these across Ireland, such as the one near Patrickswell in County Limerick; in County Clare, there is an area known simply as "the bottles," said to be frequented by a banshee; County Waterford has such a chair near Ballynaguilkee. This town also has a road by a river around which a banshee has been sighted combing her hair. County Waterford boasts a banshee rest stop near Modeligo on a nice spot overlooking River Finnisk.

A modern case from Stranorlar in County Donegal in the 1940s illustrates the question as to whether the banshee is a fairy or the ghost of a human. A man in his twenties was walking through town

---

183. Lysaght, *Irish Death Messenger*, 89–90.
184. Lysaght, *Irish Death Messenger*, 81.

one night when he was confronted by a banshee. Being a strong and brave Irishman, he decided to put as much real estate between him and the banshee as he could, and to do it as quickly as possible.

He ran toward Main Street where he saw a woman slowly approaching him. He looked closer and saw that she was someone who had died more than a year earlier. The fright was too much for him; he collapsed to the ground. When he recovered enough to stand, the ghostly woman was not there.

But now, he heard the wailing sound he assumed was from the banshee he had seen. From the distance, he determined the entity's shrieking was not meant for him, but for someone else. He just happened to be in the wrong place.

He was correct in this. He learned later that the husband of the woman whose ghost he'd seen had just died. It was time for him to join her. Evidently, she was coming to meet him.[185]

The White Cat of Drumgunniol

A very interesting description of a banshee was supplied by the great Irish writer of gothic horror, Sheridan Le Fanu. Much of his work is, sadly, somewhat forgotten today; although, during his lifetime, he was a neighbor of and a great influence on a young Irishman who also wanted to be a writer—his name was Bram Stoker.

In 1872, Le Fanu wrote one of the greatest vampire stories of all time, "Carmilla." Seemingly, his old neighbor, now the manager of the great actor Sir Henry Irving, enjoyed it and learned a great deal. In 1897, Bram Stoker wrote his own vampire novel.

Two years before "Carmilla" was reprinted in the magnificent horror collection *In a Glass Darkly*, Sheridan had turned his attention to the traditional Irish spirit of the banshee. His short story "The White

---

185. Á Cnamhsi, "Banshees, Fairies and Leprechauns."

Cat of Drumgunniol" was published in *All the Year Round*, a literary publication begun by Charles Dickens.

"The White Cat" is obviously the product of growing up in Ireland. It quickly becomes obvious that although this is a work of fiction, Le Fanu is relating a few of the many stories he had been told over his lifetime concerning the banshee. In it, he gives a very poetic description of the banshee's appearance.

In the story, the narrator relates an instance from the boyhood of a Mr. Donovan, an educator. In his youth, the teacher spent a good deal of time in an orchard sitting on a stone by the shade of a hawthorn tree, reading a book on history. He assured the reader he was wide awake when he saw the entity.

He looked up to see a peculiar woman walking down a grassy hill toward a field.

> *She wore a long, light grey dress, so long that it seemed to sweep the grass behind her … Her course lay diagonally from corner to corner of the field, which was a large one, and she pursued it without swerving.*
>
> *When she came near I could see that her feet were bare, and that she seemed to be looking steadfastly upon some remote object for guidance.*[186]

She continued in her route, completely straight with no deviation. Indeed, she would have walked right into him except that she stepped around a pond.

While she avoided that bit of water, she paid no attention to the lough she was walking toward: "But instead of arresting her course at the margin of the lough, as I had expected, she went on without

---

186. Le Fanu, "The White Cat."

seeming conscious of its existence ... walk across the surface of the water, and pass, without seeming to see me, at about the distance I had calculated."[187]

In the remainder of the story, the banshee is quite similar to the Scandinavian *fylgja* in that it materializes in animal form, an entity sometimes referred to as a fetch. In this tale, the banshee becomes a white cat.

The family banshee, in the form of a white cat, interfered with the layout of the narrator's grand-uncle, a selfish and unpleasant person. The cat even took up a position on top of the body, sitting on the corpse's face as if in triumph.

Eventually the body was buried. The narrator then reflected upon the family messenger of the grave: "No banshee ever yet was more inalienably attached to a family than this ominous apparition is to mine ... The banshee seems to be animated with an affectionate sympathy with the bereaved family to who it is hereditarily attached, whereas this thing has about it a suspicion of malice."[188]

He states that the entity takes the form of a cat as these animals are "the coldest, and they say, the most vindictive of brutes."[189]

Le Fanu was correct in his eerie tale. Sometimes the banshee appears not as a human at all, but, like the Scandinavian *fylgja*, as an animal, usually a crow.[190] This, of course, recalls the myths of the dreaded Morrigan and her connection to carrion crows who would feast on corpses after a battle. As we shall see shortly, there is an actual case from nineteenth-century Cincinnati of a banshee taking the form of a cat, although this feline is the more traditional black.

---

187. Le Fanu, "The White Cat."
188. Le Fanu, "The White Cat."
189. Le Fanu, "The White Cat."
190. Lysaght, *Irish Death Messenger*, 105.

The Hitchhiking Banshee of County Killarney

We find a bit of preternatural wisdom in a rather unexpected location. Most people are familiar with Disney's delightful Haunted Mansion attraction. Toward the end of this ride, the Ghost Host advises us to beware of hitchhiking ghosts. There is also a wealth of urban folklore concerning ghosts who hitchhike with unsuspecting motorists.

And there is at least one case of a hitchhiking banshee.

In Moll's Gap, County Killarney, there was the curious case of a man named Jeremiah Sheehan. He was driving a cart through the gap, but his mind was elsewhere. He was weighed down with sorrow as his two children were in the hospital, suffering from scarlet fever. Her chances of survival were not good.

It certainly did not cheer him up to suddenly hear the unearthly sound of a woman wailing. He knew what it was, but, of course, he did not know who the crying was for. Maybe it was for someone else. He prayed that it was so.

He sped the frightened horse on faster and faster, but no matter how rapidly the steed galloped, he could still hear the wailing. In fact, it was too loud. Filled with terror, he turned where the lamenting was coming from.

It was from his own cart—and the banshee was sitting in the back, still wailing.

Jeremiah was stuck; he certainly couldn't push her off. He had no choice but to keep going. She remained on the cart for a few miles through empty country. But as soon as they passed a cottage by the road, the wailing abruptly stopped, possibly to keep from alarming the people inside. Jeremiah turned to see the dark messenger was no longer there. He had no idea where she went, and he certainly wasn't going to look for her.

That same day, he learned his daughter had passed away from the illness.[191]

A curious variation of the banshee is found in a family in County Galway. One night in the 1800s, the lady of the house was worried as her husband was late coming home. She listened intently for the sound of the carriage, but heard nothing.

Frustrated, she opened the door and looked out on the lawn. It should be noted that in the middle of this lawn was a curious feature, a ring of differently colored grass. This unique circle was surrounded by evergreens. Some old-timers considered this a fairy circle, although no one had ever reported seeing anything unusual there. She had no time for such superstitious nonsense. There was just something a little different about the grass there … no big deal.

The wife, of course, was used to the ring; she saw it every day. It was just part of her yard. But on this night, looking out of the door for her husband, she saw what appeared to be a child rushing about in the confines of the circle. What was even worse, she distinctly heard another unseen child crying.

She had heard stories of this happening in the family in the past. It always meant a death or a terrible accident.

A servant was immediately sent down the same road where the husband's coach was to have traveled. He found him lying unconscious but still alive by the road. Obviously, he was the victim of a carriage accident.[192]

One of the most frightening of these nonhuman banshees was recorded by the German traveler Johann Kohl who visited the Emerald Isle in 1842. In County Clare, he met a woman named Cosideen. She related how she once had a strange encounter with the banshee.

---

191. Chaplin, "The Death Knock," 152.

192. Neligan and Seymour, *True Irish Ghost Stories*, 209–210.

She had seen the entity more than once in her life. But the spirit always appeared to her in the traditional form of Death. The curious thing was, Death was struggling about on two crutches. Despite the Grim Reaper's apparent handicap, whenever she witnessed this ghastly apparition, someone in her family was soon to die.[193]

Thus, we have the appearance of the banshee—sometimes an old crone of tiny size, at other times a beautiful Irish maiden combing her long golden hair. If you should happen upon either type, it is best to leave her alone.

Now, let us take a quick look at a few unfortunate people who did not.

---

193. *Western Folklore,* 275.

Chapter 6
THE SAGA
OF THE COMB

I would be a mermaid fair;
I would sing to myself the whole of the day;
With a comb of pearl I would comb my hair;
And still as I comb'd I would sing and say,
'Who is it loves me? who loves not me?'

—TENNYSON, "THE MERMAID"

There is a curious affinity between banshees and water. They will very often be seen near lakes, streams, or ancient wells or sitting on rocks by the sea. The sound of their cry often follows the course of rivers and streams.

Sometimes banshees are seen on bridges, another anomalous setting that is neither on one shore nor the other, not in the water, not on the land, not in the air. Spirits tend to be encountered in such liminal spaces, such as on the middle of a staircase as we have seen.

Tom Connolly

One such manifestation on a bridge was recorded by Yeats. Thomas Connolly was on his way home one night when he passed a bridge. There was a woman sitting on the edge, weeping uncontrollably. Although he was at first reluctant to disturb her in her time of such intense sorrow, he figured he had to do something. He walked up to her, excused his intrusion, and asked her what the problem was and if he could be of any help.

He was trying to do the right thing, but he received the shock of his life as a reward.

He realized at once that he had disturbed a banshee. He described her skin as being utterly pale, with "an' a most o' freckles on it, like the freckles on a turkey's egg."[194] Her eyes were red from crying, but he could see they were also "as blue as forget-me-nots."[195] These blue eyes were, as he so poetically put it, cold as the moon in a bog on a frosty night. He also stated that there was a lifeless quality to them, which frightened him immensely.

She did nothing to him, but simply slid off the railing, revealing that she was not a bent old lady but a creature much taller than

194. Yeats, *Irish Fairy and Folk Tales*, 118.
195. Yeats, *Irish Fairy and Folk Tales*, 118.

the tallest man. She then slipped down from the bridge and into the stream.

Poor Mister Connolly ran home as fast as his legs could carry him. The next thing he knew, Mrs. Maguire, his landlady, was standing over him trying to wake him up. She told him he had collapsed on the floor after storming in.

Confused, Tom asked if he were alive or dead. She assured him he was still among the living and asked what had caused such a fear in him.

For some reason, he did not want to reveal what he had seen. By then, it was obvious the creature he'd encountered was a banshee, and that someone in the vicinity was doomed to die very soon.

That did not take long. The very next day, he heard of the death of a neighbor, Mr. O'Nales.[196]

Banshee-Haunted Lakes, Rivers, and Wells

There are a number of lakes in Ireland that boast being the preferred hangouts of the death messenger. If you are planning your itinerary, among these banshee-haunted bodies of water are Caherglassan Lake in County Galway, Lough Allen in County Leitrim, Lough Derg in County Tipperary, Lough in Hackett County, Cloggagh Lough in County Cavan, Lough Gowna in County Longford, and many others. The aquatic phantoms also follow rivers and streams, including the Daelagh in County Clare (known as the Banshee's Brook), the Millburn in County Antrim, the Barrow in County Kilkenny, both the Shannon and the Multeen rivers in County Tipperary, and many more. It has been reported that people have heard the sound of the shrieking spirit as she follows the course of the river to her unlucky destination.

---

196. Yeats, *Irish Fairy and Folk Tales*, 117–120.

Banshees have even been associated with that lost bit of the spiritual heritage of the British Isles: sacred and healing wells. One banshee has been said to frequent St. Patrick's Well in County Carlow, while County Waterford hosts one at the well known as *Tobar na Baidhbe*.[197]

Banshees and Mermaids

The image of the banshee with her golden hair sitting on a rock in the stormy sea instantly brings to mind another supernatural creature, the mermaid. The puzzling connection between banshees and mermaids is so prevalent that some scholars believe the two legends may well have merged and borrowed from each other at some point in the past. There is no doubt that some of the attributes of the fishy maidens appear to have been transferred to death's herald.

One of these connections is found in a curious folktale from County Kerry. A man stumbled upon a mermaid and was immediately entranced by her beauty. Before she could escape, the man stole her wand, without which she would be unable to live with her people.

She begged him to return the stolen item, but he adamantly refused. Entranced by her beauty, he demanded that she transform into a full human and marry him, a request that was reluctantly granted.

Naturally, he hid the wand well, and afterward, he refused to allow her or anyone else into a certain locked room. She was a good wife and loyal to him. The couple soon had a child together, a daughter. The daughter became curious herself as to what was going on in the locked room. Was there some kind of great treasure in there? What was her father hiding?

---

197. Lysaght, *Irish Death Messenger*, 129.

One night, when no one was about, she took a candle and peeked through the keyhole into the forbidden chamber.

As a punishment for sacrilege, the little girl was struck blind. She did not live long after that, and after her death she was transformed into a banshee.[198]

The mermaidlike combing of the hair is found in many instances of sightings of a banshee. In Sleevemweel, County Carlow, a woman was lying on her deathbed, ready to leave this world. The people attending her clearly heard the screeching of a banshee just outside the window.

Some of the braver of the group went to the window and looked out. There she was, and true to form, she was combing her hair as she lamented.[199]

The connection between banshees and bodies of water is seen once again in this case of a young woman in County Cork. One night, she heard the keening and looked out the window. There, in the moonlight, she saw a woman clad completely in white sitting on a nearby bridge. She was wailing and crying, but at the same time, the lady was waving her arms toward the girl's house, as if directing something toward the home. The uncanny woman then vanished into the darkness.

It did not take long before she learned what this had all been about. The girl's father was walking on the street in the city of Cork when he stumbled. In the fall, he struck his head and died.[200]

---

198. Lysaght, *Irish Death Messenger*, 45.

199. Lysaght, *Irish Death Messenger*, 137.

200. Neligan and Seymour, *True Irish Ghost Stories*, 203.

Disturbing the Banshee

There is an old Irish saying about the proper way to deal with a ban-shee: "Let her alone while she lets you alone, for an hour's luck never shone on anyone that ever molested the banshee."[201] This would seemingly make perfect sense.

However, as we all know, there is an exceptionally large number of people who do not have sense and, as a result, do some very stupid things.

In County Westmeath near Moyleroe, three young men—Bob Smythe, James Gilmore, and Joe Flynn—all heard the banshee one night. They looked about and saw her, a woman no larger than a small child, with long red hair and a red cape, wailing pitifully.

Possibly emboldened by some of Ireland's more famous products, the stalwart trio decided to run to try to catch her. What exactly they thought they would do with her if they caught her was undoubtedly beyond their level of strategic planning.

They were fortunate. The banshee saw them coming and simply disappeared. Soon thereafter, they learned their neighbor, Mrs. Mulligan, had gone on to her reward.[202]

Stealing the Comb

One of the most ignorant things a person can do is steal a banshee's comb. There are a large number of such stories, undoubtedly folktales, concerning people who are blessed with this high grade of stupidity.

There are a few variations of this tale, as we see in this example from County Tipperary. A man was coming home about midnight, probably after having a little liquid refreshment, and heard the dreadful wailing in a field nearby. Rather than cross himself and move on

201. Keegan, "Legends and Tales," 366–374.
202. Lysaght, "Banshee Traditions," 98.

swiftly, he crept into the field to have a better look. Crouching down, he saw a woman in a long white cloak with long golden hair wailing and, at the same time, combing her hair.

For some unknown reason, he decided to charge at her to scare her. It worked; she fled and, in the process, dropped her beloved comb. Thinking he now had quite a souvenir to show the boys at the pub, he took the comb with him.

Now everyone knows that the comb is the banshee's most loved possession. He made his way home without trouble. As he slept, he was suddenly awakened by the angry cry of the banshee right in front of his house.

The effects of his liquid refreshment having worn off, he finally wised up and figured that this was not someone he would want to anger—and the stolen comb might not be such a good thing to have in his house after all. But the vicious sounds outside convinced him that opening the door and merely handing it to her might not be too safe.

Coming to a conclusion, he took a pair of tongs from the fireplace, attached the comb, and let it out under the door.

She took the comb back—and with it, half of the iron tongs. Now he definitely had something to show the boys at the pub! [203]

There are a number of these stories of people foolish enough to steal the comb of a banshee. In some of them, the frightened people turn to the advice of the sage priest for directions on how to return it and remain a while longer in this world. [204]

---

203. Lysaght, *Irish Death Messenger*, 154.
204. Lysaght, *Pocket Book*, 79.

The Comb Thief in County Offaly

One of these stories is from County Offaly. A foolish boy slinked up behind a banshee and stole her comb. He took it home, but the banshee followed. Every night, she would cry out in front of the house.

The family had no idea how to solve the problem their genius son had brought upon the household. As this was a spiritual matter, they took it to the priest. He advised them to return the item, but not to touch the entity in any way.

A solution was devised in which the comb would be passed out through the window using a pair of iron tongs. The tongs were heated in the fireplace; the comb was gripped, then gingerly put out through the barely open window.

The banshee recovered her precious comb, and, as a souvenir, she took half of the tongs as well.[205]

A rather silly variation of this tale involves an equally drunken fool from Black Cow in County Wexford. Under similar circumstances, he stole a banshee's comb, but found that her magic was a bit more powerful than he expected.

He could take the device, but he could not let go of it. What was worse, he had somehow been put on a high windowsill and could not come down. Try as he would, the comb was stuck to his hand and he was stuck on the ledge. At midnight, the comb magically left his hand. The family dutifully returned it to the rightful owner, once again using tongs.

The comb was returned, but the now sober thief was still up on the windowsill. Two days later, the family summoned the fire department, who, after laughing hysterically and shaking their heads for a few moments, were able to rescue the man.[206]

205. Almqvist, "Crossing the Border," 209–278.

206. Lysaght, *Irish Death Messenger*, 156.

The Beetle

Another variation of this tale involves a fellow who came across a banshee combing her hair. She also had a beetle, a device used for beating clothes. He rushed up and grabbed the comb and ran off. The unearthly sounds running behind him revealed that he was now being chased by the extremely angry banshee.

The phantom washer threw her beetle at him. Twice it whizzed right past his head, then as though it were a spectral boomerang, she had it again. He was running like mad, but without enough sense to simply drop the comb and make his escape.

He reached his house and flew in the door just as the creature tossed the beetle a third time. As he slammed the door shut, it struck. The crash was so loud the entire house shook. This, of course, woke up the rest of the family, who rushed downstairs to find out why their house was shaking and who was setting off artillery in the middle of the night.

He had a little explaining to do. His wife, doubtlessly after making comments that her mother had warned her against marrying the village idiot, devised a plan. They put the dreaded comb on a spade, and thus slid it out to her.

From this, they incurred great expense. Not only did they have to buy a new spade—half of it was gone—but going outside the next day, they saw the crash of the beetle had split one of the gables of their house.[207]

Finding a Comb

Sometimes, banshees seem to be a little bit careless with their prized possession. It is common knowledge taught to young people in Ireland, particularly little girls, that if they should happen to find a

---

207. Lysaght, *Irish Death Messenger*, 164–167.

comb somewhere, they should not, under any circumstances, touch it. It may have been dropped by a banshee, and they don't believe in finders keepers.[208]

A tale about this concerns the lost comb being found not by a little girl, but by a boy. He foolishly took the comb home, only to find that now the banshee was coming around crying out in the night, demanding her property be returned.

Again, advice was sought from a priest, who warned the family not to touch the creature by handing the comb out, but to use iron tongs and push the item out in that manner.

The family did this, and half of the tongs went with it.[209]

A modern example of this comes from County Laois. A family was busy cutting corn when their little girl shouted that she'd found something. It was a blue comb, lying discarded in a ditch. She was ready to claim it as her own, but her family suddenly became upset, indeed even manic. She was told not to even touch the device, as it may have come from a passing banshee, and she would certainly be back to look for it.[210]

In a dramatic variation of this folk belief, the comb used by the banshee is sometimes said to be made from a single bone of a corpse with notches crudely cut into it. How any witness would be able to move in close enough to see this is something of a mystery.[211]

208. Mac Philib, "Dublin South County," 114.

209. Almqvist, "Crossing the Border," 221–222.

210. Lysaght, *Irish Death Messenger*, 180.

211. Lysaght, *Pocket Book*, 42.

Touching the Banshee

A variation of this legend involves people making physical contact with a banshee and the mark of its fingers appearing permanently etched on them or some iron implement.

A man from County Galway, identified only as Thomas Harte's uncle, came home one night to see a woman in front of his house. Not knowing who she was or what she was up to, he walked up behind her and put his hand on her shoulder.

This was a big mistake.

The woman turned out to be a banshee—and she was not the touchy-feely type. The wraith spun around and angrily grabbed him by the forehead. She then lifted him up into the air. Just as quickly, she tossed him down. She then disappeared.

He was not terribly wounded from the encounter, but he did have a few souvenirs. The first was that all his hair had turned completely white. The second is that the imprint of the banshee's five fingers was now permanently scarred on his forehead.[212]

It is interesting to note that in these many tales of the stolen banshee comb, the thief is almost always a man, usually drunk. There are a few variants of this motif in which the thief is female. However, she is described as being particularly wild, in no way the traditional Irish view of feminine propriety.[213]

So, if you happen to see a comb lying in the grass—leave it there! Should you stumble upon a banshee combing her long hair while crying out in the middle of the night, do not bother her.

It never ends well.

---

212. Lysaght, *Pocket Book*, 72.
213. Lysaght, "Banshee's Comb," 78.

Chapter 7
THE BANSHEES IN THE UNITED STATES AND CANADA

"Adieu," they cried, "to Fatherland.
To all in life most dear!"
And when they caught the shore's last glimpse,
They shed a parting tear.
Parting tears shed for home and friends,
What bitter tears they were.

—J. A. B., "THE EMIGRANT SHIP"

Banshees will follow members of their family even if they leave the Emerald Isle and are living overseas. With so many desperate people escaping the potato famine from 1845 to 1852, both the United States and Canada received boatloads of new citizens.

Not counted on the passenger manifests were their family banshees.

No matter how much these émigré families became absorbed into the culture of their new homeland, they were still Irish, and although destitute and fleeing starvation, some were members of families still connected to the banshee. Sometimes, those who remained in Ireland, detached from their kinfolk in the New World, would hear the banshee cry when one of their separated relatives was due to die, and vice versa. It is believed that the sound of the wailing would begin at the location where the expatriate was now living, then the mournful spirit would travel across the sea to deliver her dark message to the rest of the family.[214]

Con Egan

One of these was Con Egan, a farmer in Ballydaly in County Offaly, a practical man who claimed he did not believe in the existence of the banshee. He had just put down the cows one evening when he suddenly heard a horrible screaming. Thinking that one of his family was injured, he dropped everything and rushed to the house.

No one was hurt, and all were wondering what the shrieking was. Then, his sister, Mary Anne, remembered that she did have a letter from relatives in America in her pocket, a letter that she had been carrying around all day but had been too busy to open. Perhaps, with Con at her side, it was time to take a look at it.

With a frightened look and shaking hands, she opened the letter. It was from their brother Martin who lived in the States. It bore bad

---

214. Lysaght, *Pocket Book*, 59.

news, as there was yet another brother in America, and he was quite ill and in the hospital.

It was not long before they received another message from their émigré siblings. The ill brother was dead. One may assume that after this, Mr. Egan had second thoughts about his disbelief in the family banshee.[215]

The American Civil War

The boatloads of Irish bound for the United States ended up in big city ghettos, locked in poverty and facing discrimination. Young men seeking employment to feed their families were blocked by signs stating "Irish Catholics Need Not Apply." But then a terrible war broke out, and things started to change.

There were numerous Irishmen who fought in the American Civil War. As the new immigrants struggled for acceptance in an often hostile nation, they found that fighting in its wars, risking their lives for their new nation, would help them gain acceptance. Both sides had Irish regiments who won credit and praise for their tough fighting. Some Irishmen rose to become famous generals, such as Cleburne, Gamble, Lytle, Lawler, Sweeny, and the man who struck the final death blow at the Confederacy at the Battle of Sayler's Creek, Philip Sheridan. These immigrant soldiers brought with them their culture, their values, and, in a few cases, their banshees.

There is the curious encounter of an Irishman who fought for the Confederacy. One night, he was on a ship headed to Charleston, South Carolina. As he looked over the railing at the moonlight and the ocean, he suddenly heard a woman singing in the air.

This was the last sound he wanted to hear on this voyage. Was there a Union warship nearby, moving silently through the darkness,

---

215. Lysaght, *Irish Death Messenger*, 220.

searching for blockade runners? Did it mean there would be a ship-wreck, with him onboard the ship? Was he going to die in battle?

Frightened, he asked another soldier, a fellow who was not Irish, if he heard the sound. The man looked at him with a pale expression. Yes, he had heard it too. What could it possibly be?

The first soldier answered back that his family had a banshee, and he was always taught what she sounded like—and she sounded exactly like that.

The night did not pass well, but they landed in Charleston and disembarked with no problems. Mail call came soon thereafter. He read in a letter that a cousin of his, also a soldier, had died in an attack.[216]

Another Irishman, a man named O'Hagan, was a Union sympathizer. He was not content to just join the army, he joined the US Marines. He soon found himself on a ship patrolling the coast of North Carolina, searching for rebel warships and, more importantly, the blockade runners who were keeping the Confederacy supplied.

He happened to be belowdecks one night when he heard a strange tapping at one of the portholes. Now, of course, there should never be tapping at a porthole when one is out at sea. Not wishing to waken the others until he had a better idea of what was going on, he stumbled through the dark toward the porthole. It was probably nothing, maybe just a bird.

No, it was indeed something—and it was something he certainly did not expect. There was a woman floating in the air just outside the porthole.

As he described her: "It was the face of a woman with raven black hair that fell in long ringlets about her neck and shoulders. She had big golden rings in her ears, that shone like anything as the moon-

216. O'Donnell, *The Banshee*, 136–137.

beams caught them, as did her teeth, too, which were the loveliest bits of ivory I have ever seen, absolutely even and without the slightest mar."[217]

Despite the strange sight of a lovely young lady floating above the ocean, there was one thing in particular that fascinated him above all: her eyes. "They were large, not too large, however, but in strict proportion to the rest of her face, and as far as I could judge in the moonlight, either blue or grey, but indescribably beautiful, and, at the same time, indescribably sad."[218]

As he moved closer to the porthole, she moved back a bit. She then pointed with her arm to a particular spot on the black ocean. He looked, but could see nothing there.

Then he heard the sound: the beautiful melody of an Irish harp playing in the distance. As best he could tell, the music was coming from the exact spot she had pointed to.

Then both she and the music were gone.

He knew this was the family banshee. What was she pointing to? Was there a Confederate warship out there in the darkness? What was she trying to tell him?

Of course, he could not notify anyone in charge. They would think he was mad or drunk. There was nothing he could do; he simply returned to his bunk, but had very little sleep that night, expecting a call to battle stations at any moment.

The call never came. The patrol went without a hitch. When they finally returned to port, there was a letter waiting for him. It was bad news from the Old Country; his father had died. In fact, he had, from what he read in the letter, died at the same moment he had seen the mysterious woman. Then O'Hagan understood what the

217. O'Donnell, *The Banshee*, 139–140.
218. O'Donnell, *The Banshee*, 139–140.

banshee had been pointing at. She was pointing in the direction of Ireland.[219]

A Modern Case from Boston

The years may have passed, decades, even a century—but the banshee always knows her own. In 1982, Antoinette and her family lived in a suburb of Boston. In the middle of a winter night, she was suddenly awakened by the sound of a frantic knocking at the door.

She put on a robe and rushed downstairs. Could there have been some kind of accident? She called out, asking who it was, but there was no answer. She looked out the window, but there was no one standing there. This could be a dangerous situation, but she held her breath and opened the door.

There was nobody there. It seemed awful late and cold for kids to be gallivanting around the neighborhood, knocking on doors then running away. She looked down at the snow.

There were no footprints.

This was insane. Could she have imagined it? But no, she was absolutely certain she'd heard a knocking. Being the middle of winter in Boston and quite cold, she quickly shut the door and made her way back into the house. If there were any doubts as to what she had heard, they were dispelled when she saw her daughter Pauline standing at the top of the stairs asking who was knocking. Was something wrong?

No—go back to sleep.

Antoinette took her own advice, but before too long, there was a loud knocking on the front door once again. For a second time, she rushed down the stairs, called out, then looked. No one was there.

---

219. O'Donnell, *The Banshee*, 139–140.

It was then that she had a strange feeling. Memories of stories told by gray-haired relatives were coming back to her.

Antoinette was one of the daughters of a family that, a few generations earlier, had left the Emerald Isle for America. Indeed, of all the sisters, she was the one with the least connection to Ireland. Born and raised in America, her Irish heritage went little further than wearing a bit of green on St. Patrick's Day.

What is more, she was far from religious and had little room for spirituality in her busy life. One might say that she was just shy of being a full-fledged agnostic.

However, as she sat in the kitchen contemplating the sound, she remembered those old tales from Ireland. She recalled the stories she had heard of the banshee, of mysterious balls of fire floating through a doomed person's cottage—and of another ominous sign, the death knock. But those were just old stories, silly ramblings of superstitious, simple people. They couldn't possibly…

As soon as it was a decent hour, she began to make calls to relatives. No one knew anything. She was about to breathe a sigh of relief.

That was when the phone rang. It was from Ireland. Sure enough, just as the old stories had said, there had been a death in the family. A close uncle had died suddenly from a heart attack.[220]

Canadian Cases

In a banshee tale that would make good fodder for a horror movie, there is a strange case from Canada in the 1800s. Ellen was one of two nieces of an Irish major. The girls had a houseguest from the old country, her friend Delane.

---

220. Chaplin, "The Death Knock," 135–136.

One night, Delane was awakened by the loud sound of a coach pulling up in front of the house. She heard footsteps, then the clacking sound of a brass door knocker. Curiously, she did not hear any of the servants going to open the door.

All was silence.

The next morning, she asked about the coach and the knocking. She was told that such things were impossible—the major had had the door knocker removed some years earlier. There was no knocker, and there had been no coach.

The next evening, Delane was awakened in the middle of the night by something pulling violently on her bedsheets. She raised up to see it was Ellen—and Ellen looked as though she were about to die from fright. Then Delane saw what had caused the commotion.

There was someone else moving around the room in the darkness. It was very hard to see with the moonlight coming through the windows, but both girls could see that, although impossible, it appeared to be a nun. It moved about, taking very long and quiet steps. Her head was covered, but in a moment, she turned toward them.

She focused her stare on Ellen. The two locked eyes for a moment, after which the ghostly nun walked in her strange way toward the wall. When she reached it, she "seemed to melt into the wall. At all events, it had vanished, and there was nothing where it had been standing, saving moonlight."[221]

The two, very frightened, girls were now alone.

The next morning, the girls went to the major and told him what they'd seen. Delane informed him she did not feel safe in what was obviously a very haunted house. She wanted to leave, that very day if possible.

---

221. O'Donnell, *The Banshee*, 65.

They expected an argument, or at least surprise from the major. Instead, he merely nodded and muttered that yes, perhaps it would be best if she departed. Obviously, there was a story here, and he was not willing to impart it.

Delane returned to her room and, as fast as possible, packed her trunk. She then decided that before making her departure, she and the nieces would take a final stroll through the beautiful garden. To their horror, here, on the flagstone path, in the midst of the day, they saw the apparition again.

"The sunlight falling directly on it revealed features now only too easily distinguishable of someone long since dead, but animated by a spirit that was wholly antagonistic and malicious, and as they shrank back terror-stricken, it stretched forth one of its long, bony arms and touched first Ellen and then her sister on the shoulder." [222]

Delane, who had not been touched by the specter, soon returned to Ireland. She asked some knowledgeable friends what the heck was going on with the major's family over in Canada. It was explained to her that they had a banshee; sometimes it would shriek and wail in the traditional manner, at other times it would simply appear but say nothing.

It was not much longer before sad news came from Canada. Not only had the major died suddenly, but both nieces, who had been touched by the specter, contracted an illness and had died as well. [223]

Also in Canada, in the late 1800s, there was the tragic case of the O'Grady family, immigrants who over the years had lost most of their connection to the old land. Their ancestral heritage was unexpectedly revived when, in the middle of the night, they heard a strange sound outside. It was a horrific, bloodcurdling shrieking. The

---

222. O'Donnell, *The Banshee*, 66–67.
223. O'Donnell, *The Banshee*, 62–67.

family members ran out into the yard and tried to figure out who was making such a noise. Did someone need some help? They looked about in the darkness, called out, but there was no one.

The next morning, the father and son went out in the boat. The water was rough and choppy, but the wife wasn't concerned, as they were both good sailors.

She did start to worry as the hours went by from the time they should have been back, but there was no sign of them. As the hands of the clock crept along, she spent more and more time looking out the window. She tried not to think of the cry they had heard the night before.

Near sunset, some of the local fishermen were bringing the two dead bodies up the hill toward the house. Apparently there had been an unexpected wave, and the boat had capsized. The family may have forgotten Ireland, but the banshee had not forgotten them.[224]

The Tarboro Banshee

The most famous banshee in the United States, indeed in all of North America, is found in the woods near Tarboro, along Tar River in North Carolina.

Tar River is not actually filled with tar. It is a corruption of the Tuscarora word *taw*, meaning that the waters bring good health.[225]

It did not bring good health to one patriot and a few British soldiers during the Revolutionary War.

There are several variations of this tale. One of the most popular goes like this.

In 1780, a man named Dave Warner set up a small mill on Tar River. David was known throughout the area as a Whig, and a man

---

224. Wilde, *Ancient Legends*, 136.

225. Layne, "Ghosts Said to Haunt Tarboro."

totally committed to the patriot cause. He detested the English soldiers marching through the area and would do whatever he could to
stop them, even if it meant giving his life for this new nation.

Having more than his share of bravery, he also did not seem to
mind the local legend that the river his mill was located on was the
abode of a banshee. She had her business, he had his.

By the next year, the American General Greene was leading his
forces against an experienced Lord Cornwallis who was commanding
the British army in North Carolina. A number of fierce battles had
been fought in the state, and there were more to come.

As British troops moved into the area, Dave Warner knew very
well that he would be on their list of civilians suspected of helping
the rebels. He had heard how a number of other people had been
arrested, beaten, had their property seized—and it looked like just a
matter of time before they came for him.

That time came in the dry heat of August. A neighbor galloped as
fast as he could to the mill. There was Dave, working late as he often
did, grinding the corn to help feed General Greene's army.

The neighbor told Warner that he had to vacate while he still
could; there was a small party of British scouts headed this way,
intent on arresting him. The miller remained calm, merely stating
that General Greene's army needed the food, and he was going to
keep working until the job was done.

The neighbor, a patriot himself, decided to stay and help.

It was not long before three Redcoats barged in. They grabbed
Warner and dragged him out of the mill to the bank of Tar River.
Despite this, Dave was still calm. He told his captors that there was a
banshee in the river, and if they harmed him, it would be their death.

Two of the soldiers were quite familiar with the banshee and
knew her powers. They looked at each other, not knowing what to

do. They could face cannon fire and muskets; they would charge an entrenched enemy on command—but this?

Their executive decision was to wait there with their prisoner until the commander of their regiment came along. Let him deal with the banshee.

But there was a third member of the scouting party, and he was not in the least bit superstitious. He did not want to hear any more nonsense about banshees, and knew that the commander would be furious if they held up the mission because of some silly old story that the man had probably made up on the spot.

Under his urging, the three tied up Dave, then to make sure he went under, they tied a heavy rock to him. In a moment, they tossed Dave Warner into Tar River. The rock did its job; he went under, never to surface again.

But, at the same moment, there was a shrill sound of a screeching woman coming at them across the water. The three men were now terrified. This silly old superstition was now shrieking for them.

When the commander did arrive, he was furious at what they had done. He ordered that the three of them should remain behind, work the mill to feed the British army, and not leave the area until he gave the order. With that, the British forces moved on without them.

Now the three were alone, working and living in the mill, with the knowledge that there was a very angry banshee watching them. An Irish spirit was now ready to extract vengeance on British soldiers—not a good situation for them to be in.

They remained there for a few days. During the daylight hours, they worked the mill. But when the sun set, the banshee wails would begin. The shrieking would go all night, robbing them of their sleep—and bit by bit, of their sanity.

Then, one night, a ghostly female figure appeared in the doorway of the mill, a figure clad in a flowing white gown blowing in the night breeze. She looked up and revealed a skull-like face.

The two soldiers, the ones who had wanted to wait for the commander, acted as though they were in some manner of trance. The specter started to glide away from the mill. The two soldiers slowly followed her, walking out of the mill and straight to the river's edge. From there, they just kept walking into the muddy water. Just like their victim, they drowned in Tar River. The brave one who had made fun of the superstition was now in a fetal position in the corner of the mill.

As his commander was apparently too busy with other matters to summon him, the terrified soldier remained alone at the haunted mill. He was going slowly insane. He would perform his duties during daylight, but at night, he would wander about the woods crying out for Dave Warner. The banshee was the only one to answer his cry.

Eventually, he too was found drowned in Tar River. The banshee had both predicted his death … and taken her revenge.

It is said that the banshee of Tar River is still there, and people will occasionally hear her cry at night. When they do, they know that someone is about to die.[226]

Mr. Gailor Hears a Banshee

A truly crazy banshee case occurred in Cincinnati in the Gilded Age at the City Hospital. One beautiful day in May of 1892, a Mr. Gailor walked in off the street. When the attendant asked how he could help him, the man inquired if it would be possible for someone to take him on a short tour to look at the facility.

---

226. Curran, *Mysterious Celtic*, 277–280.

It was a curious request, but a person was found who dutifully took this stranger around, showing off the medical skills of the staff and the first-rate facilities of the hospital. Mr. Gailor seemed impressed and thanked his tour guide.

By now, the attendant could resist it no longer and asked Mr. Gailor why he wanted the tour. Was his wife or another loved one ill? Was he ill?

No, he felt just fine—how could you not feel fine on such a wonderful spring day? The problem was that the other day, he had heard the family banshee wailing, and he knew he would soon be dying, probably in a hospital bed. It didn't matter that he was healthy now; the banshee had called him and he would answer. It was inevitable.

As the attendant stared in disbelief, Mr. Gailor thanked him again and walked out the door.

He was not seen again in the hospital. Whether he died quickly somewhere else, or the wail was for another member of his family, or if he was completely bonkers, is a question that will never be answered.[227]

But that was not the end of it. While the hospital workers had a good laugh and a story to tell over a few beers at one of the many Over-the-Rhine saloons, the very next day, another visitor arrived.

This one was quite welcome, at least initially. It was a black cat and seemed to be content with the new surroundings. The entire staff, from janitor to surgeon, enjoyed the company of the cat. The nurses gave it plenty of milk and food; everyone gave it a little pet as they passed by.

The night clerk, Mr. Hudson, sat in a booth with a telegraph. These were connected to the different wards. Whenever a death would take place, a signal in the telegraph would go off. Then Mr.

---

227. *Cincinnati Enquirer*, 1892.

Hudson had to go to the ward for the sad, and hopefully inconspicuous, task of removing the body.

One night, the black cat suddenly went into a screeching fit, arching its back and making a terrible ruckus, running about as if the devil had gone into him. Just as the cat stopped the unusual behavior, the death signal went off. Mr. Hudson gave the black cat a suspicious look, then went off to do his somber duty.

A few nights later, the cat did the same thing. As soon as the feline settled down, the death signal would go off.

This happened again and again. Now the hospital workers were not as happy with their ominous visitor. Somehow, the animal always went into a fit just before a patient died, as if it could sense the arrival of the Grim Reaper. To commemorate this ability, the cat was given the nickname Death.

Eventually the cat was no longer seen. It had just moved on of its own accord. No one missed it, and all hoped it would not return.

That was when some of the workers recalled that colorful Mr. Gailor coming in saying that a banshee was looking for him. Did the banshee, in the form of a witchy black cat, follow him into the city hospital? Was this seemingly harmless creature a kind of banshee itself, a spirit that the old folks called a fetch, like Le Fanu's white cat?

No one dared to speculate.[228]

The Macabre Vision of Mrs. Coleman

An even more grisly case came from Oakland, California, in the 1920s. A woman, Mrs. Coleman, happened to be walking into her house one day when she saw two of her neighbors nearby chatting. She looked again and, to her horror, saw a skeleton standing next to

---

228. *Cincinnati Enquirer*, 1892.

one of them, with his boney arm on her shoulder. A few days later, that woman was dead.[229]

There are many accounts of Irish descendants experiencing the cry of the banshee. One American encounter with the family death messenger took place on a college campus in Pennsylvania in the 1950s. Two students were walking along the walkway when one suddenly asked his companion if he heard that wailing sound.

No, his friend (who would later become a priest) replied that he had heard nothing. But his friend was quite convinced of what he had heard. A frightened look came over his face. He stated in a low voice that there was no doubt about it: he had just heard the family banshee. This was a story he had grown up with. This could only mean that his mother back in Ireland had gone to her reward.

It was not long before the sad news was received. He was absolutely correct.[230]

229. Hudson, "64 Death Omens."

230. Lysaght, *Pocket Book*, 54.

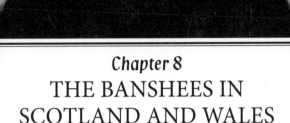

Chapter 8
THE BANSHEES IN SCOTLAND AND WALES

Before the death of any of his race, the phantom-chief
gallops along the seabeach, near to the castle,
announcing the event by cries and lamentations. The
specter is said to have rode his rounds and uttered
his death-cries within these few years, in consequence
of which, the family and clan, though much shocked,
were in no way surprised, to hear, by next accounts,
that their gallant chief was dead at Lisbon, where he
served under Lord Wellington.

—Scott, Letters on Demonology

Now this is the stuff that gothic horror is made of. Who cannot see that wild ancestor of the family MacLean galloping madly down the beach near Lochbuy on the Isle of Mull? He races past ancient standing stones as the sky above erupts into flashes of lightning, inky clouds dance about a full moon, and the waves collide against the rocky shore. It is indeed a wild, thrilling ride!

The only curious thing here is that this messenger of the grave is male. Banshees, at least in Ireland, are exclusively women. But then, this is Scotland—and the Scots have always done things their own way.

Naturally, there is a delightful story connected to this phantom horseman.

This occurred in the fourteenth century, in the midst of the time of endless warfare between the clans. Ewan was the son of Eachann Reaganach, known as Hector the Stern. Before a great battle, Ewan was walking through the forest when he spied the Scottish banshee, the *bean nighidh*, washing the bloody armor and clothing of the soldiers destined to die in the upcoming conflict.

Having been told the stories, he knew to sneak up behind her and suck at her breast. If he did so successfully, he could then ask her anything. Naturally, what he wished to know more than anything else was who would win the battle the next day.

He was successful in this curious operation. The banshee now had to answer his question concerning the outcome of the next day's battle.

Angry, the death messenger replied that if unasked-for butter was given to them with their porridge at breakfast the next morning, then victory would be his. The butter must be given without request; thus, it must be a freewill offering.

However, should there be no butter …

The next morning, Ewan and his men were assembled for breakfast. He ordered that no one should eat a bite before he gave permission. All sat there, hungry and staring at him as though he had lost his mind. Their food was in front of them, they could smell it, but they couldn't touch it.

Ewan waited for a long while, but no unasked-for butter emerged from the kitchen. Fuming with anger, he ordered his men (who still had no breakfast) to leave the table and assemble for the battle.

In the fight, not only did his side lose, but Ewan had the top of his head cut off. Since that bloody day, he has galloped at night announcing the deaths of his descendants. As a result of his insolence, he had become a banshee himself.[231]

The Bean Nighidh

The wraith that Ewan had encountered is known as the *bean nighidh*, the Scottish version of the washerwoman banshee. Scottish tales of this creature have a curious variation that is reminiscent, believe it or not, to some accounts of the American Bigfoot.

In some parts of Scotland, such as the Isle of Mull, the *bean nighidh* performs her dark washing while bare chested. Thus, she reveals that she has abnormally long breasts. Like the famous Sasquatch, she tosses the breasts over her shoulder to get them out of her way.

Now the unseen observer has a decision to make. He could steal away silently and allow the wraith to go on with her business. Or…

He could sneak up behind her. If she does not see him, "he is to catch one of her breasts, and, putting it to his mouth, call herself to witness that she is his first nursing or foster-mother (*muime cìche*).

---

231. Scotclans, "Ewan the Headless."

She answers that he has need of that being the case, and will then communicate whatever knowledge he desires."[232]

Of course, under the circumstances, the question is always the same: Whose shirt is she washing? Should she reply that it is that of an enemy … well, don't let me interrupt laundry day. But should she reply that it is the questioner or someone close, then she is stopped in her grim task.[233]

Not surprisingly, this is a rather perilous operation. If the intruder lacks stealth and is seen by the washer, she will cause him to become paralyzed.[234]

As in Ireland, the Scottish banshee is known by several names. Most prominent is a *caointeach* or a *caoineag*, signifying the weeping ghostly maiden. However, the washerwoman tradition is quite prominent. In this form she is known as the *bean nigheachain*, or more commonly, the *bean nighidh*. In this form, she is also known as the rather poetic *nigheag bheag a bhròin*, translated as "the little washer of sorrow."

This washerwoman form is well known in the Hebrides. Indeed, on the Isle of Mull, there is a stone where she was often reported as washing the shrouds or other clothing of those doomed to die. The stone has a curious burn mark on it.[235]

There is a folk belief in Scotland that is closely related to the Irish banshee in its washerwoman form. It states that if a woman dies unexpectedly, a tragic occurrence that would most likely happen in childbirth, and should she happen to have wash that is yet to be done, then the ghost of that woman would become a *bean nighidh*.

---

232. Campbell, *Superstitions of the Highlands*, 44.

233. Campbell, *Superstitions of the Highlands*, 43.

234. MacGregor, *Peat-Fire Flame*, 298.

235. Maclagan, "The Keener," 87.

She would then be compelled to wash clothes until the time she was originally fated to die. Thus, it would do well to keep up with the laundry.[236]

There are those who confuse the *bean nighe* with another Scottish supernatural entity, the *glaistig*. It should be remembered that the *bean nighe* is a *sith*, a fairy. Although both are female, supernatural, and are dressed in green, the *glaistig* is a mortal woman under an enchantment.[237]

Gille-cas-fliuch

Another banshee tale from medieval Scotland concerns a man named Gille-cas-fliuch who chanced to be walking on the shore of a loch. Suddenly, he spied an old woman washing a bloodstained shroud in the water. He also noticed that the water was turning red from the blood she was trying, in vain, to remove.

He paused for a moment, frightened. He knew darn well that this was the dreaded *bean nighidh* he had heard about since he was a boy. Gille wondered if he should turn about and try to make his way from her, unobserved. She was so intent upon her dismal work that she had not seen him—at least not yet. Then, on the other hand, he knew that if certain people had the courage, they could force the creature to reveal things, or possibly even grant wishes.

But this maiden was no wish-granting leprechaun. He did manage to sneak up behind her as she was engrossed in her task. Without warning, he clutched her hand. The hideous hag tried to break free, but despite her struggles and screeching, he held tight. He demanded three wishes from her.

---

236. Campbell, *Superstitions of the Highlands*, 43.
237. Campbell, *Superstitions of the Highlands*, 45.

She relaxed a bit. Realizing she was trapped, she asked what it was he wanted of her. The first request was obvious. He demanded to know whose bloody shroud she was washing.

She did not hesitate to answer him. With an evil smile, she revealed that it was the clothing of Clanranald, the great chieftain.

But Clanranald was Gille-cas-fliuch's lord. Being a loyal subject, he did not even bother with the other two wishes. He immediately snatched up the bloody shroud with his spear and flung it out into the loch. As the water-soaked garment sunk into the water, the crone erupted into devilish laughter. Gille ran away, rushing to the palace.

He dashed in and, once he caught his breath, told Clanranald the terrible news of what he had seen by the loch. The chieftain thought for a moment. He then ordered that a cow be killed, obviously some manner of sacrifice. After giving this order, he went down to the loch and entered a small boat. Alone, he set off toward the mainland.

He had told no one where he was going or what his mission was. It is only known that whatever his intentions were, they did not happen. He never arrived at the mainland. Nor did he ever return to his home. It would appear that just as the bloody shroud had sunk into the loch, so had Clanranald. The washer by the ford had the last laugh.[238]

Modern Witnesses of the Washer

In a much later case from Scotland, a boy and his two sisters were walking to school in the early morning when it was still dark. Suddenly, the two girls exclaimed that they could see the dreaded washerwoman. Their brother looked at where they were pointing, but he could see nothing. They were just silly girls trying to play a joke on him.

---

238. Sherwood, "Meet the Bean-Nighe."

Later, the boy who could not see the entity became ill and died. His sisters who could see the spirit remained healthy and alive.[239]

A grisly Scottish case of an encounter with the *bean nighe* comes from Cromarty in the Highlands. A young woman was walking along a trail near Loch Slin when she chanced to see a very tall woman in the water washing bloodstained clothes. Nearby on the grass were nearly three dozen other pieces of clothing, all smeared with blood.

This woman was smart and did not attempt to interrupt the specter. In fact, she turned around and ran the heck out of there as quickly as possible.

It was shortly after seeing this ghastly sight that the woman learned the roof of Fearn Abbey had suddenly collapsed in the middle of the service. Thirty-six people died in the tragedy.[240]

The Caointeach

Of course, not all Scottish banshees are washerwomen. There is a strong tradition of the wailing specter called the *caointeach*. There is this intriguing tale from the Scottish Isle of Islay in the Inner Hebrides.

A man was lying in his bed, extremely ill, preparing to leave this world. His family and friends were around him, praying and trying to give him as much cheer as they could. Outside, the weather was horrible, a cold night with pelting rain beating against the windows.

Suddenly, at the door on the side of the house that the wind was striking the hardest, there came the mournful sound of a woman wailing. Some of the people who heard the bleak sound knew immediately what it was. A few others were unfamiliar with the old beliefs and could not imagine who would be wailing at the door on a stormy night like this.

---

239. Nico, "Gaelic Folklore"; see also Maclagan, "The Keener."
240. MacGregor, *Peat-Fire Flame*.

156   Chapter 8

But one woman, not understanding what was going on, took pity. She thought it was a poor woman wandering about in the midst of a ferocious storm. She grabbed a garment and walked out of the door, on the leeward side of the house, of course.

She then called out to what she believed to be an unfortunate lady in distress: "'Come to the sheltered side, poor woman; and cover yourself with a piece of my plaid.'" [241]

She did not receive the reaction she expected. The wailing ended abruptly. Not only did it stop there, but it has not been heard in the district ever since.

This curious motif of offering a supernatural creature clothing causing them to leave is also found in a beloved folktale from the Isle of Man, a land filled to overflowing with fairy tradition. The Fenodyree, a satyrlike creature, was helping a poor farmer at night in secret. The farmer eventually figured out what was going on and naturally wished to repay his supernatural helper. Seeing how the poor thing went about unclothed, the farmer left a gift of clothing for him.

He did not receive the response he was expecting. The creature looked at the clothing, naming it off piece by piece, then dropped the gifts to the ground and walked away, leaving the farmer to fend for himself. [242]

Just like their cousins on the Emerald Isle, Scottish banshees like to sit on rocks. They are quite possessive of their stony thrones and are angered if anyone shows disrespect.

One Scotsman reached under a rock said to be frequented by the *caointeach* merely to grab a bit of flint to light his pipe. Suddenly, he

---

241. MacDougall, *Fairy Lore in Gaelic*, 214.
242. Callow, *Phynodderree*, 25.

felt a vicious slap to his face. He suffered from partial paralysis on his face as a result of the blow.[243]

A Scottish case of a *caointeach* from the Isle of Skye that occurred in 1776 is quite similar to the Irish banshee.

A group of young people, some from the Ross-Lewin family, was riding in a wagon near the ruins of the old church known as Cill Chriosd (or more commonly, Kilchrist) on the Isle of Skye. As they rode by, they heard a loud wailing. They saw, in the moonlit church-yard, a woman with long gray hair, dressed in a black cloak, running about. She was clapping her hands, crying, and making a terrible fuss. Upon seeing the people in the wagon, she fled into the ruins of the church.

They stopped the wagon and ran toward the strange scene. All was quiet now. The young men, showing their bravado for the ter-rified ladies, surrounded the roofless building so that she could not pass them. They then moved inside as a group, making certain that there was no possible avenue for her to run beyond them.

However, once they reached the inside of the ruined building, the only ones they found there were themselves. Frustrated and per-plexed, but having demonstrated their bravery for the ladies in the wagon, they continued home.

Here, they received their second surprise of the evening. Mrs. Ross-Lewin was terrified and very glad the children were finally home. She was alone in the house as her husband was away on busi-ness in Ireland.

Earlier that evening, she had heard a curious tapping sound and turned to look out of a window. To her horror, there was a raven there—tapping on the glass just as Poe's inky visitor had. However,

---

243. Nico, "Gaelic Folklore."

this one was even worse. This particular raven had glowing crimson eyes, a feature so often reported by witnesses of preternatural creatures.

Naturally, the poor woman was terrified. She wondered what the strange occurrences were, what could they possibly mean? She found out soon enough—her husband had died on his trip to Dublin.[244]

The Murder of King James I

One of the strangest assassinations in all of history may well have been that of the Scottish king James I, the only man to die partially as a result of lost tennis balls. His death was foretold to him by a woman, a woman some thought was a seer but who may well have been a *caoineag*.

One day King James, along with his entourage and guards, was riding into St. John's Town. As they approached the gate, a strange old woman, presumably a seer, approached the monarch. As the guards moved to shield the king, the woman cried out in a panicked voice that he should stop where he was and go no farther.

Then, in an ominous voice, with the guards pushing her back, she declared that if he should dare enter the city, he would be dead within a year.

Some of the men in the royal party began to laugh. It was assumed by all that she had been sampling too much of one of Scotland's most famous products. Ignoring her warning, the king proceeded through the gate, apparently sealing his doom in the process.[245]

The same woman reportedly attempted to see the king later that night, to give him more forewarning and advice. The guards, however, did not allow her to visit the monarch.[246]

---

244. Neligan and Seymour, *True Irish Ghost Stories*, 201–202.

245. Hewitt, "Banshee: Celtic Messengers."

246. Curran, *Mysterious Celtic*, 274.

James's life was an entire season of *Game of Thrones* and *I, Claudius* put together. He was surrounded by relatives who wanted his crown, who were constantly hatching plots and conspiracies. For him, the threat of assassination was very real and constant.

In February of 1437, James and his family were in his favorite town, Perth, staying at the Blackfriars monastery. One of his preferred activities during his stay was to play tennis. Apparently, he was not Wimbledon material as he was losing many of his balls in a sewer drain. Frustrated, he ordered that the conduit be sealed over with a sturdy grating. Little did he know that in doing so, he had just fulfilled the prophecy made by the strange woman.

On the night of February 20, 1347, he was in his nightclothes, sitting in a room with his wife and some of the lady attendants. Suddenly, there was a disturbance outside and the sound of coaches approaching. He ran to the window and saw a group of men jumping out of the coaches and charging into the monastery.

He knew immediately what this meant. His first instinct was to check that the door was secure. However, apparently there was a confederate working in the monastery, or possibly this was the work of an earlier visitor, most likely Robert Stewart. The bottom line was that someone had tampered with the lock; the door could not be secured against the quickly approaching assassins.

The king ran into another room, seeking a way to escape his murderers. He checked the windows to see if they could make their way out onto the roof and attract help. But the windows were too solid; there was no chance of getting out that way.

He felt completely ensnared when he happened to notice the privy. That was his escape! He removed the floorboard and climbed down into the pipe of the privy, intending to make his way out through the pipes onto the yard.

He would have ... had it not been for one small detail. He had just had the tunnel secured with a heavy grate. He was now completely trapped in his nightshirt in a privy, certainly not the most distinguished way to confront his attackers.

Meanwhile, in the outer chamber, the women were struggling to keep the door secure. One of the women, Catherine Douglas, had been straining to hold the door shut. When the attackers forced their way through with axes and levers, she suffered a broken arm.

The assailants finally stormed in and began to search the rooms for the missing king. Queen Joan, who was also injured in the attack, denied having any knowledge of where her husband was. Then the attackers said they should ignore the women and look for their target before the guards were alerted and confronted them.

As the assassins left, so did the queen. She was able to grab her son and make her way to safety.

The assassins were brutal, but like most criminals, they were not particularly smart. Even though they could see there was no way out, they could not find the king. Perhaps he had made his getaway before they entered the monastery. They turned around to leave.

The king was no genius either. Hearing their footsteps leave, he now found himself stuck in the tunnel. He called out to the women to come help him extricate himself. The problem was that he said that just a little bit too early. One of the attackers heard his cry for help, then immediately realized what they had overlooked. The gang did an about-face and returned to the room.

Seeing that the floorboard had indeed been moved, they opened it and found their target. Sir Robert Graham, a longtime enemy of the king, struck the first blow with his dagger. Others followed, stabbing the monarch over and over. The king did his best to fight back, but it was hopeless. The assassins continued to slash at him until finally he was dead. His corpse would reveal no less than sixteen knife wounds.

However, by now the alarm had been raised, mostly by the fleeing queen. The attackers fled just as the people of Perth were arriving to help the king.

The conspirators fled the scene, but they were quickly apprehended. A few of them spent some quality time in the torture chamber, where they revealed the entire plot. Soon all involved were executed.[247]

There is no doubt that King James should have listened to the old lady. Her prophecy that he would not live for another year had come true.

The Aberdeenshire Banshee and Others

One Scottish banshee with a bad attitude likes to have a little snack. Evans-Wentz mentions two hills in the Aberdeenshire Highlands. Each of these hills had a well. A banshee dwelled there and demanded a sacrifice. Travelers going through the area by the two hills would have to leave a barley cake at each of the wells. If they neglected this token offering, the banshee would become angry and some manner of disaster would certainly befall them on their journey.[248]

Other Scottish banshees were more protective and would sometimes be of assistance to their families. There are even reports of the spirits helping their descendants make the correct moves at a game of chess.[249]

---

247. Abernethy, "The Assassination of King James."

248. Evans-Wentz, *Fairy Faith*, 437.

249. Scott, *Letters on Demonology*, 296.

Another interesting tale from Scotland involves a beautiful *sith* who took on the form of a banshee. Thomas of Ercildoune encountered the fascinating young woman by an Eildon tree. She revealed herself to be none other than the queen of the fairies.

She took him to the Otherworld, where his excursion turned sour. She transformed into a corpselike banshee before his eyes.

> *The hair that hung upon her head,*
> *The half was black, the half was grey,*
> *And all the rich clothing was away*
> *That he before saw in that stead;*
> *Her eyes seemed out that were so grey,*
> *And all her body like the lead.*[250]

Now we will put the golf clubs and the kilt away and move south to Wales.

Wales

In Wales, we find the Hag of the Dribble (*Gwrach y Rhibyn*): "She is said to come after dusk, and flap her leathern wings against the window where she warns of death, and in a broken, howling tone, to call on the one who is to quit mortality by his or her name several times, as thus: a-a-n-ni-i-i-I [*sic*]! Anni."[251]

The phrase "leathern wings" obviously implies this grisly wraith is a batlike creature, or a hideous woman with bat wings.

There is the folktale of a man, undoubtedly more than a little bit tipsy, staggering home one night, when he saw a woman turned away from him. With all the romantic charm that a drunk can muster, which

250. Campbell, *Superstitions of the Highlands*, 45.

251. Croker, *Fairy Legends*, 116.

is never as much as they think, this Don Juan staggered up to her and made some comments that were, to put it mildly, inappropriate.

It was then that he found out he had made quite a mistake. The apparition turned around and faced him, displaying her deathly hideousness.

For his part, the Welsh Cassanova collapsed in fear. When he was able to raise himself from the dirt, he saw he was still alive and that the creature was no longer there. Brushing himself off, he walked away a much wiser man—and, for the record, a great deal more sober.[252]

Wirt Sikes and the Llandaff Hag

The celebrated journalist Wirt Sikes, in 1876 appointed the US consul to Wales, was tireless in collecting the vanishing Welsh fairy lore. He relates what one man told him in 1878 of an encounter with the death hag.

The witness had no trouble remembering the bizarre events of that night; they were things he could not possibly forget. He even remembered the date as being the fourteenth of November.

He was visiting a friend and was staying in an upper-floor room in the village of Llandaff. Around midnight, he was startled awake by the blood-chilling sound of some kind of creature screeching just outside of his window. It didn't sound like any bird he was familiar with, or ever wanted to meet.

As he jumped up from the bed, he could hear something rattling against the glass, as if trying to force its way in. Then, as he rushed across the bedroom floor, the sound stopped. He looked out of his window, and to his absolute horror, he saw the *Gwrach y Rhibyn* in its infernal glory.

---

252. Sikes, *British Goblins*, 217.

He described the ghastly specter: "A horrible old woman with long red hair and a face like chalk, and great teeth like tusks, looking back over her shoulder at me as she went through the air with a long black gown trailing along the ground below her arms, for body I could make out none."[253]

When the monster glanced back at the witness, she made yet another horrific screeching sound. Apparently, she did not appreciate an audience. She then flapped her leathery wings against the window below his and flew away. But she did not go far.

The witness stared into the darkness and watched as the wraith traveled a bit more and flew into the Cow and Snuffers Inn. He continued to watch for a long time, but he did not see the demonic creature reemerge from the inn.

The next day, he learned that Llewllyn, the innkeeper for the last seventy years at the Cow and Snuffers, had died during the night. He also commented that it was not the newcomers to the area who experienced visits from this horrific being, but rather, the old folks like the unfortunate innkeeper.[254]

The Welsh Harpy of Death

The biggest difference between the *Gwrach* and the Irish banshee is that she has wings. As mentioned above, she will beat these flapping leather wings against the window of the dying person, all the while calling out the name of the person, extending it in a ghostly voice.

The *Gwrach* is the hag of the dribble, this "dribble" referring to fog. Like her Irish cousins, she is connected to water, whether it is a body of water such as a river or the sea or just moisture in the air. She

---

253. Sikes, *British Goblins*, 217–218.
254. Sikes, *British Goblins*, 217–218.

will stand concealed in the fog or in some lonely, haunted spot and wail her death warning.

If there is one thing that all accounts agree upon, it is that she is incredibly ugly: "The spectre is a hideous being with dishevelled hair, long black teeth, long, lank, withered arms, leathern wings, and a cadaverous appearance."[255] She is certainly the last thing anyone would want to encounter lurking in a dense fog in a secluded glen.

One would think that someone as repulsive as this leather-winged hag would not be particularly lucky in love. However, according to Welsh legend, she had a husband; and if it can be believed, he was even uglier than her.

Ancient Mythology—Afagddu and Taliesin

According to the blending of ancient Celtic myth and folklore, we find that the name of this husband was Afagddu, also known as Avagddu or Morfran. His name translates as "utter darkness," and thus he was probably a primeval deity similar to the Greek Erebus.

There is very little known of him as a god—his worship was probably not particularly popular—but there is quite a tale about him in a human form.

According to the Arthurian legend, he was the son of the hag Ceridwen. She could see that his chance of securing a proper wife was somewhat limited as no one could stand to look upon his ghastly appearance. While she could not change his exterior form, the witch decided to work some magic to give him the gift of inspiration. This might attract at least one maiden, most likely one with poor eyesight.

The mystic procedure was quite complicated and involved stirring the cauldron for the magic period of a year and a day. But as

---

255. Sikes, *British Goblins*, 216.

she had other things to do, she hired a local boy, Gwion Bach ap Gwreang, to do the stirring.

It went well for a while. But toward the end, when the mixture was almost finished, Gwion stirred a bit too hard and splashed some of the hot liquid onto his hand. Naturally, he licked his finger where it was burned.

Three drops had spilled upon him. As it turns out, three was the magical number. If one would consume just three drops, they would have the precious gift of inspiration. But to drink more was death—everything else in the cauldron was poison. By licking the burn, he received the gift. "And the instant he put those marvel-working drops into his mouth, he foresaw everything that was to come, and perceived that his chief care must be to guard against the wiles of Caridwen, for vast was her skill. And in very great fear he fled towards his own land."[256]

Thus, the boy became the celebrated bard Taliesin, while Afagddu remained hideous and utterly uninspired. There is an old insult in Wales to say that someone is as ugly as *Gwrach y Rhibyn*.

There is also some belief that the *Gwrach y Rhibyn* does not merely content herself with announcing deaths, but is, at times, a kind of vampire. There are tales of her attacking children, infants, and bedridden elderly, drinking their blood. She does not drink so much that she kills them, just helps them along their way.[257]

The Cyhyraeth

The Irish banshee is said to move about in its wailing, sometimes following the course of rivers. There is also a Welsh version of this.

---

256. Guest, *Mabinogion*, 471.

257. Pfeifle, "Gwrach y Rhibyn."

It is called the *cyhyraeth*, or the death sound. Unlike the *Gwrach*, this specter is heard but never actually seen.

The actual sound is very similar to the Irish counterpart, a ghostly woman wailing in the night air. However, this entity will take the route of the final journey of the doomed person, going from home or church to the cemetery, stopping at the place of soon-to-be burial.[258]

In the old churchyard at St. Mellons, a boy passing by heard the *cyhyraeth* one night. Having more courage than sense, he stopped to listen. It was then that he noticed something very unusual. The sound came first from one spot, then another, and finally stopped at a third. This made absolutely no sense, but it could not be denied that he had heard it.

A few days later, a funeral did indeed enter the burial grounds. The coffin was carried to one spot, but the old sexton rushed up and informed them that there was already someone buried there in an unmarked grave. Undaunted, the funeral party carried their dreadful burden to a second spot, but once again, they were informed that this land was also taken. Becoming a bit frustrated, the pallbearers lifted the coffin onto their aching shoulders a third time and went to yet another spot. The sexton nodded that this was a good place. The coffin had indeed stopped at three different places in the churchyard, just as the *cyhyraeth* had predicted.[259]

There is a detailed description of the sound of the *cyhyraeth* from a man named Joshua Coslet. According to Mr. Coslet's testimony, there are many similarities between the Welsh *cyhyraeth* and the Irish banshee. The cry is, of course, quite sad and mournful, and is heard most often before stormy weather. Also, like its Irish cousin, the warning is given in groups of three. However, the first of the three

258. Owen, *Welsh Folk-Lore*, 302.

259. Sikes, *British Goblins*, 221.

would be at full strength, the second would be weaker, then the third would sound like the last gasps of a dying person.

The terrible sound starts some distance from the house but moves ever closer. It is stated that in the coastal region of Glamorganshire, the sound begins out at sea. It comes ashore and will then follow a stream or, if necessary, a road to the house of the dying person.

But there is something different and quite interesting about the lament of the *cyhyraeth*. It sounds like the groaning of that particular dying person. "A person 'well remembering the voice' and coming to the sick man's bed, 'shall hear his groans exactly like' those which he had before heard from the *Cyhyraeth*." [260]

The informant stated that at one time the *cyhyraeth*, unlike the Irish banshee that only wails for its family, would announce the deaths of everyone in the district, particularly those on the southeastern area of River Towy. [261]

The Interrupted Game

Evidently the *cyhyraeth* is a stickler for propriety. In the village of Bedwellty, there was a wake for a four-year-old child who had recently died. While the parents were devastated with grief and the neighbors were saddened, two men seemed to forget where they were.

They must have thought they were sitting at their local pub as they began playing cards, drinking, and talking very loudly, and not always with the most appropriate vocabulary. A number of people tried to ask them to behave more respectably, but they were ignored.

It soon became apparent that it was not merely the living who were becoming annoyed. Everyone heard a ghostly groaning at the

---

260. Sikes, *British Goblins*, 18.
261. Sikes, *British Goblins*, 18.

window. The cardplayers ceased their game when this happened, and just that quickly, the groaning stopped as well.

The two men behaved themselves for a while, but soon they could not stand up to the temptation and began their game again. As soon as the cards were dealt, the groaning returned as well.

By now they decided that some neighborhood smart aleck was playing a trick on them. They decided to go out to investigate, and to give the miscreant a little lesson in manners (as if either of them was qualified for such a task).

That is when their brilliant plan fell apart. Each one told the other to go outside. No, each one wanted the other to go out. It would appear that, suddenly, they were not so certain that the sound came from a human agency.

There was a dog present, and the cardplayers had the brilliant idea to send the dog out. He would frighten the intruder away, and they could go on with their game in peace. The dog gave them a look as if to say, "Are you out of your mind?" The dog, having more sense than the humans, would not budge. He knew darn well what was out there.

With this, the two men looked at each other, then one quietly put the cards back into his pocket, where they stayed for the rest of the evening.[262]

---

262. Sikes, *British Goblins*, 222–223.

Chapter 9
OTHER
DEATH MESSENGERS
IN IRELAND

In haunted glens the meadow-sweet
Flings to the night wind
Her mystic mournful perfume;
The sad spearmint by holy wells
Breathes melancholy balm.

—TODHUNTER, "THE BANSHEE"

Besides the traditional banshee screaming in the middle of the night, there are other heralds of the Grim Reaper in Irish lore. One of the most frightening to see on a dark and stormy night is a black coach drawn by headless horses. This is the dreaded *cóiste-bodhar*, or more commonly, the coach-a-bower. To see it is like hearing the banshee—someone is going to die, but the question is who.

The Dullahan and the Coach-a-Bower

Sometimes, this dark conveyance is driven by a *dullahan*, a gloomy death spirit who carries his head in his arm. This demon is said to be a remembrance of the Celtic fertility deity Crom Dubh. It is believed that this phantom was the inspiration for the Headless Horseman in Washington Irving's classic tale, "The Legend of Sleepy Hollow." [263]

In 1807, two sentries who were posted at the gate of St. James Park literally died from fright. While they were still alive and on duty, they were watching for the appearance of an intruder. There had been reports of a topless woman coming by and scaling the rail fence to enter the grounds at night.

One can reasonably assume that they had to fight their fellow soldiers to merit being given this assignment. But it was not as they expected. They should have remembered the old military adage: never volunteer.

They did not realize they were dealing with a female *dullahan*. To their dismay, the woman did indeed show up that night; and, as promised, she was topless—including her head! [264]

Sometimes, it is said that a more traditional banshee will be riding in the coach-a-bower. One particularly grisly bit of folklore states

---

263. Weber and Clements, "Headless Horsemen."
264. Yeats, *Irish Fairy and Folk Tales*, 116.

that if someone should happen to see the omnibus pass, the banshee will toss a bucket of blood on them.[265]

In 1806, in County Limerick, there was an appearance of the phantom coach. Ralph Westropp was lying on his deathbed in the house. His three sons, Ralph, William, and John, had summoned the doctor and were now sitting outside talking, waiting for the physician's brougham to arrive.

Suddenly, they heard the sound of a coach coming at full speed down the dirt road in front of the house. One of the brothers scurried down the steps to open the gate for him. He certainly was in a hurry.

But to his surprise, a coach dashed right past the house. Thinking that somehow the doctor had forgotten where they lived, the young man ran down the lane, shouting for him to come back. He knew that the conveyance couldn't go too far as the road ended a little bit beyond the house.

But when he reached the end of the road, he found, to his amazement, that there was no coach. Where could it have gone? Perplexed, he and his brothers woke up the lodge's keeper, who not only assured them that he had not opened the gate for any coach, but even showed them the key kept secure underneath the pillow on the bed he was anxious to return to.

Quite confused, the brothers returned home. To their relief, the coach with the doctor in it pulled up shortly afterward and parked properly in front of their house. When asked about the strange incident, the doctor could only assure them that he did not drive down the lane earlier.

---

265. Harris, "*Daoine Sidhe.*"

It did not matter how many times he drove there, as Mr. Westropp was beyond his care. He died that night. Then the sons understood what the first coach was.[266]

A few years later in 1821, another death coach was encountered in County Clare. Young Cornelius O'Callaghan had been extremely ill and had traveled in a vain attempt to restore his health. It did not work, and now he was returning to the family manor. If he had to die young, then he might as well do it in his own bed.

Knowing that he was soon to arrive, two of the servants were waiting up for him. Late in the night, they heard the sound of a coach stopping in front of the house. One of the servants went out with a light to open the coach door and, if necessary, help Cornelius into the house.

Instead of greeting his young master and welcoming him home, the servant let out a terrified scream. When he opened the coach door, there was a skeleton grinning out at him. The servant collapsed in a faint. When he found himself being helped up, there was no sign of a coach.

Soon the real coach arrived, and inside of it, young Cornelius. He had made it back just in time, as he did not live long after that night.[267]

In County Clare, one night a man from Annaghneale was walking down a road when he heard the sound of a coach behind him. He did not even look around, but merely stepped off to the side to allow the vehicle to go by him safely.

But to his surprise, the coach stayed right behind him and did not pass. Now he did turn around to see what was back there, and he saw the dreaded phantom coach. He was even able to behold the coach-

266. Neligan and Seymour, *True Irish Ghost Stories*, 207.

267. Neligan and Seymour, *True Irish Ghost Stories*, 207.

man, something he never wanted to see. As he told it later to anyone who would listen, the driver was merely a splotch of inky darkness.

By now, completely terrified, he began to run. However, he was quite safe, as the coach had not come for him; it had a different destination.

He turned and watched in amazement as the coach turned off the road and drove right over a wide ditch and even over a stone wall. It was presumably headed toward the village of Fortanne.[268]

Another coach-a-bower sighting was from a servant of the Macnamara family. In 1876, he was checking things on the property late at night when he suddenly heard the sound of a fast-approaching coach.

Unlike the others, he knew immediately what it was. He had heard stories of this while sitting by the peat fire since he was little; and thanks to that informal education, he knew exactly what to do.

The servant ran ahead on the road, opening all three gates. He reached the third one just in time, and threw himself on the ground, burying his head in his arms so as not to gaze upon the passing conveyance or its cursed driver.

It is the long-held belief that when one encounters this phantom, one must do everything possible to speed it on its way. A sane person certainly does not want it to be delayed, lest it stop in front of one's house. Should it do this, it may just pick up an extra passenger before continuing its journey.[269]

Of particular interest in this account is the fact that the servant threw himself on the ground and covered his eyes. This is the same precaution as those who accidentally find themselves witnesses of the approach of the Wild Hunt. They, too, must hit the ground and

---

268. Westropp, "A Folklore Survey," 193.

269. Neligan and Seymour, *True Irish Ghost Stories*, 208.

not watch as the spirits go by. Should they look up at the host of the dammed, there is a good chance they might be swept along with them.[270]

It is interesting to note that we find almost the same belief halfway around the world, in the pre-Christian lore of Hawaii. Here, it is held that on certain sacred nights, a ghostly procession of ancient kings and mighty warriors will rise from their graves or from the sea and move in an eerie torchlit procession to some sacred place. To see this parade, commonly called the *huaka'i pō* (night marchers), is extremely dangerous. Any accidental witness must immediately fall to the ground, facedown, and cover their head to prevent glimpsing the phantoms. Some say that they must lie on their back and pretend to be asleep. To fail to do this would cause the leader to shout out an order for the witness to be speared. If the unfortunate victim has any ancestors in the parade, they will escape with their life. Otherwise, they are killed on the spot.[271]

This dark conveyance is spoken of outside of the Emerald Isle. In Wales, it is known as the *ceffyl heb un pen.*[272]

It is said that on occasion, a banshee will ride in the coach-a-bower. A tale of this comes from County Laois. An unidentified man, rather wealthy, who had rejected Catholicism and embraced the Protestant faith, was a fellow with a bit of an attitude. He did not believe in any kind of supernatural lore, especially not the banshee.

One morning, his elderly housekeeper, Moya, informed him that she had heard both the banshee and the coach-a-bower the night before. He dismissed it as superstitious nonsense, then said that he was headed into town to conduct some business. He would be back early.

---

270. Lecouteux, *Phantom Armies*, 44.

271. Beckwith, *Hawaiian Mythology*, 164.

272. Sikes, *British Goblins*, 216.

Moya begged him not to go, but he would hear none of it. While in town, he met an old friend; the two went to the pub to have a drink and relive old times. Although he did not expect to stay in town very long, it was growing dark when he finally left for home.

What he did not notice amid his reminisces were the two men sitting at a table nearby, quietly watching and listening to him. They could see that he had money, and from the conversation, they knew the road he would be taking to return home.

He never made it.

After the horse returned riderless with a bloody saddle, one of the servants grabbed a lantern and went out to look. He found the dead body lying by the side of the road, a bullet wound in his head, his money and expensive watch gone.

But the story did not end there. The body of the murdered man was to be picked up by his brother. It would take a few days for him to arrive. In the meantime, two local men were hired to stay with the corpse as custom dictated.

However, to everyone's surprise, the banshee and the coach-a-bower were heard yet again, seemingly circling the house. One of the men, who also did not believe in superstition, figured that it was thieves or vandals they were hearing, not a banshee and the death coach. He grabbed his gun and, along with his terrified companion, went outside to drive away the intruders.

There they saw the dreaded coach and its occupant. The coach was "drawn by six headless, sable horses, and the figure of a withered old hag, encircled with blue flame, was seen running nimbly across the hay-yard. She entered the ominous carriage, and it drove away with a horrible sound. It swept through the tall bushes ... and as it disappeared, the old hag cast a thrilling scowl … and waved her flesh-less arms at them vengefully." [273]

Soon thereafter, old Moya died. The banshee and the coach had come for her.

The Irish Woman in White

In an Irish version of the German *Weiße Frau* (we will spend some quality time with her in the next chapter), in County Laois, there is the legend that the death of members of a certain family is predicted by the appearance of a woman in white. Doors open by themselves as the ghostly woman glides in. [274]

There is a similar woman in white in County Limerick, haunting Kilcosgriff Castle. She is supposed to appear before a family member dies, thus assuming the role of the traditional banshee, although she appears inside of the building.

It is believed that she is the wife of the Lord Langford who died in the 1800s. Her last reported appearance was in 1914. [275]

There is quite a story behind this particular haunting. In the early 1700s, William Langford returned unexpectedly to the castle while on leave from the army.

His surprise visit was at an inconvenient time, as there were many guests staying there. He did not mind. As his room was being used by one of the visitors, he said he would stay in what was known as the Haunted Chamber. Not surprisingly, no one else was staying there—but William did not believe in silly ghost stories.

In the middle of the night, he was awakened by the figure of a woman in a white nightgown walking silently about the chamber car-

273. Keegan, "Legends and Tales," 374.

274. Neligan and Seymour, *True Irish Ghost Stories*, 209.

275. Massey, "13 Shades of Fear."

rying a lit candle. So, the room was haunted after all. He pretended to be asleep and watched what was happening. The woman in white blew out the candle, then lay down in the bed right next to him.

He reached over and found that it was no phantom but a real flesh-and-blood woman lying in the bed next to him; and despite what he may have thought initially, it became obvious she was utterly asleep.

He reached over, felt her hand, and saw there was a ring on it. Wishing to have a little fun on his leave, he gently removed the ring and placed it on his own finger.

After a while, the woman rose, relit the candle and, just as quietly as she'd entered, left the room, gently closing the door behind her.

The next morning, William went to breakfast, wearing the ring prominently so that all the guests could see it. One very attractive young woman, by the name of Gertrude St. Ledger, saw the ring. Her jaw opened, her eyes were wide in shock, and she nearly fainted. She left the table immediately, obviously quite distressed.

Later, she approached William and said that the ring was hers and demanded to know how it came to be on his finger. Had he violated her privacy and come into her room last night? Is that how the Langford family showed hospitality to their female visitors?

He explained that, no, it was quite the other way around. As he told her what had happened the previous night, a guilty look came over her. She confessed that she had a tendency to sleepwalk, which by now William had already figured out. But, sleepwalk or not, she wanted her ring back.

With a smile, he removed the jewelry and said she could not only have the ring, but have him as well, which would involve another ring to add to her collection. This must be one of the strangest marriage proposals of all time. Even stranger, she smiled and said yes.

Gertrude soon became Mrs. Langford in 1703. Years later, as she lay dying, she told those assembled that she was not going to leave her beloved castle, but that she would appear to warn her family whenever a death was imminent.

Since then, she has been seen numerous times. In 1856, she was seen by the head of the household as she was walking about outside. He did not comprehend that she was a ghost, but the dog did. The dog began howling.

He ran outside onto the lawn to follow her. Seemingly unaware that he was coming after her, she walked into a stable. He followed close behind, but when he opened the stable door, she was nowhere to be seen, and there was no other way to leave the building. She had vanished.

He was shocked. Could this be the lady in white he had always heard about—the one who predicted deaths in the family? It was not long before he received his answer. Soon afterward, he learned his father had passed away in Miltown Malbay.

Gertrude could, on occasion, act as a regular banshee. Years later, a woman in white was heard crying and wailing in the garden on what was known as the Lovers' Walk. The young man of the house heard this and called out to her, but she did not respond. He ran outside and followed her toward a laurel bush. Once again, she had delivered her message and vanished. That same evening, the young man's grandmother died.

By 1889, the young man's father was suffering from a terrible illness and was not expected to survive. Family members were shocked to see the white woman glide down a hallway and suddenly vanish. He ran to his father's room but found that he was already dead.

The final case, from 1914, was the death of Crawford Langford who lived in Glenville. He had just returned from a fruitless visit to some doctors in Dublin and was invited to stay at the abbey in Rathkeale. While there, his condition became critical and he could travel no farther.

The same witness who years earlier had seen the lady in white in the hallway and on the Lovers' Walk was sitting in his bedroom where his brother lay dying. Suddenly, the door opened of its own accord and the familiar white lady floated in. She bent over the dying young man, then looked at the brother and smiled.

The witness stated that he wanted very much to speak to her, but he could not talk in his shocked state. A few days later, the brother died.[276]

Other Irish Death Omens

It is very bad luck to break a mirror, but for another County Laois family, it is tragic. Their belief is that a death in the family is always presaged by a mirror suddenly shattering for no explicable reason.[277]

One of the manifestations of the death messenger in Ireland and elsewhere is the appearance of a ball of fire floating slowly through the air. In the 1800s, a lady in County Cork was lying in bed, extremely ill. The family was downstairs going about their business when they suddenly heard the mother scream as if someone were killing her.

They raced up the stairs and found her in bed, a look of total horror on her face. To their amazement, her eyes were following something. They looked to where she was staring, but they could see nothing. After a few minutes, she calmed down and informed the frightened family that there was a family tradition that before one of them would die, a floating ball of fire would be seen. That was exactly what she had just seen drifting through her bedroom.

---

276. Neligan and Seymour, *True Irish Ghost Stories*, 210–214.

277. Neligan and Seymour, *True Irish Ghost Stories*, 209.

They had heard this story handed down as well. They were worried that the omen had been for her, that she would not recover from this illness. However, they soon received word that it was not her, but her brother.[278]

Another spectral light, that of the Scanlan family, also functions as a banshee. It is quite interesting as there is a weird tale of its origin, one that involves a miracle from a saint.

In the sixth century, Scanlan Mor was suspected of treason and imprisoned by Aedh mac Ainmire, the high king. As part of his punishment, he was weighed down with ponderous fetters. St. Columcille, also known as Columba, was visiting the area. (Yes, this was the same St. Columba who turned away an attack of the Loch Ness Monster.) He asked the king to show mercy and free Scanlan. Aedh adamantly refused.

The saint was calm and replied that despite this stubbornness, the prisoner would indeed be released that very night. That evening, a brilliant light suddenly appeared over the keep. Inside, where the prisoner lay weighed down with his cruel bindings, a mysterious voice ordered Scanlan to rise and shake away his fetters. He did, and the chains fell off him. Then, led by an angel, he simply walked out of the prison.

Since then, mysterious lights would be seen before a member of the family died. Quite often, these are seen as pillars of fire, sometimes wearing a crown; other times, they are balls of fire floating about. William Scanlan reported seeing the light on top of a hill on the night one of his aunts died.[279]

It has long been known that certain prehistoric sites are places of profound mystical power. These ancient locations include neo-

---

278. Neligan and Seymour, *True Irish Ghost Stories*, 217.

279. Neligan and Seymour, *True Irish Ghost Stories*, 217–219.

lithic burial mounds, stone circles, dolmens, standing stones, and holy wells. These settings are often reputed to be the abode of fairies. These are spiritual crossroads where the barrier between this world and the Otherworld is a bit thinner. Supernatural occurrences are often reported in these spots.

Thus, it should come as no surprise that another death messenger in Ireland includes a mysterious voice said to come from a prehistoric stone monument, the cairn Dungiven.

The Vampire Abhartach

It is said that twice a year, on the haunted nights of Samhain (Halloween) and May Day Eve, what the Germans refer to as *Walpurgisnacht*, a brave (or particularly stupid) person may approach the burial place. A mysterious voice will then boom out from the world below, naming all the people in the area who are destined to die before the next Samhain or May Eve.[280]

It comes as no surprise that the region near this cairn is said to be haunted by dark spirits and fairies. There is even a delightful vampire story here. Even though it does not relate directly to the banshee or other death messengers … how can I resist?

In ancient times, when the exploits of Cuchulainn were breaking news, two men were fighting for lordship. A particularly savage warrior named Cathrain killed his rival, Abhartach. Through this act of violence, he became the new chieftain.

But there was a slight problem in this transfer of power: his opponent was not about to take this lying down. Abhartach, although dead, was soon reported to be wandering about the villages at night as a *dearg dur* (the red blood drinker), sustaining its vile existence by satiating itself on the blood of the common people.

---

280. Curran, *Mysterious Celtic*, 76.

The local folks were understandably not too happy about this development. They demanded something be done about this. The new chieftain consulted a wise druid, who advised him to make a sharp weapon of a yew branch and thrust it into the heart of the walking corpse.

Thus Cathrain fought his opponent for the second time, and won again. With the yew stake driven through his heart, the vampire Abhartach walked no more.[281]

In County Cavan, near the village of Blacklion, there is a standing stone that is said to cry out the names of people who are doomed to die.[282]

There is an entire lake in County Donegal, Lough Naman Finn, which is also said to call out the names of those destined to die soon.[283]

The Gormanston Foxes

Before we take our leave of the Emerald Isle, we must consider one last herald of the Grim Reaper. Possibly the strangest, and in a dark way a bit humorous, is the death prediction in County Meath. While most banshees are either old hags looking like walking corpses or attractive young women combing their long hair, the death messengers attached to the Gormanston family are real foxes.

Literally—they are foxes!

The legend states that back in the 1600s, Lord Gormanston was out foxhunting. He ran across a vixen with her young, nursing. Rather than kill her, he deflected the hunt so that she and her young would survive.

---

281. Mullan, "Derry's Haunted Spots."

282. Curran, *Mysterious Celtic*, 76.

283. Curran, *Mysterious Celtic*, 76.

That act of charity set up a curious bond between foxes and the family. For some reason, the animals became banshees and mourners. For numerous generations following, they would appear at the estate at Gormanston Castle when the head of the family was dying or had died in some other place.

This sounds like something that would be told over a beer at a local pub, the tale growing with each telling. The strange thing is that it has actually happened right into recent times.

In the year 1860, another local nobleman, Lord Fingall, was on his horse and ready to go out with the hounds for a little foxhunting. One of the local people just laughed and told him he would come back empty-handed. All the foxes were elsewhere that day.

That "elsewhere" was Gormanston Castle, as Jenico, the lord, was in bed dying. All that Lord Fingall caught that day was fresh air and exercise. The man was right; the foxes were busy elsewhere. Curiously, on their way to mourn their human leader, the foxes had walked right through the middle of frightened poultry—but they never touched a single one.

Sixteen years later, it was recorded that Edward Gormanston, the thirteenth of his line, was ill. He seemed to be well on the way to recovery. However, the yard, especially under his window, was suddenly filled with every fox in County Meath. In true banshee form, they began to howl, and did so all night.

The recovery that they believed the lord was experiencing turned out to be short lived. He was dead by morning. The doctors and the family may have been mistaken, but the foxes knew.

In 1907, Jenico, the fourteenth lord of the manor, went to his reward. His son was sitting with his father's body in the chapel when he heard a curious sound just outside. He opened the door, and there in the moonlight was a very large fox and several other foxes with him. They had come to pay their respects as well.

In 1925, with the death of the head of the family, the foxes were back at the chapel. The mourning brother became irritated and tried to drive the foxes away—probably not the smartest thing to do. The foxes paid him little mind and kept their vigil on the lawn until sunrise.

In 1940, the lord of the manor was fighting in the early days of the war, part of the disastrous conflict at Dunkirk. That night, although the family knew only that there was fierce fighting and a desperate evacuation there, the lawn was suddenly filled with crying foxes. Sure enough, the terrible telegram came shortly after, stating how the lord had fallen in battle.

Another Lord Gormanston fought in the Second World War. He was officially listed as missing in action. For years the family waited, hoping and praying he would be found alive.

It did not happen. After the legal requirement of seven years had passed, the nobleman was declared legally dead. It was assumed he died in combat and his body was never found. His widow remarried.

A groundskeeper at the castle kept looking about and said quite openly that the marriage was a mistake. The lord had to be alive, as the foxes had not appeared.

Everyone thought he was a superstitious fool who enjoyed too much time in the pub. Despite their criticism, he insisted that the foxes knew, and the lord was definitely alive somewhere. If he were dead, as had happened with the Dunkirk death, they would have been on the castle grounds wailing as they always did.

The groundskeeper was right. Just like the plot of a bad soap opera, in 1952, the missing Gormanston suddenly showed up one day. He had survived the war but had lost his memory, which only recently had returned.

The estate was donated to the Franciscans, who turned it into a boarding school. Two years later, there was a night when the faculty and students were frightened to death. Even though the castle was now a school, no one had told the foxes. They showed up on the lawn, making a terrible racket. Inside the manor, lights were flicking on and off of their own accord. The next day, it was reported that the head of the Preston family, now the lord of the family, had passed away while visiting Tasmania.

The foxes always know.[284]

---

284. French, "Gormanston Foxes."

Chapter 10
OTHER DEATH MESSENGERS

Out—out are the lights—out all!
And, over each quivering form,
The curtain, a funeral pall,
Comes down with the rush of a storm,
While the angels, all pallid and wan,
Uprising, unveiling, affirm
That the play is the tragedy, "Man,"
And its hero, the Conqueror Worm.

—Poe, "The Conqueror Worm"

Death has sent his emissaries out into all nations. Sadly, we must now leave the Emerald Isle and visit a few of the banshee's kith and kin throughout the globe. We will start in Wales.

The Tolaeth and the Drychiolaeth

Closely related to the *cyhyraeth* is the *tolaeth*. This often comes from a carpenter's shop late at night when everyone is gone. It is the sound of a coffin being made. When people passing by hear this coming from the darkened workshop, they know someone in the neighborhood will die very soon.[285]

There are a number of worldwide superstitions related to this. In some cases, a strange light appearing in a closed and dark carpenter's shop is a sign that he is soon to be working late fashioning a coffin. Or, while the establishment is open, if the carpenter hears the sound of sawing and hammering with no one there, he knows he will soon be making those same sounds fashioning a coffin.[286]

Very similar to this is the grisly *drychiolaeth*. This apparition is once again heard but not seen; in this case, it is the sound of some part of the funeral, an auditory preview of a somber event that is yet to happen.

Reverend Owen gives a detailed account of one such *drychiolaeth* encounter involving some railroad workers sitting in the parlor of a lodging house in the Penderlwyngoch farm. The men were sitting by the fire in a room, smoking and chatting. Everything seemed normal.

Suddenly, they heard a commotion from the farm dogs outside. Naturally, these hounds always barked when a person was approaching who they did not know. But this barking was intense. What is

285. Owen, *Welsh Folk-Lore*, 303.

286. Bergen, Beauchamp, and Newel, *The Journal of American Folklore*, 12–22.

more, it was not angry and threatening, but somehow frightened. Then, for no apparent reason, the barking abruptly ceased.

The railroad men looked at each other in wonder. Then the strange sounds began.

They could clearly hear the back door being opened. There was a mass of footsteps, the sound of men walking in the house struggling while carrying something heavy. The sound continued as the footsteps entered the parlor next to their room. They could hear something being laid down. It sounded like a dead body.

Then all was silence.

The men looked at each other, stood up, and, grabbing a light, moved cautiously to the parlor where they had heard the sound. They were frightened of what sight might have greeted them there.

But there was nothing. Not only had nothing been laid down, there were no footprints on the floor. Well, there may not be any footprints inside of the house, but there would certainly be some outside. They went out the back door, but there was no trace of anyone having walked around.

But one piece of evidence was there for them to see: the dogs who had barked so furiously were now cowered down, too frightened to move.

The men made their way back to the room with the fire, asking each other what they had just experienced. They could not all have imagined the exact same thing—and the terrified dogs were evidence that something had happened. The Welshmen in the group did not have to ask or question. They knew exactly what the sounds were, and what they meant.

Sadly, the very next day, one of the men who had sat by the fire died in an accident. The other men carried the body back to the farmhouse—and made the exact same sounds they had heard the night before.[287]

The Corpse Candle

One of the most often sighted death manifestations in Wales is the dreaded *canhywllah cyrth*, the corpse candle. These are dim, flickering lights that will appear before the house of a person soon to die or along the road where the funeral will soon take place.

Sometimes, the eerie light will appear at the spot a person is destined to die. There is one case in which a river had recently flooded but was slowly receding. Of course, as is the case in any flood, the current is always extremely strong and there is deadly debris, oftentimes hidden below the surface of the water.

Near the village of Llanglar, several of these apparitions were seen on the river, as witnessed by numerous people.

As the waters were going down, a young woman wished to wade across the water, just as she had always done. However, the old folks warned her against this, stating that they had seen the candles there and, with the rough current, it was far too dangerous. Being young and strong, she laughed at this and headed into the water.

A bit later and farther downstream, they pulled her drowned body from the water.[288]

At Aberglasney House in Dyfed, around 1630, there was a tragedy predicted by the spectral flames.

A room was being remodeled, and to help the walls dry, a coal fire had been lit. There was very poor ventilation. Some of the people in the house saw what they thought was a small group of corpse candles

---

287. Owen, *Welsh Folk-Lore*, 301.
288. O'Donnell, *The Banshee*, 169.

in the room, but no one paid too much attention. It was probably some manner of reflection from the fire.

That night, five of the maids decided they were going to sleep in that room. No one thought anything of it. However, the next morning when they didn't report for duty, some of the staff went up to wake them up. This didn't make sense—they were good workers. How could they all oversleep?

The answer was simple. They were not resting, but dead. They had quietly suffocated from the coal fumes as they'd slept their final sleep. The curious lights were indeed the dreaded corpse candles.[289]

Also in Dyfed, in Carmarthen, William John was riding his horse down a country lane when he saw a terrible apparition. He did not see just some vague candlelight; he was so close that he could make out the image clearly. It was a bright candle being held by a dead woman lying on a bier. Suddenly, the corpse lady turned her head and grinned at him. Then the ghastly vision faded away.

Poor William was so frightened he literally fell off his horse. As he lay on the road, he contemplated what he had just witnessed. He knew the woman he had seen. He also knew that she was very much alive and seemingly in good health.

But these things never lie. Before long she became ill, and soon after that, she was dead. As a mourner, William saw her body, without the flaming candle, lying on a bier—just as he had seen it in his vision.[290]

Some young men, out for a holiday of mountaineering, were walking through the countryside of Penthryn in Powys, Wales. They were headed for the ferry. But as the river came into view, they were horrified to see that the ferry-house was covered in flames—and

289. Mann, "Dyfed Ghosts."

290. O'Donnell, *The Banshee*, 171.

there was no one standing outside. Was the family trapped inside a burning building?

The young men rushed to the edifice, but when they arrived, there was no fire. The structure stood as it always had with no signs of burning. They could not understand it—they were all certain they had seen flames around the house.

The ferryman came out as usual and took them across the river. Amid the voyage, they told him what had happened. He seemed puzzled; no, there were no flames. Must have been some trick of the sunlight.

Later, when the party reached Barmouth, they sat in a pub talking to some other travelers. To their surprise, these other people had seen the same flames at the ferry-house earlier. When they'd rushed up to help, the flames were completely gone.

To have the exact same thing happen twice to two different groups of witnesses? This was no trick of the sun! By then, the young men were starting to speak in a low voice about the corpse candle. No … it couldn't possibly be.

But it could be. A few days later, after some heavy rains upriver, the waterway erupted into a flash flood. The same ferryman who had taken them across died while trying to maneuver his boat through the wild current and debris.[291]

The Ghostly Voice of Aberhafesp

A curious tale from Aberhafesp concerns the thirteenth-century church dedicated to St. Gwynog. It is said that if one goes in there at the witching hour on *Nos G'lan Geua'* (Irish Samhain, or Halloween), one will hear a ghostly voice announce a death for the coming

291. O'Donnell, *The Banshee*, 171.

year. (It should be remembered that Samhain was originally a New Year's festival.)

A couple of young fellows, after consuming a little liquid fortitude, sneaked into the church on the haunted night and sat in the stillness and the dark waiting for the voice to foretell the passing of someone. Soon, the stillness was interrupted—not by a ghostly voice, but by one of them snoring.

His friend was about to wake him but decided to let him rest. He stayed awake, sitting in the darkness, listening for a spectral message … and he received one. The phantom voice did indeed speak to him, and it named the person doomed to die. It was the friend sitting next to him, sound asleep.

When he caught his breath, he woke up his friend, but naturally did not reveal what he had heard. No, nothing had happened; he'd heard nothing.

A few weeks later, the doomed friend was a pallbearer for another person's funeral. The dead man had perished of a contagious disease. The unwary pallbearer contracted the illness, and soon the prophecy of the voice was fulfilled.[292]

Fad Felen

Throughout the world, pestilent disease has been personified, such as the German *Pest Jungfrau*, the Assyrian god of the southwest wind Pazzuzzu, the Greek Stymphalian birds, and countless others. In Wales, there is a curious case involving the death-bringing plague and the danger of looking at him.

In the sixth century, Wales was suffering from a disease they called the Yellow Plague (most likely bubonic plague, as the Roman Empire was suffering through the same disease in what was dubbed

---

292. Owen, *Welsh Folk-Lore*, 170.

the Great Plague of Justinian). The sickness was personified as a horrible monster known as the *Fad Felen*.

This scourge had been predicted by the poet Taliesin, who'd stated that the plague-bringing demon would emerge from the marsh of Rhianedd. At Rhos Church, the king Gwynedd tried to look at the beast through the keyhole.

It would appear that his curiosity was satisfied, as he soon died from the shock.[293]

Scotland

Moving north to Scotland, as if a regular banshee wasn't bad enough, a Scottish case from the 1930s is even more disturbing. It involved a ghostly arm that appeared emerging from the wall. While it was signaling to the family, it would also knock things over to seize people's attention. As if a spectral limb appearing from a wall isn't conspicuous enough, it has to knock over a lamp?

Sure enough, a death always followed the appearance of the arm.[294]

The Bloody Hand

Rather than an entire arm, another bizarre bansheelike spirit from Scotland is the *Laimh-dhearg*, the Specter of the Bloody Hand. This dark entity is connected to the Stewart family.

As the story goes, Robin Oig, son of the baron of Kincardine, was hunting one day. Having killed a hind, he sat down and began to prepare it. However, his *sgian-dubh* (single-edged knife) that he had set down was nowhere to be seen. Frustrated, he pulled another knife out of his belt, but the moment he laid it down, it too vanished.

---

293. Sikes, *British Goblins*, 214.

294. Hudson, "64 Death Omens."

It was difficult, but he was able to complete his task without his proper tools.

Later, as he walked by Loch Morlich, he was confronted by a strange man who had a bloody hand. He asked Robin to be more "sober" in the forest, then gave him back his knives.[295]

This bloody hand later became the family banshee. He would appear to certain men of the family and challenge them to a duel. It did not matter if the person accepted or refused the challenge—that person was doomed to die soon.[296]

As if one death messenger was not sufficient, Kincardine Castle also has a ghostly lady who wears fairy green. She sits under her favorite tree and will wail for the person who is soon to die.[297]

The Drummer of Cortachy

Another very bansheelike phantom in Scotland is the celebrated Drummer of Cortachy who haunts Cortachy Castle near Kirrimuir. According to the legend, the countess of Airlie was having a torrid affair with a drummer in her husband's service. Before long, her cuckolded husband found out about this.

He had a poetic way of dealing with this lustful percussionist. He had his guards stuff the young man into his drum, then toss the instrument off of the tallest turret. The drummer did not immediately die; before he expired, he was able to pronounce a curse on the family. He vowed he would return to announce their deaths.

He was good to his word. His ghostly drumming was heard in the hallways before the death of his illicit lover, the countess, and has been reported many times thereafter.

295. McIntyre, "Shadow of Cairngorm VI."

296. O'Donnell, *The Banshee*, 161.

297. McIntyre, "Old Scottish Customs."

The English writer Catherine Crowe stated that her friend, Margaret Dalrymple, was a guest in the castle in 1848. During the night, she heard the strange drumbeats going up and down the halls, then suddenly stopping.

The next morning, she asked her host what the strange sound was all about. The earl suddenly became pale and did not answer the question. Obviously, it was something that he did not want to discuss, so the matter was dropped in favor of lighter subjects. Margaret was later told by a servant about the ghostly drummer. He stated that it was a death prophecy, so naturally, it was not a topic the family liked to discuss.

The prophecy of the drummer, once again, was true. It was rumored that a piece of paper was found in the study with the name of a countess written on it. That same countess died within a few months.[298]

The Ghostly Piper of Duntrune Castle

It should come as no surprise that if there is a Scottish death messenger drummer, then there must also be a piper. And there is; he is said to be connected to the MacDonalds.[299]

There is, of course, a good story connected to this phantom musician. He haunts Duntrune Castle, which is located on Loch Crinan in Argyll. It is the oldest continuously occupied castle in Scotland.

In 1645, the MacDonald clan, supporters of the English King Charles I, took the stronghold from their rivals, the Campbell clan, who supported parliament. They knew that most of the troops from the Campbells were in the field elsewhere, so the castle would not be heavily guarded.

---

298. *Edinburgh Evening News*, "Ghostly Drummer."
299. O'Donnell, *The Banshee*, 162.

Once the castle was taken, the MacDonalds also had to go into the field in search of their enemy. Leaving only a small number of men to defend their newly acquired stronghold, they left. One of the handful of defenders was a piper.

The Campbells learned that their castle had been taken and returned in force. They soon retook their fortress. Most of the MacDonald defenders were summarily executed, but the piper was spared. He now had to play his music for the other side.

One day, the chieftain of the MacDonalds was seen in a small boat crossing the loch, apparently unaware that the castle was once again in the Campbell hands—he was rowing into a trap.

The piper, loyal to his chieftain, went up on the battlements and piped a tune of welcoming. The Campbells paid this little mind—yeah, they had a welcome for him. But when the boat was close enough, the musician suddenly changed his repertoire to the Piper's Warning.

The MacDonald chieftain knew immediately what this music meant, and at the last moment, turned the boat around, escaping with his life.

The loyal piper, however, was not so fortunate. The chieftain of the Campbells had the man's hands cut off, after which he bled to death.

But he did not leave Duntrune Castle. He is the piper who still haunts the ancient hallways and chambers, along with something that causes a great deal of poltergeist activity.[300]

Hairy Hands and Bodach Glas

One of the strangest death messengers from anywhere in the world is "'the girl with the hairy left-hand' which haunts Tulloch Gorms,

300. *Bagtown Clans*, "Top 10 Haunted Scottish Castles."

and gives warning of a death in the Grant family, like the Banshee in many old houses in Ireland, the *Bodca-an-Dun* in the family of Rothmarchas, or the spectre of the bloody hand in that of Kinchardines."[301]

A fascinating bansheelike entity from Scotland is the *Bodach Glas*, the dark gray man. To see him is a portent of death, as described in this sighting by a nobleman who was playing a game of golf at St. Andrews.

"The Earl of E, a nobleman alike beloved and respected in Scotland, and whose death was truly felt as a national loss, was playing on the day of his decease on the links of St. Andrews at the national game of golf. Suddenly he stopped in the middle of a game, saying, 'I can play no longer, there is the Bodach Glas, I have seen it for the third time; something fearful is going to befall me.' He died that night at M. M., as he was handing a candlestick to a lady who was retiring to her room."[302]

There is a great deal of folklore behind the *Bodach Glas*; one story depicts him as a kind of evil Santa Clause. In this form, he is a goblin who will climb down the chimney, and rather than leaving presents and snacking on a cookie, he finds naughty children and carries them away, much like the Teutonic Krampus.

There is little doubt that this "old man" is actually an ancient pagan deity who never left. He is connected in lore to a stone monument known as *Tigh nam Bodach*, located in the remote area of Gleann Cailliche. This glen in Perthshire is named after Cailleach, who was both a fertility goddess and the spirit of winter. She was believed to be the wife of the old man Bodach.

---

301. Henderson, *Northern Counties of England*, 344.

302. Henderson, *Northern Counties of England*, 344.

There is a very curious death portent at Gordon Castle at Moray. On the grounds is a massive willow tree. There is a family belief that if anything should harm that tree, such as a strike by lightning or branches coming loose, a person in the family will die.[303]

The Oxenham Bird

As we have now had enough Scotch whiskey and fresh air from the Highlands, we will now leave Scotland and journey south to England. Here we find a curious bansheelike creature haunting the Oxenham family. This emissary for the grave takes the form of a white bird and is constantly seen by family members before they die. The family was located in Devon, once known as Devonshire, that rocky area of southwest England so famous for its prehistoric megaliths and rich folklore.

The apparition began with a disastrous wedding. Margaret Oxenham was a beautiful and desirable young woman. She had many suitors. At long last, she decided upon a wealthy landowner we know only as Bertram.

Unfortunately, before the wedding could take place, there was a tragic accident involving a head injury to Bertram. He survived, but his mind was in shambles. Now being completely insane, there was no way he could enter matrimony.

Margaret was brokenhearted, but in time, she found another man, Sir John of Roxanclave. He proposed and, as her options were running out, she accepted.

On the day of her wedding, wearing her beautiful gown, she was waiting in a dressing room. Suddenly, there was the apparition of a white bird floating above her.

---

303. O'Donnell, *The Banshee*, 164.

The avian specter vanished. Margaret, quite disturbed by what was obviously some kind of omen, went on with the ceremony anyway. She and her intended husband had just reached the altar when Bertram, having escaped from those who were supposed to be caring for him, rushed in. He ran up to Margaret and, before she or her intended husband could say anything to stop him, plunged a knife into her heart. As she fell down dead, her white gown stained crimson, he took the same knife and plunged it into himself.[304]

Since then, the ghostly white bird who appeared before Margaret has haunted the Oxenham family, announcing their deaths.

The famed folklorist Baring-Gould wrote of this apparition at length, mentioning the deaths of John Oxenham, Mary Oxenham, the infant son of John, Elizabeth Oxenham in the seventeenth century, and William Oxenham, who looked upon it in defiance.

"It first was seen outside the window, and soon afterwards by Mrs. Oxenham in the room, which she mentioned to Mr. Oxenham, and asked him if he knew what the bird was. 'Yes,' says he, 'it has been upon my face and head, and is recorded in history as always appearing to our family before their deaths; but I shall cheat the bird.' Nothing more was said about it, nor was the bird taken notice of from that time; but he died soon afterwards."[305]

It would appear that Mr. Oxenham did not cheat the bird.

The Deathbird

Arundel Castle in West Sussex also has an avian death messenger to go along with its other ghosts (those would be the Blue Man who hangs out in the library, a woman in white reputed to be the ghost of a young woman overcome with grief who died by suicide, and, natu-

---

304. Sandles, "The White Bird."

305. *Devonshire Characters*, 256.

rally, the earl of Arundel himself, who built the castle in the eleventh century). This death messenger also takes the form of a large white bird, usually said to be an owl.[306]

Film buffs will recall that in the opening scene of Murnau's 1922 classic vampire film *Nosferatu*, at the very beginning of the film, there is a written line, "Nosferatu, does this word not sound like the death-bird calling your name at midnight?" What exactly is Murnau talking about here?

The tradition of this "deathbird," an avian death messenger, is not peculiar to these two families. There is a Welsh legend of a ghastly creature known as the *aderyn y corph*, the corpse bird. This uncanny creature manages to fly even though it has no wings. It also has no feathers, which would make it look rather like a plucked chicken floating about. That may sound humorous at first, until one stops to picture it.

This weird specter flies right up to the door of the doomed person and calls out "come, come!"[307]

Other English Death Messengers

One of the most curious animal death portents is that of the Clifton family in England. Before there is a death in the family, a large sturgeon will swim up River Trent until it reaches the area of the manor. It will swim around in a circle, then depart.[308]

One would definitely not want to see the death messenger that haunts the squires of Worcestshire. Similar to the herald mentioned

---

306. Dyer, *Ghost World*, 222; see also *Fringe Paranormal*, "Arundel Castle."

307. Sikes, *British Goblins*, 213.

308. Earp, "Spotlight."

above in Scotland, it appears as a ghostly arm coming through a wall.[309]

A literary death messenger haunts the Byron family. Yes, that would be the same family that sired the great poet, Lord Byron.

This apparition takes the form of a black monk. During the reign of King Henry VIII, Catholic property was seized, including the ancient Newstead Abbey, in Nottinghamshire. This was granted to the Byron family.

Soon afterward, a monk in black began to appear when members of the family died.[310]

One dark omen that is mentioned in many cultures is the belief that a dog can sense the arrival of the spirit of death and will begin a mournful howl. On December 9, 1871, the prince of Wales was lying at Sandrigham, dreadfully ill. That night, a dog began to howl. The act was so important that the newspapers reported it.

In Germany we find the same belief: "I read lately of a dog in a German village which was supposed to have announced so many deaths that he became an object of general terror, and was put to death."[311]

We can thus safely assume that since that day, no one has died in that village.

Brittany

Crossing the Channel to France, we arrive at the region of Brittany. Here, one finds that mysterious megalithic complex known as Carnac and a countryside overflowing with folktales. Many of these legends and beliefs are of a dark tone. It should come as no surprise that

---

309. O'Donnell, *The Banshee*, 165.

310. BBC, "The Five Ghosts."

311. Conway, *Demonology*, 1:134.

this fairy-haunted region should have a few of its own, particularly grim, versions of the death messengers.

One of these is quite similar to the washerwoman type of banshee, but with a decidedly evil twist. W. Y. Evans-Wentz, in his classic *The Fairy Faith in Celtic Countries*, gives a description of this dark entity: "The phantom washerwomen of Brittany are known as les *lavandières de nuits*; or in Breton, *cannered noz*. They are not heard very often, but they are terrifying when a lone traveler at night stumbles upon them."

Anyone who stumbled upon the specter had a big problem. If he were detected, it could mean his life. The specter "would ask a certain passer-by to help them to wring sheets, he could not refuse, under pain of being stopped and wrung like a sheet himself. And it was necessary for those who aided in wringing their winding sheets to turn in the same direction as the washerwomen; for if by misfortune the assistant turned in an opposite direction, he had his arms wrung in an instant."[312]

They would not do this merely out of spite. These ghostly laundresses were condemned to their grim task for hundreds of years. However, should they be fortunate enough to force some mortal into service, then have that person wind the wrong way, they would be freed from their penance.

He comments that these women are undergoing a kind of purgatory, some for the heinous sin of having murdered their own children.

Ankou

Evans-Wentz continues, discussing the similarities between the Irish banshee and the dreaded reaper himself, Ankou. He relates how Ankou will leave his cart and stroll up to the front door of the house.

312. Evans-Wentz, *Fairy Faith*, 216.

He would then call out the name of the person whose soul he was to collect. He states that every family, around that mysterious mega- lithic structure of Carnac in the Morbihan district, has some story to tell concerning a visit from Ankou.

That does indeed mean everyone. In Ireland, as we have seen, only members of certain select families receive the attention of the lady of the mound. But for Ankou, everyone who lives—and dies— in the region is eligible for one of his nocturnal visits.

Evans-Wentz relates a number of other death manifestations and omens in Brittany. Referring to the work of Le Braz, *La Légende de la Mort*, he mentions such eerie manifestations as disembodied hands floating about and poltergeist activity. There are also "death-candles or torches, dreams, peculiar bodily sensations, images in water, phan- tom funerals, and death-chariots or death-coaches as in Wales."[313]

The figure of Ankou is certainly one of the darkest we will encounter, although whether he is the messenger of death or if he is Death personified is up to debate. It is from this entity that we derive our modern character known as the Grim Reaper, including the carrying of a scythe. The one major difference, however, is that the modern Death personification is a skeleton who wears a black hood; Ankou is manlike and wears a wide-brimmed hat, one which will hide his ghastly face.

Ankou rides at night over the dark lanes of Brittany in a coach that screeches from a lack of grease. He is often followed by his assis- tants: two skeletons.

In his office as death messenger, anyone who hears the shrill creaking of his cart is doomed to ride in it soon—very soon, for he

---

313. Evans-Wentz, *Fairy Faith*, 220.

will often stop right in front of the house and, as a phantom, walk right in and claim the soul of the doomed person on the spot.[314]

There is an interesting variation of this in which we see that serving as Ankou is only a temporary assignment. Each year, the very first person in a district to die is doomed to become Ankou for the rest of the year. This is similar to the motif in Victor Sjöström's 1921 Swedish horror film *The Phantom Coach*, in which the last person to die on New Year's Eve will have to drive Death's coach throughout the new year.

Ankou has a herald of his own, the Death Bird, known locally as *Labous*, also referred to as an "ankou." This is assumed to be an owl, but no one who has ever heard it has lived to tell the tale.[315]

To this day, people will still make food offerings to Ankou, obviously to encourage him to keep a good distance away. Milk and crepes are left for him, particularly in late October and November, the time around Samhain when he is said to be the most active. Some old churchyards even have special holders for people to leave the traditional offering to keep the messenger of Death at bay.[316]

In one of the greatest horror films ever made, Carl Dryer's 1932 masterpiece *Vampyr*, we see a shot of a character wearing the wide-brimmed hat of Ankou and carrying a scythe. He is sitting in a boat ready to cross the water, possibly the Styx, destined for the world beyond. The viewer should note that the boat is not moving—the figure of the Dark Reaper Ankou is merely sitting, waiting for his passengers, who he is certain shall come to him.

314. Oxford Reference, "Ankou."

315. Badonne, "Death Omens," 99.

316. Sutherland, "Ankou."

Teutonic Death Messengers

Further east on the continent, the Teutonic nations such as Germany, Austria, and Switzerland, among others, have a particularly eerie death messenger, the *Weiße Frau*, or "white woman." There are countless legends and gothic horror stories of this spirit, the ghostly woman in white gliding down darkened hallways in an old manor. Sometimes these spectral maidens will merely announce an upcoming demise, others take an active role and lure their victims to their deaths. There are so many of these tales that only a few examples of haunted German castles and remote Austrian manors will be needed. We will start at the top.

Up until the First World War, the most powerful family in Germany was the ruling dynasty of the Hohenzollerns. The power of this house ended, as did so many other royal families with the abdication of Kaiser Wilhelm II on November 9, 1918. It should come as no surprise that a dynasty as old and as powerful as this would have their own *Weiße Frau*.

In 1628, this spectral lady appeared to a princess of the Hohenzollerns in the palace at Berlin with a grim warning: "*Veni, judica vivos et mortuos; judicum mihi adhuc superest*"—that is to say, "Come judge the quick and the dead—I wait for judgment."[317]

After she recovered from the shock, the princess who witnessed this apparition tried to find the identity. She scoured all the family portraits. Finally, at the castle of Neuhaus, she found two that looked like the ghost she had seen: one was a long-dead princess; the other, the equally dead countess of Orlamunde.[318]

As it turns out, the princess was right with the second one.

317. O'Donnell, *The Banshee*, 151.
318. *The Queenslander* (May 11, 1933), 34.

Years later, another princess, this one married with young children, was staying at the Neues Palais. One of the young children ran out on a terrace after hearing a mysterious woman in white sitting out there playing a harp. However, when the young prince reached the balcony, the harpist suddenly vanished.

The child ran back into the room and told his mother what he had seen. Now both walked out onto the terrace, and sure enough, the harpist was there again, playing her instrument.

The princess did not like trespassers, especially around her children. She raised her walking stick to help encourage the interloper to leave. However, as soon as she raised the device, it flew out of her hand and off the terrace. The strange harpist gave them an evil smile, then did not walk, but rather glided across the balcony to the edge. She simply disappeared right in front of them.

By now, the princess had figured out that this was the famed Hohenzollern *Weiße Frau*. There had been talk in the family about this ghost for generations. Interestingly, the talk also included mention of a hidden treasure.

She was further convinced that the harp-playing phantom had appeared right over the spot where the treasure was located. It was time to do some digging. She brought in workmen who excavated the terrace. To her delight, they did indeed uncover an underground vault.

The princess had the workmen step aside and, grabbing a lantern, she went down the ladder alone to see what was down there. She didn't want any of the workers taking free samples of gold coins.

As it turns out, there was no gold down there. But what was there caused the princess to scream, drop her lantern, and rush through the darkness back to the ladder.

Instead of treasure, there was a skeleton—a skeleton chained by an iron collar to the stone wall.

The kaiser himself ordered his aides to find out who she was. After some intense research of the palace records and local histories, they learned the horrific truth of what they had found. As the princess had guessed years before, the skeleton was indeed that of the countess of Orlamunde, a woman famous for her beauty.

The margrave of Brandenburgh had taken this young beauty as his mistress with the sincerest promises that someday soon he would make her his wife. As a result of this affair, she bore him two illegitimate children. However, now the margrave was concerned that these two children would have some claim to an inheritance. They were a problem.

Taking a cue from the Mexican *La Llorona*, the uncaring countess poisoned both of her children. She then went to the margrave, announced what she had done, and said that there were no more obstacles to him marrying her.

Well, there was this little matter of infanticide, and one can also surmise that he did not wish to actually marry this woman, just use her. As punishment for her unspeakable crime, she was chained to a wall in the vault and sealed up to die a ghastly death.

The Hohenzollern *Weiße Frau* made a bansheelike appearance at the death of the dynasty. She was sighted at the famous Potsdam Neues Palais in 1914, just as Kaiser Wilhelm was giving the orders that would help plunge the world into a wasteful bloodbath—and, in the process, destroy the power of his dynasty.[319]

With true German efficiency, the Hohenzollern *Weiße Frau* even tells the time.

In the Bohemian *Jindrichuv Hradec* (Castle Neuhaus), a princess was in a hallway in front of a mirror trying on a hat. She noticed out

---

319. *The Queenslander* (May 11, 1933), 34.

of the corner of her eye that there was someone there. Thinking that it was one of the maids, she calmly asked what time it was.

A spectral voice, almost mocking, replied, "*Zehn uhr ist es irh Liebden*! It is ten o'clock, your love!"[320] The princess spun about and saw that it was no maid standing next to her, but the infamous lady in white, the ghost she had heard about all her life.

The princess died shortly thereafter.

Other Teutonic White Ladies

Teutonic white ladies have a great deal in common with their Irish cousins. It is related by O'Donnell that the Germans have a wide variety of death messengers connected to various families. With some households, "the phenomenon is a roaring lion, in others a howling dog; and in others a bell or gong, or sepulchral toned clock striking at some unusual hour, and generally thirteen times."[321]

Of course, no matter what form the supernatural harbinger takes, the meaning is exactly the same. Someone in the clan is about to leave this world, or possibly, there is about to be some manner of terrible misfortune.

Teutonic folklore has no shortage of death messengers. The mountainous Tyrol region has a particularly unnerving one, a ghostly lady who says nothing but stares in the window. One would certainly not want to glance out of a window at night only to see a wraithlike face staring back.

Of course, the *Weiße Frau*, often with a white veil covering her face, is similar to the banshee. Even closer to the Irish counterpart is the *Klage-weib* (mourning woman).

---

320. O'Donnell, *The Banshee*, 151–152.
321. O'Donnell, *The Banshee*, 156.

"On stormy nights, when the moon shines faintly through the fleeting clouds, she stalks of gigantic stature with death-like aspect, and black, hollow eyes, wrapt in grave clothes which float in the wind, and stretches her immense arm over the solitary hut, uttering lamentable cries in the tempestuous darkness."[322] Whatever home she has stretched her arm toward, one of the inhabitants has no more than a month to live.

The Klagmuhme and the Bihlweisen

Even more closely related to the Celtic banshee is the Teutonic spirit known as the *Klagmuhme*, a word meaning "the wailing aunt." There are variations of this such as *Klagemutter*, the weeping mother. Like her Irish cousins, she will go to a doomed person's house but not enter it. She will then wail sorrowfully, and leave.[323]

There is a macabre legend that comes from the farm country around Augusta, Georgia. Every so often, folks will report seeing a man dressed in old-fashioned clothing, all black, plowing a field. There are two horses connected to the outdated plow. However, there are no marks on the ground where the plow has gone.

Local people have no idea who he was, only that to see him means there will soon be funeral bells ringing in the area.[324]

This curious American legend has roots in the Altmark region of Germany. Reverend Moncure Daniel Conway, in his classic work on demonology, mentioned this area as being the home of that ghastly spirit troop known as the *Bihlweisen*.

The reverend relates how there is a group of black-clad men with scythes going through the field cutting away. There are, however, two

---

322. O'Donnell, *The Banshee*, 156–157.

323. Grimm, *Teutonic Mythology*, 3:1135.

324. Curran, *Mysterious Celtic*, 286.

very unusual things about their appearance. The first is that no matter how hard they cut, none of the grain would fall.

The second curious thing is that the reapers have no heads!

The local people know their appearance signifies that there will soon be a terrible disease affecting the community. It might strike the cattle—or it might strike them.[325]

The Habsburg Birds

One of the most bizarre death messengers is the tale of the curse of the Habsburg family of Austria. This once minor royal family rose to great power by intermarrying with the right people. Once they had ascended the ladder of regal success, they closed ranks and began to marry only members of their own family, causing some problems genetically.

But one of their biggest problems was with a messenger of doom, the raven.

It all began in the thirteenth century with the count of Altenburg going hunting one day in the Swiss Alps. He rode off alone and wandered a bit too close to some nesting eagles. The young count suddenly found himself being attacked by a flock of extremely angry birds of prey. There seemed to be no possible chance for him to survive this unusual threat except to call out for the help of God. He prayed as hard as he ever had in his life, all while trying to swipe away the massive birds.

Apparently, God heard his prayer. From seemingly nowhere, a massive murder of ravens appeared and attacked the eagles. The aerial battle gave the count enough time to make his escape.

---

325. Conway, *Demonology* 1:267–268.

As the ravens had saved his life, he wanted to repay them. He had a tower built to house his inky-feathered saviors. He named the new bird sanctuary *Habsburg*, meaning "tower of prey."

For a while, his family took good care of their raven friends. His family soon bore the name of this curious tower, a family destined to great power and even greater tragedy.

Things would have probably gone differently had it not been for an idiot descendant who, a century later, took a good look at the tower and decided it would be a wonderful site for an entire castle to reflect the growing wealth and power of the family. The only problem was all those birds.

He should have left the ravens alone. Instead, he had them driven away, sometimes by having his reluctant servants shoot them. The former avian protectors now became portents of doom. Angry at the betrayal, supernatural ravens, known in Germany as *Turnfalken*, would appear at Habsburg death and tragedy over the centuries to come.[326]

There was plenty of tragedy in this family to keep the birds busy. There were numerous battles fought over the centuries. When the Habsburg side was destined to lose, the ravens would appear. They also made an appearance at the execution of Marie Antoinette, the 1867 execution by firing squad of the French-installed emperor of Mexico Maximilian I (who was the Habsburg archduke Ferdinand Maximilian), and the 1853 assassination attempt on Franz Joseph I, which he survived. His wife, Empress Elisabeth, did not. Of course, the birds appeared in Sarajevo in 1914 when the Habsburg archduke Franz Ferdinand and his wife, Sophie, were assassinated. This murder was the spark, but not the true cause, of the First World War. That

---

326. Stepko, "Role Ravens Played."

conflict brought down the Habsburg dynasty once and for all. One can just hear the ravens crying out for the Habsburgs, "Nevermore."[327]

Hans Holzer related a variation of this legend. The Habsburg family in Vienna resided at the opulent palace known as *Schönbrunn*. There had been a legend lasting for centuries that when the birds left the grounds of the palace, the time of the family's power was over.

These were not crows, but rather common blackbirds. There were countless blackbirds on the grounds for centuries. However, within two years of the assassination of the archduke in Sarajevo and the slaughter of the First World War, all the blackbirds simply flew away.[328]

The Lower Saxony Premonition

A vision of one's own funeral is certainly a terrifying experience. There is a macabre case from the German state of Lower Saxony in which a man was employed as a field laborer by a farmer. In the middle of the night, the field hand dreamed there was a coffin lying in state on the threshing floor. He moved closer to it to see whose body was lying there—but for some reason, he could not recognize the features.

He took a scissors and cut off a portion of the corpse's hair where it would be quite visible. He figured that in the morning, he would see who had a recent haircut and know that this was the person he had seen in the coffin.

The next morning at breakfast, he looked at all the other field-workers. Everyone looked normal; no one had their hair cut in a weird way.

327. Stepko, "Role Ravens Played."

328. Holzer, *Habsburg Curse*, 124–125.

Relieved, the field hand went off to wash up. It was then that he saw his reflection in the mirror. His hair was cut in that strange way...he had seen his own body in the coffin on the threshing floor.

He immediately decided this was not a particularly healthy place for him to be working. He told the farmer that he was leaving right away. The farmer did everything he could to convince the man to remain—he was one of his best workers. But without revealing the reason for his unexpected departure, the field hand left.

A few years later, he was back in the same town and ran into his old employer. By now, he felt he had escaped the prophecy and accepted an invitation to dinner at the farmhouse. Obviously, the farmer wanted his old worker back, and was wining and dining him.

He never worked another day. While visiting the farm, he suddenly became extremely ill and died. His body was placed in a coffin exactly as he had seen in his vision.[329]

Italy and the Donati Family Visitor

Italy has a very peculiar banshee haunting the Donati family. Jacopo Donati was the head of one of the most wealthy and powerful Venetian families. However, his wealth and influence could do nothing to help his son, who was lying in bed desperately ill. Despite all the doctors could do, each day the boy was drawn closer to the grave.

One night, Jacopo was in bed when he was roused by a strange sight. "The door of his chamber opened and the head of a man thrust in. Knowing that it was not one of his servants, he roused the house, drew his sword, went over the whole palace."[330]

To his surprise, the hallways were already filled with some of the members of his household staff. The same head of a man had

329. Lecouteux, *Witches*, 135.

330. Dyer, *Ghost World*, 229.

appeared to them as well, and they were seeking the intruder. Despite the exhaustive search, no stranger was found in the manor.

The next day, they understood the identity of the unwelcome visitor. The boy died.[331]

Death Birds of Asia

Across the globe on the island of Sri Lanka, we find another avian messenger of death. It is known as the *ulama* (screamer) or the *yak kurulla*, the Devil Bird. To hear its eerie wail on a night while walking through the jungle is a sign of imminent death.

Naturalists have determined that the sound is caused by a species of owl. However, the cry is not only humanlike, but it resembles that of a person being tortured.[332]

There is a ghastly legend as to where this creature came from. A man and his wife lived in the remote rainforest. The woman gave birth to a child, but the husband, whose grip on sanity was apparently not too tight, believed it was someone else's.

One day he went completely mad, and while his wife was out, killed the baby and cooked it. He then, pretending that nothing was wrong, served some of the meat to his wife.

As she ate, he laughed manically and told her what she had just consumed. She screamed in horror and ran off into the jungle. Ever since then, unlucky people ready for death will hear her wail.[333]

Not too far away, on the north island of New Zealand, there is mention of another death messenger in the form of a screaming bird. It is called the *hakawai*. To hear the cry of this bird is a sign not just of death, but of war.

---

331. Dyer, *Ghost World*, 229.

332. *Taranaki Herald*, "Devil Bird of Ceylon," 2.

333. Perera, "The Devil Bird."

Over the years, a number of people known as muttonbirders would go off into the rainforest at night seeking the newly hatched seabirds. However, as soon as they heard the ghastly sound of the *hakawai*, they would drop what they had collected and rush back to their huts as fast as they could.

These folks also had to watch out for another supernatural avian enemy, the *poukai*. It is said that this massive bird likes to eat humans.[334]

La Llorona

A surprising addition to the list of death messengers is one of the most famous folk characters of all time: *La Llorona*.

It is said that to see her or hear her mournful wail as she searches for her children is a certain sign that death or another disaster will soon befall the unlucky witness.[335]

The basic story is very well known and has many variations. To quickly summarize it for anyone not familiar with this dark spirit, she is the ghost of a Mexican señora, usually named Maria. Maria was a beautiful woman and, in some versions, wanted to marry a wealthy man.

The man was quite willing to marry this gorgeous lady, but there was one slight problem: she already had two children. Maria decided to fix this problem by taking her little children to the river and drowning them.

She returned to the man saying that she was now free to marry him—there were no more children to interfere with their life together. But rather than embracing her in love, he recoiled in absolute horror at what she had done.

---

334. Baraniuk, "The Animals."

335. Curran, *Mysterious Celtic*, 277.

Since then, her ghost wanders about, crying mournfully (the Spanish word *Llorona* is from *llorón*, meaning "weepy") and calling out for her murdered children.

Another variation of this story is that she married the wealthy man and bore him two children. At first, he was a loving husband, but as she grew older and her looks faded, he paid less and less attention to her. Soon he would go out drinking and carousing; at times, he would be gone for weeks. When he returned, he would merely visit his children but pay no attention to his rejected wife.

Finally, in a fit of jealousy, she took the children down to the river for a bath. There she held them both under the water until they drowned. Rather than finding the happiness she was seeking, she was executed for her crime.[336]

Now she wanders the city streets late at night, crying and seeking her children, bringing death to those who are unfortunate enough to hear her.

There are many people who assert they have seen this spectral woman. The Lujan family in New Mexico in the 1930s chanced to notice a woman dressed all in white crossing the road by their property. They had no idea where she had come from, as they did not see anyone walking down the road, nor did they see any vehicle let her out.

As they continued to observe her, the family could not help but notice that she seemed to be gliding rather than walking. Then she just vanished.

The family looked at each other in wonder. Then, before they could rub their eyes, she reappeared, but much farther away near a creek.

Then she disappeared, this time for good.[337]

---

336. Weiser-Alexander, "La Llorona."

337. Dimuro, "The Legend of La Llorona."

Just as in the Irish banshee we see the shadow of the earlier Celtic goddesses, there are those who believe this is the same with *La Llorona*. The best candidate for this is the Aztec goddess Cihuacōātl, known as the Serpent Woman. She was, ironically, a powerful fertility goddess. Like the modern counterpart, she was dressed in a white robe and wandered through the night wailing. She was closely connected to mothers and midwives.

She was said to have a group of ghostly followers known as the *cihuateteo*, women who had died in childbirth. They would haunt crossroads, waiting for their victims. They loved to kidnap children. They would also cause disease in children and insanity or even possess them. Naturally, Aztec mothers would warn their children about going out at night for fear of the *cihuateteo*.

There is another Aztec goddess who may be the origin of the death-bringing *Llorona*: Chalchiuhtlicue, the Jade-Skirted One. While she is also connected to childbirth, she is primarily a goddess of the sea and lakes. One of her favorite pastimes is to capsize fishing boats and drown men.[338]

Some historians speculate that there may well be an actual person connected to the *Llorona* legend. This would be the slave girl known as *La Malinche*. She rose from her position as a slave to become the interpreter for the conquistador Hernán Cortés, finally achieving her freedom and later the title Doña Marina. While she was definitely a real-life person, there is a dark story, for which there is no documentation, that she murdered the children of Cortés.[339]

We see in the folk belief of *La Llorona* an echo of the familiar classical myth of Medea, the evil woman who murdered her own

338. Mingren, "Aztec Water Goddess."
339. Dimuro, "The Legend of *La Llorona*."

children to be with her lover, in her case the hero Jason. It didn't go well for her, either.

Now we turn our attention to one of the strangest death messengers of all.

Chapter 11
THE DOPPELGÄNGER

"Ah," said the distinguished visitor, "I thought you wouldn't recognize me, now that I've put real flesh on my body and wear clothes. I don't suppose you ever expected to see me in such fine condition. Don't you know your old shadow?"

—ANDERSEN, "THE SHADOW"

One entity with many connections to the Celtic banshee is the Scandinavian *fylgja*. In Norway it is often referred to as a *fölgie* or a *vardögr* and usually appears in animal form; in Sweden it may be referred to as a *välnad* or *värd*.[340]

Like the Celtic counterpart, it will also sometimes rattle door-knobs to warn a family of an impending death. As we shall see a little further on, these Nordic entities may also appear as doppelgängers, literally a double of the person. This is a terrible manifestation, for to see such an entity is a certain sign of impending death.[341]

Fylgja literally means "the female follower." The spirit, a psychic double, may not be limited to simply one specter. There may be several *fylgjas* connected to a single person.[342]

These entities may be utilized by shamans. During this time, the sorcerer would appear to be dead. It is vitally important that no one disturb the body during this period, or the *fylgja* may not be able to reunite with it.

An example of this is seen in *The Saga of the Lakevale Chiefs*. Ingimund's magic amulet has been stolen. He employs three Sami (Lapp) shamans to locate the amulet, which he believes is in Iceland. They go into a trance and appear dead for three nights. When their spirit doubles return to their bodies, they sigh deeply to revive themselves.

They then say their journey had been very difficult, but they are able to give Ingimund exact information about the area in Iceland where the amulet was hidden.[343]

Like the banshee, the *fylgja* is connected to certain families and follows only them. They will, as the name implies, remain loyally

---

340. *Atlas Mythica*, "All about Fylgja."
341. *Atlas Mythica*, "All about Fylgja."
342. Lecouteux, *Witches*, 45.
343. Lecouteux, *Witches*, 34.

with these clans, even when the offspring move to other lands.[344] The *fylgja* takes on other attributes as well, being not only a messenger of death but also a protective spirit over the entire family.[345]

The spirit is closely connected to afterbirth at one's arrival in this world and is especially prominent in babies who are born with a caul, a membrane that, at birth, will sometimes cover a newborn's face or head. These people, according to many cultures, are already blessed with fortune and luck. Some old beliefs state that they can never drown.[346]

Some of their darker attributes are identical to their Irish counterparts. They will be the heralds of death or sometimes a great disaster. To announce this, they will wail and lament in the voice of a woman. They have been known to tap on or rattle windows, exactly like the traditional banshee. The *fylgja* have even been reported as playing a harp.

Sometimes they do not go about alone but are divided into two beings: "They sometimes haunt in pairs, a kind spirit and an evilly disposed one attending the fortunes of the same family; and they keep exclusively to the very oldest families."[347]

The *fylgja* has been known to appear in animal form and could appear both in dreams or in real life. The entity appears in a number of the ancient sagas, in which it is often quite similar to the ultimate "fetch," the valkyrie.

---

344. Lysaght, *Irish Death Messenger*, 63.

345. Lysaght, *Irish Death Messenger*, 55.

346. Griffiths, "Listening to the Caul."

347. O'Donnell, *The Banshee*, 159.

The Gisli Saga

We see this in *The Saga of Gisli*, written in the thirteenth century about events that occurred in the tenth century. This saga, dealing with the conflict between the old pagan beliefs and the new Christian religion, depicts the clash in the form of two women. The pagan faith is depicted by a valkyrielike *fylgja*, while the other appeared more like an angel.

In the saga, Gisli has a vision of a hall in which there are seven fires burning, some brightly, others dying out. This is a perfect description of the spiritual life of the Viking society at the time.[348]

It is considered to be very unlucky to have a vision or a dream of one's *fylgja* as a woman riding a gray horse. It is similarly dire to dream of them inviting the sleeper into a house. These are certain signs of approaching death.[349]

And that is exactly what happened to Gisli. The good woman ironically was riding a gray horse, a dreadful omen of death. She took him to a great house and revealed that this was the place where he would die. Her darker companion placed a bonnet covered in blood on his head, thus revealing the violent manner of his upcoming death.[350]

"'Again I dreamed,' says Gisli, 'that yon wife came to me, and bound round my brow a bloody hood, and washed my head first in blood, and poured blood over me, so that I was all over gore.'"[351]

He continued in verse, describing the dark prophecy of his death:

---

348. Atlas Mythica, "All about Fylgja."

349. Timmons, "Sleep Myths."

350. Lecouteux, *Witches*, 45.

351. DaSent, *Gisli*, 191.

She, methought, her face all flushing.
Bathed my locks in reddest blood. Flames of light so
rosy blushing,
Woden's balm so bright and good Still I see her fingers
glowing,
Bright with gems and blazing rings,
Steeped in blood so freely flowing,
Welling from the wounds of kings.[352]

Thorsteinn Falls

A curious feature of the *fylgja* is that they are so present in this world it is even possible to trip over them.

A seven-year-old boy named Thorsteinn ran, as children of that age will do, into a room. Seven-year-olds run everywhere. But this time, the boy—for no apparent reason—suddenly fell facedown on the floor.

When he raised his head, he saw the adult in the room, a man named Geitir, was laughing hysterically over the boy's clumsiness. This was quite embarrassing, but the young man stood up, brushed himself off, and went on with things. However, he could not understand why he had tripped over nothing—and why the man had been laughing so hard. Finally, he could stand it no more and asked.

Geitir gave him an answer he did not expect: "'I saw, what you did not see, as you burst into the room, for there followed you a white bear, running in front of you, but when it saw me it remained stationary, and you stumbled over it.'"[353]

---

352. DaSent, *Gisli*, 191.

353. Baring-Gould, *Book of Folk-Lore*, 90.

The white bear, of course, was Thorsteinn's *fylgja*. Thankfully, it was not predicting death at this time.

Njalls Saga and the Song of Doom

In *Njalls Saga* we find a vision of a group of women, like the Irish *badbhh* appearing to Donogh O'Brien at Lough Rasg, sitting at a loom filled with heads and entrails of dead men.

The grisly vision occurred on the sacred day of Good Friday to a man named Daurrud. As he was walking down a road, he saw a group of twelve well-dressed men on horseback. The fellow travelers were making their way toward a building.

He lost sight of them for a moment, but they did not reappear. Curious as to who they were and what their business was, he made his way to the building. There was a long vertical slit of a window, common in medieval buildings. He walked up and peeked in, wondering if he would see the riders.

He did not. But what he saw terrified him: "There were women inside, and they had set up a loom. Men's heads were the weights, but men's entrails were the warp and wed, a sword was the shuttle, and the reels were arrows."[354]

The group sang a long song of death and slaughter, of which there is only time here to repeat a portion:

See! warp is stretched
For warriors' fall,
Lo! weft in loom
'Tis wet with blood;
Now fight foreboding,
'Neath friends' swift fingers,

354. DaSent, *Burnt Njal*.

Our gray woof waxeth
With war's alarms,
Our warp bloodred,
Our weft corseblue.
This woof is y-woven
With entrails of men,
This warp is hardweighted
With heads of the slain ...
When they speed the shuttle
How spear-heads shall flash! [355]

Leaving Scandinavia on that happy note, we will take a quick jaunt back to Wales. It is hard to imagine a more frightening apparition of death than to witness one's own self as a corpse.

The Lledrith

One very creepy death messenger from Wales is the *lledrith*, a vision of a person as a corpse seen by the same person—who is very much alive. "It never speaks, and vanishes if spoken to. It has been seen by miners previous to a fatal accident in the mine." [356]

One such encounter happened to a miner on an average day. As he went about his duties, he suddenly had a vision of his own body lying motionless, crushed and covered in blood. The corpse of himself was in a tramcar, surrounded by ghostly miners and being carted out of the mine.

This may have been dismissed as an overactive and rather morbid imagination, except for one undeniable bit of verification. The miner's

355. DaSent, *Burnt Njal.*
356. Dyer, *Ghost World,* 370–371.

dog saw the same exact thing. The terrified hound ran off, leaving a howl in his wake.

The miner would have liked to have joined him, but that was not possible. Thinking it over, he decided there was nothing he could do about the situation, so he might as well continue his work. If it was his time, then it was his time.

Not long afterward, a rock plummeted from the ceiling. It struck the miner, but it only broke his arm.

He recovered from the accident and kept waiting for the big tragedy. However, as the days passed, nothing happened. He came to the conclusion that the tragedy the *lledrith* had predicted was the broken arm. Everything was fine, no need to worry.

But there was.

After a few days, another rock was suddenly dislodged from the ceiling; this one was much larger than the first. It struck him directly, and he was crushed to death.

Then, just as the *lledrith* had predicted, his broken and bloody body was placed on a tramcar by his fellow miners and rolled out of the mine.[357]

The Doppelgänger

This eerie phantom is a variation of a creature reported throughout Europe, the *Doppelgänger* (German: "double walker"). It is very bad fortune to see one's double wandering about on its own and is most certainly an omen of imminent death.

The Irish refer to this manifestation as a fetch. There is a great deal of lore associated with it, as its appearance can mean different things. It is described as "a mere shadow, resembling in stature features, and dress, a living person well known to the beholder. If the

---

357. Dyer, *Ghost World*, 370–371.

apparition appears in the morning a happy longevity for the original may be confidently predicted; but if it appears in the evening the immediate dissolution of the living prototype may be as surely anticipated. When the fetch appears agitated in its movements a violent or painful death is indicated for the doomed prototype, who is known at the time to be labouring under some serious illness." [358]

Consider the reaction of the young people experiencing this phenomenon in the famous Rosetti watercolor *How They Met Themselves*. A couple strolling in a forest is suddenly face-to-face with their own selves doing the exact same thing. As this means certain death, the young mortal woman has fainted dead away. The man has drawn his sword, but this will do him no good. The eerie doubles have a strange glow around their bodies and are staring intently and without emotion at their mortal counterparts.

It is interesting to note that the characters depicted in this famous work of art are the artist and the woman he had just married, Elizabeth Siddal. In fact, they were on their honeymoon as he was working on it.

Rosetti was apparently obsessed with this idea of the double. His home was filled with numerous mirrors. Ironically, his new wife died of an overdose of laudanum just two years after the painting was completed. This dark work of art, partially created on her honeymoon, was truly a prediction of her death. [359]

Göthe and Shelley

Several cases have been recorded of people seeing their *Doppelgänger*, usually, but not always, resulting in death. One of the most famous is the case of the great German philosopher Göthe.

---

358. Wood-Martin, *Traces of the Elder Faiths*, 1:370.

359. Wilks, "'How They Met Themselves.'"

When the scholar was a younger man, he chanced to be riding a horse along a path leading toward Drusenheim. Everything seemed normal, until he had a strange vision, one he saw with his physical eyes and with his mind.

The eerie vision was of himself, but older. His double was riding towards him but on a different horse, and was dressed in gray clothing that he did not own.

He shook his head to dispel this strange sight, and it worked. When he looked back, the mysterious double had somehow vanished.

It was eight years later that Göthe found himself riding a horse down that same road. It was then that he realized that the horse was the same color that he had seen in his vision, and that he was now wearing the exact same clothing that he had seen! He had somehow been given a vision of himself in the future.[360]

The most infamous case of a *Doppelgänger* appearing right before a death is the bizarre case of the poet Percy Bysshe Shelley in 1822. His wife, Mary Shelley, recorded that a friend, Mrs. Williams, had seen Percy strolling along the street, walking past the witnesses on a terrace. He passed a few times in the same direction, but there was no way for him to do this. Of course, this was his double.

Shelley had seen visions of his double a few times in his life. Towards the end, he had a vision of his *Doppelgänger* appearing to him and asking, "How long do you expect to be content?"[361]

The vision of the *Doppelgänger* seen from the terrace was on June 15. On July 8th, Shelley drowned in a boating accident in the Gulf of La Spezia.[362]

It is curious to note that Shelley had written about the *Doppelgänger* in one of his most famous poems:

---

360. Von Goethe, *Autobiography*, 433.

361. *Whitby Uncovered*, "The Whitby Doppelgänger."

362. Shepherd, "Full Fathom Five."

They shall be told. Ere Babylon was dust,
The Magus Zoroaster, my dead child,
Met his own image walking in the garden.
That apparition, sole of men, he saw.
For know there are two worlds of life and death:
One that which thou beholdest; but the other
Is underneath the grave, where do inhabit
The shadows of all forms that think and live,
Till death unite them and they part no more.[363]

There is a curious case of a *Doppelgänger* not predicting death, but rather, by its presence, preventing one.

Christoph Willibald Glück

The famed opera composer Christoph Willibald Glück was residing for a short time in the Flemish city of Ghent. One evening, he was returning to his lodgings, walking calmly down the street, his mind, as always, filled with musical ideas and how to convert them into opera. When he chanced to come out of his reverie, he took notice of a man walking a distance ahead of him.

At first, he paid him little mind and wanted to return to the musical problem he was trying to solve. But there was something about this man that kept drawing his attention. He finally looked up to put the matter to rest.

The man looked quite familiar. Was it someone he had met at some gathering, someone important enough that he should speak to him? Curiously, no matter where he went, the man was calmly walking ahead of him, as if they were headed to the same place. But Glück was headed home, so it could not be.

---

363. Shelley, *Prometheus*, 191–199.

Then he noticed the man looked extremely familiar. They were even wearing the exact same clothes. This made no sense. Things became particularly unnerving when the stranger turned a corner, and the composer had a better view of him. To his horror, he saw that the man he was inadvertently following was himself. This man walking ahead of him was an exact double of his own person!

He certainly wasn't about to run up and speak to him now. In fact, he slowed down a bit.

As expected, the man turned up the walkway to the lodging Glück was staying at. The double casually reached into his pocket, pulled out a key, and opened the door. He went in and calmly shut the door behind him.

The real Glück stood alone on the sidewalk, feeling the key in his pocket—the same pocket the double had produced his key from—wondering what to do. He had heard stories…

Finally, the composer decided the best course of action was to make a quick exit. He turned around and rushed away from the building. He went to the home of a friend and begged permission to remain there for the night, explaining that he was too frightened to return to his own lodging. The request was, of course, granted.

The next day, a very nervous Glück returned to his accommodations. He found that over the night, a heavy beam had collapsed just above his bed, crashing into it. If he had been lying in the bed, he would have been crushed to death.

However, by the strangest of circumstances, the bed was empty that night.[364]

---

364. Baring-Gould, *Book of Folk-Lore*, 93.

The Japanese Ikiryō

A similar entity is spoken of in the folklore of Japan. Here, the phantom is known as an *ikiryō*, and it is said to leave the body of a living person and appear in a ghostly form to others. This sometimes happens before a person is to die. There are reports of soldiers some distance away appearing in uniform to their families, then vanishing. After this, the grieving relatives were certain to receive word of that person's death.[365]

We read of this entity in the classic Japanese work *The Tale of Genji*. In the Edo period (1603–1867), this condition was listed as an actual disease. It was classified as *rikonbyō*, translated as "detached soul syndrome."[366]

It is curious—and more than a bit unnerving—to think that sometimes the messenger of death ... is ourselves.

---

365. Meyer, "Ikiryō."
366. Meyer, "Ikiryō."

Chapter 12
OMENS OF DEATH

Because I could not stop for Death—
He kindly stopped for me.

—DICKINSON,
"BECAUSE I COULD NOT STOP FOR DEATH"

Beyond the supernatural appearance of a death messenger such as a banshee or *fylgja*, there are countless superstitions regarding the passage from life to the grave. Not everyone hears a banshee's cry warning them of an upcoming departure, but there are plenty of portents to inform you that the Grim Reaper has someone in your family on his to-do list. Folk beliefs also supply plenty of rules that should be followed to ensure a safe transition from this world to the next.

In 1889, a trio of scholars, Fanny D. Bergen, W. M. Beauchamp, and W. W. Newell compiled a long list of death omens for *The Journal of American Folklore*. The majority of these superstitions are American, but as this is a nation of immigrants, most of them are remnants of the lore that had been brought here from other cultures, beliefs still firmly held in the Old Country. While the list is far too long to go into every single item mentioned, here is a sample of what they put together over a century ago. Unless otherwise noted, all the following superstitions are from that unique article.

Mirrors

Common mirrors become extremely dangerous when there is a death in the household. Besides using them to check your hair, looking glasses can be used for divination and often are considered to be entryways to the Otherworld—you can ask Alice about this.

When a death has occurred in the household, the soul of the departed may initially be wandering about the former residence in a confused state. There is a danger that the lost spirit will be attracted to the reflection in the mirror and become trapped there, unable to continue their journey to the world beyond.

According to Jewish belief, the soul can enter a mirror or any shiny object with a reflection.[367] Thus, it is a good idea to put a cover-

---

367. Krystyna, "Cover Mirrors After a Death?"

ing over the looking glass or turn the mirror to the wall. In fact, some believe that just seeing one's reflection in a mirror in a house where a death has recently occurred may be a portent of one's own imminent demise.

There is an unsettling belief that, sometimes, the face of a deceased person can be seen very faintly in an old mirror. Remember that before your next trip to the antique store. Should three people look in a mirror at the same time, one of them is doomed to die shortly.

Mirrors can be a danger for the living as well as the dead. It is said to be a grave spiritual danger to have a large mirror facing the bed. When one sleeps, according to ancient belief, the soul leaves the body and travels about. When it returns to the home, it may become confused with the reflection of the sleeping body and enter the mirror image instead.

Babies should not be allowed to look into a mirror until their first birthday, undoubtedly a belief generated by the tragic amount of infant mortality in earlier times.

Mirrors can be used for evil sorcery, as we see in the classic fairy tale of Snow White. Magic mirrors appear in numerous different traditional stories from many cultures. You don't have to be the evil queen to utilize this power. A related belief is that a mirror can be used for fortune-telling on Samhain, the original and darker version of our modern Halloween. Young women may, on this night, receive a vision of their future husband.

The prescribed way to do this is to take an apple (a fruit associated with the Celtic Otherworld), a knife, and a lit candle into a darkened room that has a prominent mirror. The apple is then sliced into nine pieces. The girl will eat only eight of these pieces. The final piece is tossed to the mirror. Her future husband will appear in the glass and catch the piece.

A variation of this does not use the mirror, but has the young ladies wrap a ribbon around the apple, toss it out of the window, then wind it back in while reciting the Lord's Prayer. An even simpler method is to simply hold the candle in front of the mirror at midnight on Samhain. In the reflection, the future husband will appear standing just behind the girl, looking over her shoulder.

For those who would like to see these practices in action, there are countless images of these mirror Halloween rites on vintage postcards.

Incidentally, the dreaded curse of breaking a mirror, itself an omen of upcoming death, can be avoided with the following ritual. First, the shards of glass must not be picked up immediately. One should wait a few hours.

Then, every single tiny bit of broken glass must be collected. This is taken out of the house in the moonlight and buried. It is a good idea to take some salt on this chore and toss it over your left shoulder, to keep the devil away … and don't even think of saying Bloody Mary three times.[368]

Clocks

The Journal list continues with the necessity of stopping clocks when a death has occurred in the household. It is not enough to simply unplug an electric one or still the pendulum on an analog model. The clock must be reset to the actual time of death and stopped there. To allow it to continue running invites the soul of the deceased to remain in the home, thinking that nothing has changed as time is still going on. One can see an example of this in the book and film *Fried Green Tomatoes*.

Related to this is the belief that, should a broken or long-stopped clock suddenly start running or worse, chime, a death will soon

---

368. *Mirror History*, "Broken Mirror."

occur; also, as seen in *A Christmas Carol*, should a bell ring of its own accord, it is announcing the arrival of Death (or Jacob Marley).

Other Death Omens

Sextons should note that leaving a recently dug but unfilled grave open over a Sunday will mean that another person will die before the next Sunday. Similarly, if it rains on a new grave, there will be another death in the family within a year's time.

Here is one we don't have to worry too much about today: it was a death portent to see a hearse being pulled by a white horse. We can see here the central European origins of this belief, as in Bohemia it is still held that white horses are death omens.

In ancient Rome, to dream of someone in white garments is a presage of death. Corpses, of course, were buried in white shrouds. As we have seen, banshees would sometimes appear in white cloaks.

There is an old saying about tardy people, "He'd be late for his own funeral." In parts of Ohio, there is a belief that if some lazy person arrives late for a funeral, and the procession has already left, there will be a death in that household. Once the late person has joined the funeral procession, it is very dangerous to count the number of vehicles making that sad journey.

The last individual a dying person looks at before crossing over will be the next one to die. Similarly, it is held in New Hampshire that if the dying person calls out someone's name, that person will soon be joining them on their dark journey.

A curious Greek belief states that, should a pair of scissors be left open near the dying person, it means that St. Michael's mouth is open and he is ready to escort the person to the judgment. (St. Michael is the archangel said to preside over the weighing of the soul; he is there to keep the devil from putting his thumb on the scales.)

A hostess planning a dinner party should be careful not to have thirteen people seated at a table. To be safe, keep the number to twelve; everyone else goes to the kiddie table.

Another deadly superstition connected to dinner parties and banquets, according to beliefs in Massachusetts: either the first one to stand up or the last one to sit down will die within a year. This could get a bit awkward…

Never set a dishrag on a doorknob.

Do not carry a tool, especially a spade or a sharp tool like an axe, through the house by placing it on your shoulder.

There are a number of superstitions concerning women trying on or wearing a black hat (the 1889 article includes bonnets, but they are now rather out of style). This is clothing worn by women in mourning, thus to wear these head garments means that, within a year, they will be worn for a funeral.

People with seasonal allergies should note a Vermont belief that sneezing before breakfast on a Sunday is an omen of death.

Lying down on a table will mean that you will be lying in a coffin within a year.

Opening an umbrella in a house is a sign of an upcoming demise.

A common belief is that a sudden shiver means someone has just walked over the spot that will be your grave. It is also said that a cat walked over your grave, as seen in Val Lewton's classic horror film *Cat People*.

Should a candle flame turn blue, it means that Death is approaching. A variation of this, the one I learned in childhood, is that the blue candle flame denotes the presence of a ghost.

A Massachusetts belief states that three lights placed in a row denote an upcoming death.

If freshly baked bread reveals cracks on the top, there will be a death. In a case from Shropshire, England, a man went into his kitchen when his wife was out. He saw the freshly baked bread and the cracks in it. Panicked, he rushed out in search of her. He found her dead.

If window shades suddenly fall down, a death is sure to come.

A flower blooming out of season, such as the roses in the marvelous 1934 film *Death Takes a Holiday*, is a sign of upcoming death. Similarly, fruit trees bearing fruit out of season denotes death.[369]

This trio of folklorists collected so many death omens that their article had to be included in a second part in the next edition of the journal. Here are some examples from part two.

This one is exceptionally eerie. If a rocking chair suddenly starts to rock on its own, a dead member of the family has returned to help guide someone in the household to the world beyond.

Starting to cut fabric for clothing on a Friday means that, unless the entire bit of clothing is sewn on that same day, the person it is intended for will die. It is similarly believed that it is an omen of death or disaster to start sewing a quilt on a Friday.

One should never do wash on New Year's Day, for that will wash away a family member or friend.[370]

There are innumerable other omens of death. For example, should a cat lie on the foot of a bed, the person who sleeps there will die. A cat crossing the path of a funeral means another member of the family will soon be following.

Seeing a group of crows is an omen of death. It is interesting to note that a group of crows is called a murder.

To have a dream of an owl is a sign of approaching death. Similarly, dreaming of muddy water has the same meaning.

---

369. Unless otherwise noted, these examples are from Bergen, Beauchamp, and Newel, *The Journal of American Folklore*.

370. Bergen, Beauchamp, and Newel, *The Journal of American Folklore* (April–June), 105–112.

A bird tapping on the window is an announcement of death. As we also know from a famous *Twilight Zone* episode, having a bird fly into the house and land on a bed is a sure sign that one is going to die. This is the same case for seeing a white moth in the house.

In Central and South America, there is a belief that black butterflies are portents of death. Sometimes, they are considered a lost soul wandering about.

If a beetle walks over your shoe, death will follow.

It is held in Sussex, England, that to see any white animal at night is a sign of approaching death. (In the *Mabinogion*, the *Cŵn Annwn*, the hounds of Annwn, were owned by the king of the dead, Arawn. These canines were milk white with bloodred ears.)

A cedar tree dying in the yard will presage death for someone in that household.

A holdover from the time when funerals were held in the home: should a corpse remain in the house over Sunday, there would be another death in the household within a year.

Should a picture depicting a family member, either photograph or artwork, suddenly fly from the wall, then that person is destined to die soon.

Breaking a glass while making toast is a sign of death.

This one is generally not relevant today. Seeing a crown (circle) of feathers in a featherbed or in a feather pillow is a certain sign of fast-approaching death. Witches are said to cause feather crowns in beds, strangling the victim as they sleep. People who believe they are being attacked by witchcraft often tear apart their featherbeds searching for these devilish devices. If found, the rings have to be sprinkled with salt then tossed into flames.

Should you burst into song at the dinner table while others are eating, it is a call for Death. It is also very bad manners.[371]

Asia, Africa, and South America

In Korea, there is the curious belief that circulating fans will cause death, particularly if they are used in a room with a closed window.[372]

In Japan, if one should happen to see a hearse go by, it is necessary to hide your thumbs in the palm of your hand. This is to prevent Death from coming to your parents, or presumably other members of your family. It is also said to keep spirits away.

Interestingly, similar to the prohibition in Ireland, there is also a Japanese proscription against picking up a comb that you may find. To take the item is to invite Death.[373]

In many parts of Africa, the custom of covering mirrors is observed. However, to make absolutely certain that the spirit of the dead person does not become too comfortable in the old home, that person's bed is also removed.[374]

According to my son, who has traveled extensively and taught in East Africa, giving a living person a gift of flowers is to wish for them to die. The flowers are for funerals.

In Brazil, it is an omen, or an invitation, of death to place one's flip-flops on the floor upside down.[375]

While we are in Brazil, be careful at night that you do not hear the cry of a ghostly bird, a death messenger known as the *Urutau*. This is another in a long line of tales of love gone bad, but this time, it is neither the fault of the woman nor the man.

---

371. This part of the list, unless otherwise noted, is from Hudson, "64 Death Omens."

372. Tetrault, "13 Omens of Death."

373. Lord, "Japanese Superstitions."

374. Ruddock, "Death Rituals in Africa."

375. *Aventura do Brasil*, "Superstition Brazil."

A young woman was desperately in love with a handsome young fellow, but he did not respond to her advances. Of course, she was brokenhearted. Her father saw this and took matters into his own hands.

He murdered the young man for causing his daughter such pain. But then, he saw that she had witnessed this crime. It was no problem—he simply transformed her into a bird.

She flew off and is now crying out at night predicting death for others.[376]

This one from Turkey is mind-boggling; it does not deal with an omen of death, but rather, of deaths that have already occurred. It involves common chewing gum. Apparently, in Turkey, some believe that after the sun has gone down, the chewing gum will turn into the flesh of corpses. Thus, by chewing it, one is practicing cannibalism![377]

In China, one would wish to avoid the number four. As thirteen is unlucky in the West, four is similar to the Chinese word for death, and, as we see in the Disney film *Turning Red*, is thus associated with the end of life.[378]

The Death Omens of Abraham Lincoln

One can certainly not consider the subject of death omens and superstition without at least a quick look at one of the most famous mortality portents of all time, the eerie circumstances surrounding the assassination of the sixteenth president of the United States, Abraham Lincoln.

Possibly the very first indication of the tragedy yet to unfold was the appearance of a Doppelgänger. Before his inauguration, Lincoln

---

376. Martins de Melo, "The Shroud Shredder."

377. Leigh, "Eight Bizarre Superstitions."

378. Leigh, "Eight Bizarre Superstitions."

chanced to see his reflection in a mirror. He was horrified to see himself as two separate images, one very different from the other. One was him as he normally was. The second, however, was five shades paler, looking more like a corpse.

He told his wife, Mary, about the vision. She was terrified, saying that it was a sign of future events. He would be elected for a second term, and he would die before this term expired.[379]

The ghostly double image would reappear on occasion; Lincoln would try to summon it, but it would not materialize except at its own will. His wife's grim prophecy was correct. He was indeed elected for a second term.

It was then, when victory in the war was about to be achieved, that Lincoln had his infamous dream. In it, the reelected president believed he heard mourning and wailing in the White House. Curious, he made his way downstairs and looked around. Everything seemed to be normal, but he could still hear the lamenting.

He went from room to room, finally stopping at the East Room. Here, he saw funeral candles and a catafalque, an ornate piece of furniture used to support a body or a coffin. Upon this lay the body of a man, his face covered in a black cloth.

Two soldiers in blue stood at rigid attention as honor guard. A group of mourners was nearby; this was the sound he had originally heard. He looked at one of the soldiers and demanded to know who was lying here dead in the White House.

He was told, "The president. He was killed by an assassin." With that, Lincoln woke up and could not return to sleep.[380]

Lincoln had another dream just before his assassination. He was standing on a boat, being taken across the water to a misty, dreamlike

---

379. Rogers, "Linclon's Doppelganger."
380. Rogers, "Linclon's Doppelganger."

destination. He thought that it was a good omen, as many of the events had been good of late.

Finally, on Good Friday, the terrible war was over. Mary reminded him that they had plans to go to Ford's Theater to see the Laura Keene production of *Our American Cousin*. Lincoln did not want to go, however his appearance at the theater had been announced to the press and people would be there to see him.[381]

The sixteenth president did indeed take the boat journey his dream had foretold. However, there is another story to be told about that terrible night, one which is not often spoken about. It reveals just how cursed the events of that evening were, and how they brought tragedy upon all who were in that theater box.

Lincoln had requested a number of dignitaries to attend the play with him, including his star general Ulysses S. Grant. However, Grant's wife could not stand to be around Mrs. Lincoln, and an excuse was made.

Finally, the invitation was extended to an army major, Henry Rathbone, and his fiancée Clara Harris. Then came the night of the tragic event. John Wilkes Booth waited in the unguarded hallway for the part of the play he knew was coming. A solitary actor, playing a rustic, was giving a comedy soliloquy. Booth knew everyone's attention would be focused on the stage and the funny lines.

Booth was armed with a derringer and a large knife. He shot Lincoln in the back of the head. As soon as the shot rang out, Major Rathbone jumped from his seat and started to grapple with the assassin. Booth then took the knife and gave Rathbone a series of deadly wounds.

This action delayed Booth's ability to escape the way he came. The only way out was to jump on the stage, a leap that broke his

---

381. Rogers, "Linclon's Doppelganger."

leg. Shouting *"sic semper tyrannis,"* the Confederate sympathizer and presidential assassin limped away. He knew the way backstage and was able to make an escape.

Lincoln was taken across the street to a boardinghouse where he died the next morning.

The Darkness Follows: Major Rathbone

The forgotten part of this tragedy concerns Major Rathbone. The officer, severely wounded, was able to recover, at least physically. Soon, there were rumors and vicious gossip that he did not do enough, and could have somehow prevented the assassination, or at the very least overpowered the actor. In truth he had done everything he possibly could and had the scars to show for it—but logic holds little meaning to a gossip.

He married Clara and the two had children. Finally, he could take no more of the gossip and left the United States for Europe.

There was a dismal piece of clothing packed away in that luggage. Clara had, for some morbid reason, kept the bloodstained white dress she had worn that fateful evening. It was kept in the back of a closet, a ghastly keepsake. Then, one night, she clearly saw the ghost of Abraham Lincoln in the vicinity of the closet.

In true Edgar Allan Poe style, she had the closet bricked up—but she still did not destroy the dress. Years later, her son had the dress burned. He said there was some kind of curse on it.

He may have been right. Major Rathbone suffered from what may be today classified as survivor's guilt. On every April 14, he would experience terrible pain from where the scars of his battle with Booth were. He was plummeting slowly into insanity.

In 1883, on Christmas Eve, his mind completely slipped. He shot his wife, then tried to stab himself, essentially recreating the horrible events of eighteen years earlier.

It was exactly reenacted. His long-suffering wife died from the gunshot, but once again, Rathbone survived the knife wounds. He was locked away in an insane asylum for the rest of his days. He died in 1911 and was buried in Germany next to the wife he had murdered.[382]

The Phantom Funeral Train

While we're talking about the Lincoln assassination and the supernatural, there is room for a quick mention of one of the most famous ghosts in the United States, the Lincoln funeral train.

This train follows the same route the actual train took, carrying the body of the fallen president back to Illinois. Not only have there been multiple witnesses observing this phantom, but people have actually sat in lawn chairs by the tracks and waited for the ghostly conveyance—and they have not been disappointed.

Inside the open cars, the witnesses could clearly see a number of soldiers in Union blue standing about. These soldiers are all skeletons. Also clearly visible is the ornate coffin, bearing the body of the fallen president.

While some may wish to dismiss this as an urban legend, despite the vast number of witnesses over the years, there is one phenomenon associated with it that is even harder to explain. When the ghost train passes, all the clocks in the area near the tracks stop. This has been attested to over and over, even in households that had no idea the Otherworld express was coming through; and, as we have just seen, a clock stopping is one of the many omens of death and tragedy.

The ghostly train has not been seen in a few decades. Apparently, the fallen president and the skeletal soldiers have, at long last, reached their destination.

---

382. Smith, "Haunted Major."

CONCLUSION

AND now, farewell! the fairy dream is o'er:
The tales my infancy had loved to hear,
Like blissful visions, fade and disappear.

—CROKER, FAIRY LEGENDS

Thus does our journey come to an end as well. We began this odyssey with a senseless act of murder, joined the wild ride of a nobleman without a head galloping along the Scottish shore. We end it with a tale of violence, murder, and madness, from presidents to peasants. Through it all, we have heard the dark cry of the banshee.

Is there a meaning behind the wailing and shrieking of this ancient Celtic spirit? Whether it is an old hag crying out on a windswept hill, a crone washing bloody clothes in a stream, or a lovely maiden sitting on a windowsill singing a mournful song while combing her long golden hair, the message is the same.

You are not home. This world is not the destination, but rather, like that sparrow flying through the banquet hall, it is just part of a grand and magnificent journey.

So, if you hear a woman wailing on the night wind, say a quick prayer for whoever the cry is destined for—it might be for you. If you go out the front door one morning to pick up the paper, and your lawn is filled with foxes …

Well, at that point, just go back to bed!

BIBLIOGRAPHY

Ã' Cnamhsi, Padraig. "Banshees, Fairies and Leprechauns—Donegal's Folklore, Part of What We Are." *Donegallive*, May 14, 2012. Accessed August 28, 2023. https://www.donegallive.ie/news /arts-culture-entertainment/37959/Banshees—fairies-and -leprechauns-.html.

Abernethy, Susan. "The Assassination of King James I of Scotland." *The Freelance History Writer*, May 25, 2013. Accessed August 21, 2023. https://thefreelancehistorywriter.com/2013/05/24 /the-assassination-of-king-james-i-of-scotland/.

"Áine." *Oxford Reference*. Accessed September 3, 2023. https://www .oxfordreference.com/display/10.1093/oi/authority .20110803095357651;jsessionid=7B620C6EBB83EAF96F 06CD472AAD26EA.

"All about Fylgja: Norse & Viking Guardian Spirit Animals." *Atlas Mythica*. Accessed August 21, 2023. https://atlasmythica.com /fylgja-norse-viking-guardian-animal-spirit/.

Almqvist, Bo. "Crossing the Border: A Sampler of Irish Migratory Legends about the Supernatural." *Béaloideas* 59 (1991): 209– 278. https://doi.org/10.2307/20522388.

"Ankou." *Oxford Reference*. Accessed September 3, 2023. https:// www.oxfordreference.com/display/10.1093/oi/authority .20110803095414434?rskey=DyDjde&result=2.

Archdeacon, Matthew. *Legends of Connaught: Irish Stories*. Dublin: John Cumming, 1839.

Badonne, Ellen. "Death Omens in a Breton Memorate." *Folklore* 98, no. 1 (1987).

"Banshee." *Ireland's Lore and Tales*, November 23, 2020. Accessed August 29, 2023. https://irelandsloreandtales.com/2020 /11/23/banshee/.

"The Banshee." *The Dublin Penny Journal* 3, no. 109 (August 2, 1834).

Baraniuk, Chris. "The Animals We Have Mistakenly Thought of as Evil." *The Independent*, January 2017. Accessed August 28, 2023. https://www.theindependentbd.com/arcprint/details/78474 /2017-01-30.

Bardan, Patrick. *The Dead-Watchers, and Other Folk-Lore Tales of Westmeath*. Westmeath: Privately printed at the *Westmeath Guardian*, 1891.

Baring-Gould, Sabine. *A Book of Folk-Lore*. London: Collins'-Clear-Type-Press, 1913.

"The Battle of Clontarf in Irish History and Legend." *History Ireland*, September/October 2005. Accessed August 29, 2023. https://www.historyireland.com/the-battle-of-clontarf-in -irish-history-and-legend/.

"Battle of the Boyne." *National Army Museum*. Accessed August 31, 2023. https://www.nam.ac.uk/explore/battle-boyne.

Bawn, Derek. "Cnoc Aine." *The Modern Antiquarian*, November 23, 2005. Accessed August 28, 2023. https://www.themodern antiquarian.com/site/7737/cnoc_aine.html.

Beckwith, Martha. *Hawaiian Mythology*. New Haven, CT: Yale University Press, 1940.

Bergen, Fanny D., W. M. Beauchamp, and W. W. Newel. *The Journal of American Folklore* 2, no. 4 (January–March 1889).

"Broken Mirror—Is Breaking a Mirror Bad Luck?" *Mirror History*, 2023. Accessed August 31, 2023. http://www.mirrorhistory .com/mirror-facts/broken-mirror/.

Brooks, Noah. *Washington in Lincoln's Time*. New York: Rinehart, 1971.

Callow, Edward. *The Phynodderree and Other Legends of the Isle of Man*. London: J. Dean & Son, 1882.

Campbell, John Gregorson. *Superstitions of the Highlands & Islands of Scotland*. Glasgow: James MacLehose and Sons, 1900.

Chaplin, Kathleen. "The Death Knock." *New England Review* 34, no. 1 (2013).

Cincinnati Commercial. August 26, 1876.

Cincinnati *Enquirer*. August 26, 1876.

———. May 13, 1892.

———. May 27, 1892.

Colum, Padraic. *A Treasury of Irish Folklore*. New York: Crown Publishers, 1967.

Conway, Moncure Daniel. *Demonology and Devil-Lore*. Vol. 2. New York: Henry Holt and Company, 1879.

Croker, T. Crofton. *Fairy Legends and Traditions of the South of Ireland*. London: William Tegg, 1862.

"Corcomroe Abbey." *The Illustrated Dublin Journal* 1, no. 31 (April 5, 1862): Library Ireland, https://www.libraryireland.com/articles /CorcomroeIDJ/index.php.

Cuchulain of Muirthemne: The Story of The Men of The Red Branch of Ulster. Translated and edited by Augusta Gregory. London: John Murray, 1902.

Curran, Bob. *Mysterious Celtic Mythology in American Folklore*. Gretna, LA: Pelican Publishing Co., 2010.

Daly, Eugene. "The Legend of Clíona." *West Cork People*, March 2021. Accessed August 28, 2023. https://westcorkpeople.ie /columnists/the-legend-of-cliona/.

Dasent, George Webbe. *The Story of Gisli the Outlaw*. Philadelphia: J. B. Lippincott and Co., 1866.

———, trans. *The Story of Burnt Njal*. London: 1861. *Sagadb.org*. Accessed September 3, 2023. https://sagadb.org/brennu-njals _saga.en.

"The Death-Place of an Irish hero." *Irish Identity*. Accessed August 29, 2023. http://www.irishidentity.com/stories/cuchulainn .htm.

"Devil Bird of Ceylon." *Taranaki Herald* 54, no. 13444, 11 (April 1907).

Devonshire Characters and Strange Events. London: John Lane, 1908.

Dimuro, Gina. "Inside the Legend of La Llorona, the Vengeful Spirit of the Southwest." *All That's Interesting*, September 2022. Accessed August 28, 2023. https://allthatsinteresting.com/la -llorona.

Dyer, T. F. Thiselton. *The Ghost World*. London: Ward and Downey, 1893.

Earp, Joseph. "Spotlight on the River Trent." *Our Nottinghamshire*, July 2013. Accessed August 28, 2023. http://www.ournotting hamshire.org.uk/page_id__1085.aspx.

"England's Haunted Arundel Castle." *Fringe Paranormal*, July 29, 2011. Accessed August 28, 2023. https://fringeparanormal .wordpress.com/2011/07/29/englands-haunted-arundel -castle/.

Evans-Wentz, W. Y. *The Fairy Faith in Celtic Countries*. New York: Oxford University Press, 1911.

"Ewan the Headless." *Scotclans*. Accessed September 3, 2023. https://www.scotclans.com/pages/ewan-the-headless.

Faraday, L. Winifred. *The Cattle-Raid of Cooley (Táin Bó Cualnge): An Old Irish Prose-Epic*. London: David Nutt, 1904. Accessed August 17, 2023. http://adminstaff.vassar.edu/sttaylor/Cooley /Faraday/Contents.html.

"The Five Ghosts of Newstead Abbey." *BBC*, November 13, 2014. Accessed August 28, 2023. https://www.bbc.co.uk/nottingham /content/articles/2008/10/08/newstead_abbey_ghosts _feature.shtml.

Fitzgerald, David. "Popular Tales of Ireland." *Revue Celtique*, tome IV (1879–1880).

"Fráech." *Oxford Reference*. Accessed September 4, 2023. https:// www.oxfordreference.com/display/10.1093/oi/authority .20110803095831973.

French, Noel. "Gormanston Foxes." *Meath History Hub*. Accessed August 28, 2023. https://meathhistoryhub.ie/gormanston -foxes/.

Ganley, Ellen. "Why Medieval Ireland Was Known as the 'Island of Saints.'" *Maynooth University*. Accessed August 30, 2023. https://www.maynoothuniversity.ie/research/spotlight -research/why-medieval-ireland-was-known-island-saints.

"Ghost Stories Special Part 3 Banshee Tales." *Derry Journal*, October 30, 2014. Accessed September 3, 2023. https://www .derryjournal.com/news/ghost-stories-special-part-3-banshee -tales-2260476.

"The Ghostly Drummer of Cortachy Castle." *Edinburgh Evening News*, March 24, 2017. Accessed September 6, 2023. https:// www.edinburghnews.scotsman.com/whats-on/arts-and -entertainment/the-ghostly-drummer-of-cortachy-castle -602310.

Griffiths, Lawn. "Listening to the Caul." *East Valley Tribune*, October 2011. Accessed August 28, 2023. https://www.eastvalley

tribune.com/spirituallife/listening-to-the-caul/article
_19d1013b-6a3d-5e0c-8955-9872ed982382.html.

Grimm, Jacob. *Teutonic Mythology*. Translated by James Steven Stallybrass. Vol. 3. Mineola, New York: Dover Publications, 2004.

Guest, Charlotte. *The Mabinogion*. London: Bernard Quaritch, 1877.

The Folk Revival Project. "Six Authentic Recordings of Keening from Ireland and Scotland (1955–1965)." YouTube video, 18:39, February 12, 2023. Accessed September 3, 2023. https://www.youtube.com/watch?v=vgts7_b1JWY.

Harris, Marissa. "*Daoine Sidhe*: Celtic Superstitions of Death within Irish Fairy Tales Featuring the Dullahan and Banshee." *Texas State University*, May 2017. Accessed August 28, 2023. https://digital.library.txstate.edu/bitstream/handle/10877/6701/Harris_Marissa_Thesis.pdf?sequence=1.

Henderson, William. *Notes on the Folk-Lore of the Northern Counties of England and the Borders*. London: Peyton and Co., 1879.

Hennessey, W. M. *The Ancient Irish Goddess of War*. Royal Irish Academy, 1870: Sacred Texts. Accessed August 29, 2023. https://sacred-texts.com/neu/celt/aigw/aigw01.htm#fn_1.

Hewitt, Les. "The Banshee: Celtic Messengers of Death." *Historic Mysteries*, December 2015. Accessed August 29, 2023. https://www.historicmysteries.com/banshee/.

Hore, Herbert, and David Mac Ritchie. "Origin of the Irish Superstitions Regarding Banshees and Fairies." *The Journal of the Royal Society of Antiquaries of Ireland* 5, Fifth Series, no. 2 (June 1895).

Hudson, Beth "64 Death Omens: Real or Folklore?" *Currant*, August 13, 2020. Accessed August 29, 2023. https://www.getcurrant.org/post/death-omens.

J. M. "A Brilliant Idea." *All Ireland Review* 2, no. 7 (March 2, 1901).

Joyce, P. W. "Irish Sorcerers and Sorcery." In *A Smaller Social History of Ireland*, 1906: Library Ireland. https://www.libraryireland.com/SocialHistoryAncientIreland/II-V-4.php.

Keegan, J. "Legends and Tales of the Queen's County Peasantry." *The Dublin University Magazine* 14 (September 1839).

"The Keening Tradition." *The Keening Wake*, 2023. Accessed August 29, 2023. http://www.keeningwake.com/keening-tradition/.

Krystyna, Klaudia. "Why Do Some Cultures Cover Mirrors After a Death?" *Cake*, June 2022. Accessed August 29, 2023. https://www.joincake.com/blog/covering-mirrors-after-death/.

Layne, Niki. "Banshee, At Least 2 Ghosts Said to Haunt Tarboro." *The Enterprise*, August 28, 2021. Accessed August 29, 2023. https://restorationnewsmedia.com/articles/columns-enterprise/banshee-at-least-2-ghosts-said-to-haunt-tarboro/.

Lecouteux, Claude. *Phantom Armies of the Night: The Wild Hunt and Ghostly Processions of the Undead*. Rochester, VT: Inner Traditions, 2011.

———. *Witches, Werewolves and Fairies: Shapeshifters and Astral Doubles in the Middle Ages*. Rochester, VT: Inner Traditions, 2003.

Le Fanu, Joseph Sheridan. "The White Cat of Drumgunniol." 1870. Haunted Crossroads. Accessed August 29, 2023. https://www.hauntedcrossroads.com/stories/joseph-sheridan-le-fanu/the-white-cat-of-drumgunniol-joseph-sheridan-lefanu/.

Leigh, Lex. "Eight Bizarre Superstitions from Ancient History." *Ancient Origins Reconstructing the Story of Humanity's Past*, January 1, 2023. Accessed August 17, 2023. https://www.ancient-origins.net/myths-legends-europe/superstitions-0017734.

"Lough Gur." *Emerald Isle*. Accessed August 28, 2023. https://emeraldisle.ie/lough-gur.

Lord, Cassandra. "Japanese Superstitions: Good and Bad Omens." *Tokyo Weekender*, June 2022. Accessed August 29, 2023. https://www.tokyoweekender.com/art_and_culture/japanese-culture/japanese-superstitions-good-bad-omens/.

Lysaght, Patricia. *A Pocket Book of the Banshee*. Dublin: The O'Brien Press, 1998.

———. "The Banshee's Comb (MLSIT 4026): The Role of Tellers and Audiences in the Shaping of Redactions and Variations." *Béaloideas* 59 (1991): 67–82. https://doi.org/10.2307/20522377.

———. *The Banshee: The Irish Death Messenger*. Boulder, CO: Roberts Rinehart Publishers, 1996.

———. "Irish Banshee Traditions: A Preliminary Survey." *Béaloideas* 42/44 (1974): 94–119. https://doi.org/10.2307/20521375.

MacDougall, James. *Folk Tales and Fairy Lore in Gaelic and English Collected From Oral Tradition*. Edinburgh: John Grant, 1910.

MacGregor, Alasdair Alpin. *The Peat-Fire Flame: Folk-Tales and Traditions of the Highlands & Islands*. Edinburgh: The Moray Press, 1937.

Maclagan, R. C. "'The Keener' in the Scottish Highlands and Islands." *The Folk-Lore Journal* 25 (1914).

MacKillop, James. *The Canadian Journal of Irish Studies* 17, no. 2 (December 1991).

Mac Philib, Séamas. "Dublin South County to North Inner City: An Urban Folklore Project 1979–1980." *Béaloideas* 74 (2006): 103–121. http://www.jstor.org/stable/20520902.

Mann, Darren. "Dyfed Ghosts, Folklore and Forteana." *The Paranormal Database*, 2023. Accessed September 3, 2023. https://www

.paranormaldatabase.com/wales/Dyfed.php?pageNum
_paradata=3&totalRows_paradata=123.

Marshall, Jessica. "Listen: The Ghostly Tale of Lincoln's Funeral
Train in Albany." *Times Union*, October 2021. Accessed August
30, 2023. https://www.timesunion.com/news/article/eagle
-podcast-ghost-story-lincoln-funeral-train-16518643.php.

Martins de Melo, Thiago. "The Shroud Shredder, the Urutau, the
Yyami Oxorongá and the Wrong and the Death Omens That
Dominate Contemporary Brazil." *Celeste*, December 2022.
Accessed August 31, 2023. https://select.art.br/the-shroud
-shredder-the-urutau-the-yyamioxoronga-and-the-wrong-and
-the-death-omens-that-dominate-contemporary-brazil/.

Massey, Ann. "13 Shades of Fear: Ireland's Most Colourful Female
Ghosts." *Spooky Isles*, March 2015. Accessed August 29, 2023.
https://www.spookyisles.com/ireland-female-ghosts/.

McAnally, D. R., Jr. *Irish Wonders*. New York: Weathervane Books,
1888.

McIntyre, Alastair. "*In the Shadow of Cairngorm* VI: The Lochs and
Their Legends." *Electric Scotland*. Accessed August 28, 2023.
https://www.electricscotland.com/history/cairngorm/6.htm.

———. "Old Scottish Customs." *Electric Scotland*. Accessed September
6, 2023. https://electricscotland.com/history/customs
/chapter18.htm.

Meyer, Matthew. "A-Yokai-A-Day: Ikiryō." *Matthew Meyer, The
Yokai Guy*, October 2013. Accessed August 31, 2023. https://
matthewmeyer.net/blog/2013/10/30/a-yokai-a-day-ikiryo/.

———. "Ikiryō." *Yokai.com*, October 30, 2013. Accessed August 31,
2023. https://yokai.com/ikiryou/.

Mingren, Wu. "Navigating the Realm of an Aztec Water Goddess and One of the Five Suns." *Ancient Origins*, July 6, 2018.

Accessed August 31, 2023. https://www.ancient-origins.net /myths-legends-americas/chalchiuhtlicue-0010325.

Mullan, Kevin. "Derry's Haunted Spots Detailed—Hauntings, Vampire and Lough Monster at Paranormal Zones." *Derry Journal*, October 2021. Accessed August 31, 2023. https://www .derryjournal.com/heritage-and-retro/heritage/derrys-haunted -spots-detailed-hauntings-vampire-and-lough-monster-at -paranormal-zones-3432725.

Neligan, Harry L., and St. John Drelincourt Seymour. *True Irish Ghost Stories*. Dublin: Hodges, Figgis & Co., 1926.

Nico. "Gaelic Folklore (10): Scottish Banshees." *The Birds of Rhiannon*, June 12, 2019. Accessed August 28, 2023. https:// nicovleeuwen.blogspot.com/2019/06/gaelic-folklore-10 -scottish-banshees.html.

O'Donnell, Elliot. *The Banshee*. London: Sands & Co., 1920.

O'Hart, John. "The Battle of Clontarf AD 1014." In *Irish Pedigrees; or the Origin and Stem of the Irish Nation*. Vol. 2. 1892: Library Ireland. https://www.libraryireland.com/Pedigrees2/battle -of-clontarf.php.

"Ordnance Survey Letters by John O'Donovan and Eugene Curry, 1839: Parish of Drumcrehy (c)." *Clare County Library*. Accessed August 28, 2023. https://www.clarelibrary.ie/eolas/coclare /history/osl/drumcrehy3_lough_rasg.htm.

Owen, Elias. *Welsh Folk-Lore*. Werham: 1887. Project Gutenberg, December 12, 2006. Accessed August 21, 2023. https://www .gutenberg.org/files/20096/20096-h/20096-h.htm#page170.

Perera, Raveen Harith. "The Devil Bird—Ulama." *Medium*, August 26, 2020. Accessed August 31, 2023. https://raveenp.medium .com/the-devil-bird-ulama-755851ad32a5.

Pfeifle, Tess. "Gwrach y Rhibyn—Astonishing Legends." *Astonishing Legends*, March 12, 2019. Accessed August 17, 2023. https://

astonishinglegends.com/astonishing-legends/2019/3/12
/gwrach-y-rhibyn.

Publications of the Modern Language Association of America 56, no. 1 (March 1941).

The Queenslander (May 11, 1933).

Rogers, Lisa W. "Bad Omen #1: Lincoln's Doppelganger." *Lisa's History Room*, March 3, 2009. Accessed August 21, 2023. https://lisawallerrogers.com/2009/03/03/abraham-lincoln-the-omen/.

Ruddock, Vilma. "Death Rituals in Africa: Cultural Beliefs and Burial Traditions." *Love to Know*. Accessed August 31, 2023. https://www.lovetoknow.com/life/grief-loss/death-rituals-africa.

Sandles, Tim. "The White Bird." *Legendary Dartmoor*, March 2016. Accessed September 3, 2023. https://www.legendarydartmoor.co.uk/2016/03/26/white_bird/.

Scott, Walter. *Letters on Demonology and Witchcraft*. New York: Harper and Brothers, 1836.

Sellar, A. M. *Bede's Ecclesiastical History of England*. London: 1907. Project Gutenberg, December 17, 2011. Accessed October 16, 2023. https://www.gutenberg.org/files/38326/38326-h/38326-h.html#Pg102.

Shelley, Percy Bysshe. *Prometheus Unbound: A Lyrical Drama in Four Acts*. London: C & J Ollier, 1820.

Shepherd, Lynn. "'Full Fathom Five the Poet Lies': The Death of Percy Bysshe Shelley." *Wordsworth Grasmere*, July 2014. Accessed September 3, 2023. https://wordsworth.org.uk/blog/2014/07/08/full-fathom-five-the-poet-lies-the-death-of-percy-bysshe-shelley/.

Sherwood, Joseph. "Meet the Bean-Nighe: The Scottish Clothes-Washing Omen of Death." *A Little Bit Human*, June

2022. Accessed September 3, 2023. https://www.alittle bithuman.com/meet-the-bean-nighe-omen-of-death/.

Sikes, Wirt. *British Goblins: Welsh Folk-Lore, Fairy Mythology, Legends and Traditions*. London: Sampson Low, Marston, Searle, & Rivington, 1880.

Simms, Katharine. "The Battle of Dysert O'Dea and the Gaelic Resurgence in Thomond." *Dal gCais* 5 (1979): *Clare County Library*. https://www.clarelibrary.ie/eolas/coclare/history /battle_dysert_odea.htm.

Squire, Charles. *Celtic Myth & Legend Poetry & Romance*. London: The Gresham Publishing Co. Limited, 1905.

Smith, Gene. "The Haunted Major." *American Heritage*, February/ March 1994. Accessed August 24, 2023. https://www.american heritage.com/haunted-major.

Stepko, Barbara. "The Fateful Role Ravens Played in Cursing One of Europe's Oldest Royal Dynasties." *Vintage News*, November 7, 2018. Accessed September 3, 2023. https://www.thevintage news.com/2018/11/07/hapsburg-raven-curse/?Exc_D_Less ThanPoint002_p1=1.

Stokes, Whitley, trans. *The Destruction of Dá Derga's Hostel Epic and Saga*. New York: Harvard Classics P. F. Collier & Son, 1910.

———, trans. *The Hostel of Da Choca*. Royal Irish Academy: 1879. *Pagesperso*, August 30, 2009. Accessed September 3, 2023. https://sejh.pagesperso-orange.fr/keltia/version-en/da-choca .html.

———. "The Second Battle of Moytura." *Revue Celtique* 12 (1891).

"Superstition Brazil—From Warts on the Fingers to the Eighth Month." *Aventura do Brasil*, November 2019. Accessed September 3, 2023. https://www.aventuradobrasil.com/blog /superstition-brazil-from-warts-on-the-fingers-to-the-eighth -month/.

Sutherland, A. "Ankou: Breton Angel of Death That Delivers Souls to the Underworld." *Ancient Pages*, July 2021. Accessed September 3, 2023. https://www.ancientpages.com/2021/07/18/ankou-breton-angel-of-death-that-delivers-souls-to-the-underworld/.

Tetrault, Sam. "List of 13 Omens of Death in Different Cultures." *Cake*, February 2022. Accessed August 29, 2023. https://www.joincake.com/blog/omens-of-death/.

The Táin. Translated by Thomas Kinsella. Oxford: Oxford University Press, 2002.

Timmons, Jessica. "Sleep Myths: The Fylgja." *Sleepopolis*, October 2022. Accessed September 3, 2023. https://sleepopolis.com/education/sleep-myths-the-fylgja/.

"Top 10 Haunted Scottish Castles." *Bagtown Clans*, February 22, 2021. Accessed August 21, 2023. https://bagtownclans.com/index.php/2021/02/22/top-10-haunted-scottish-castles/.

Von Goethe, Johann Wolfgang. *The Autobiography of Goethe. Truth and Poetry: From My Own Life*. Translated by John Oxenford. London: George Bell and Sons, 1897.

Weber, Sara, and Aedín Ní Bhróithe Clements. "Headless Horsemen in American and Irish Legend." *University of Notre Dame*, October 2020. Accessed September 3, 2023. https://sites.nd.edu/rbsc/headless-horsemen-in-american-and-irish-legend/.

Weiser-Alexander, Kathy. "*La Llorona*—Weeping Woman of the Southwest." *Legendsofamerica.com*, April 15, 2019. Accessed August 17, 2023. https://www.legendsofamerica.com/gh-lallorona/.

Wells, Mari. "Some Irish Vampires." *Mari Wells*, April 10, 2013. Accessed September 3, 2023. https://mariwells.wordpress.com/2013/04/10/some-irish-vampires/.

Western Folklore 7, no. 4 (October 1948).

Westropp, Thos. J. "A Folklore Survey of County Clare." *Folk-Lore* 21 no. 2 (1910).

"The Whitby Doppelgänger." *Whitby Uncovered*, December 2017. Accessed September 3, 2023. https://whitbyuncovered.word press.com/2017/12/01/the-whitby-doppelganger/.

Wilde, Jane Francesca Elgee. *Ancient Legends, Mystic Charms, and Superstitions of Ireland*. Boston: Ticknor and Company, 1888.

Wilks, Robert. "'How They Met Themselves': Pre-Raphaelitism and the Double." *Pre-Raphaelite Reflections*, January 2014. Accessed September 3, 2023. https://dantisamor.wordpress.com/2014 /01/14/how-they-met-themselves-pre-raphaelitism-and-the -double/.

Wood-Martin, W. G. *Traces of the Elder Faiths of Ireland: A Folklore Sketch a Handbook of Irish Pre-Christian Traditions*. Vol. 2. New York: Longmans, Green, and Co., 1902.

Yeats, W. B. *Irish Fairy and Folk Tales*. New York: The Modern Library, 1918.

To Write to the Author

If you wish to contact the author or would like more information about this book, please write to the author in care of Llewellyn Worldwide Ltd. and we will forward your request. Both the author and the publisher appreciate hearing from you and learning of your enjoyment of this book and how it has helped you. Llewellyn Worldwide Ltd. cannot guarantee that every letter written to the author can be answered, but all will be forwarded. Please write to:

Steven J. Rolfes
℅ Llewellyn Worldwide
2143 Wooddale Drive
Woodbury, MN 55125-2989
Please enclose a self-addressed stamped envelope for reply,
or $1.00 to cover costs. If outside the U.S.A., enclose
an international postal reply coupon.

Many of Llewellyn's authors have websites with additional information and resources. For more information, please visit our website at http://www.llewellyn.com.

NOTES